New Testament Spirituality

New Testament Spirituality

Michael Green
and
R Paul Stevens

Eagle
Guildford, Surrey

British Library Cataloguing-in-Publication Data. A catalogue
record for this book is available from the British Library

Published by Eagle, an imprint of Inter Publishing Service (IPS)
Ltd, 59 Woodbridge Road, Guildford, Surrey GU1 4RF.

All Scripture quotations used by Michael Green, unless otherwise
noted, are taken from the *Holy Bible, Revised Standard Version*,
and by R Paul Stevens, unless otherwise noted, are taken from the
Holy Bible, New International Version.

Typeset by The Electronic Book Factory Ltd, Fife.
Printed in the UK by HarperCollins Manufacturing, Glasgow.

ISBN No: 0 86347 113 7

CONTENTS

FOREWORD

Christians have a great gift to offer the world in all matters of spirituality. It is our New Testament. There is nothing quite like it. It is the greatest gift we can provide for people who are fed up with the hand-to-mouth existence of mere appetite. It is the perfect gift for people who are bored with the head-trip existence of mere intellect. It is the exactly right gift for people who have gone stale on second-hand religion.

Spirituality. The word promises something. Sometimes it seems to promise everything. In a world like ours, where there is much disappointment and much unhappiness, it is understandable that the word is much used. For the word, 'spirituality', suggests that there is more here than meets the eye, and that this 'more' might be just the ticket to a life that has some zest and beauty and worth to it. But the word in itself is hardly more than a hint, a 'hint followed by guesses'. And the guesses proliferate exponentially.

Meanwhile Christians have in their keeping this document, *The New Testament*, that has all the marks of the real thing. They have been reading and meditating on it for nearly two thousand years. Every kind and sort of Christian has tested it against every kind and sort of circumstance and condition of living and stood up to give witness to its validity. Tested against the reality of actual lives, it turns out to be not another of many 'guesses' about spirituality, but spirituality itself. Instead of reading *about* spirituality, getting careful definitions or elaborate descriptions of it, we come upon spirituality in action. Reading the New Testament, we are immersed in the intricate tangle of human life as it is entered, addressed, confronted, saved, healed, and blessed by the living God – God's Spirit breathed into human lives. Spirituality.

It is the great responsibility and privilege of Christians today to place this proven and essential source document on spirituality in the hands of those who are bewilderingly searching through a welter of spiritualities for something authentic, something true.

This present book is the lively product of two professors who teamed up to teach Christian spirituality to classrooms of graduate students from all over the world, using the New Testament as their text. The international character of the students in the classroom – Africans, Asians, Europeans, North and South Americans – keeps this teaching from being unconsciously reduced to the cultural predispositions of the affluent middle-class. And the activist character of the professors prevents this teaching from drifting off into anything remotely resembling self-indulgence or narcissism. Michael Green and Paul Stevens are nothing if not *involved* – committed both personally and vocationally to an evangelical integration of church and world, prayer and discipleship, learning and marketplace. It is quite wonderful to be taught by professors who not only pray what they read in the New Testament but live what they teach from it.

Eugene H. Peterson
James M. Houston Professor of Spiritual Theology
Regent College, Vancouver

INTRODUCTION

More than a century ago Nietzsche proclaimed the death of God, and revelled in it with a mixture of awe and elation. The advances of the natural sciences, the growth of scepticism, the prevalence of pluralism and relativism are just a few of the reasons why we might be tempted to believe he was right. But if we were to heed his siren voice, if we were to go along with the materialism which has been the prevailing world-view in the West for nearly 250 years, we would show ourselves to be gravely out of touch with modern men and women. For an amazing change is taking place all around us. Spirituality is coming into its own again.

Of course, this has always been true in the Two Thirds World. They have never had any doubts about the reality of spiritual forces which we cannot see but which are nonetheless both real and powerful. We are not surprised to find it there. But in sophisticated First World countries? That is the remarkable phenomenon which we are witnessing in our day.

Look, most notably, at the collapse of communism in Eastern Europe. Communism, whose basic tenet was atheistic materialism, has failed to deliver. It has not met either the physical or the spiritual needs of the millions under its heel. And in the past few years we have witnessed one of the turning points of history, when this vast, erroneous system has been decisively rejected by the whole Communist bloc with the exception of Cuba and China – and it will not be long before they follow suit. At the heart of the liberation movements which

overthrew Communism was a belief in the lasting value
of men and women because they are not mere products
of blind forces which brought them into being but care
nothing for them. Nor are they merely the stuff of
which evolutionary history is made on its way to the
fulfilment state. They have intrinsic value, because they
are the creatures of a personal Creator God. It was
that conviction which fired the majority of *refusniks*,
with Alexander Solzhenitsyn towering among them. The
Church was undeniably and visibly at the heart of the
revival of the human spirit which so dramatically brought
about the fall of communism.

Nearer home, a number of factors are bringing about
a new quest for spirituality. They are conveniently, if
quixotically, referred to under the umbrella name of
'post-modernism'. And they are a reaction against the
barrenness of the materialistic world-view which has
both freed and enslaved the human spirit since the
Enlightenment. Mankind was freed from a great deal
of irrationalism and superstition at the Enlightenment,
and for that we must be grateful. But at the same time
the human race was enslaved to patterns of endemic
scepticism, dismissal of God, and the enthronement of
reason above all else.

The rationale of this procedure has always seemed to
me to be bizarre: if we sprang from plankton and have
no future but extinction, whence does reason gain such
pre-eminence? At all events, we became obsessed with
man's origins, and neglected his destiny. We became
fixated by analysis, and oblivious of synthesis. Questions
of purpose and meaning fit uneasily into an atheistic
world-view, and it was this, no less, that the rationalism
of the Enlightenment was offering us.

Now the revolt is on. Perhaps it began with the exis-
tentialism of Sartre, Camus, Kafka and their friends in
and after the Second World War – impatient of history
and philosophy and passionately concerned to express
personhood and find meaning in life even if, as most of
them believed, no ultimate purpose or meaning existed.

Postmodernism is its heir, however, in being profoundly dissatisfied with the explanation of life offered by materialists and rationalists. They are too clinical, too cold and impersonal, too monochrome and far too inadequate to explain the beauty, the mystery of life in all its fulness. A radical reassessment is afoot: the spiritual can no longer be left out of account.

Many paths have been taken by this new quest for spirituality. Some have looked to the East, with its monism, its doctrines of karma and reincarnation, and its ultimate losing of the self in the impersonal One. Some have taken the trip within, either by drugs or by transcendental meditation and its derivatives. Some have gone for the various forms of the human potential movement, confident that we have within ourselves, if only we can tap them, all the resources we shall ever need of soul and spirit. Some have turned to magic and the occult: it has not had such a recrudescence in the West for three hundred years. But by far the most prevalent, fast growing and seductive spiritual force today is the New Age movement, combining as it does so many elements from other faiths in its basic pantheism. This is not the place to examine this most fascinating, experiential and anti-rational world-view which in a few years has penetrated the media, education, medical practice, feminism and the cadres of the occult. But it is undeniably one of the most serious competitors which Christianity has had to face since the days of the Gnostics, who were in many respects its forbears.

Amid this welter of divergent spiritualities (mutually contradictory but united in their rebellion against the attempt, exerted by rationalism for far too long, to extinguish faith in the supernatural) what has been happening in Christian spirituality? Three strands have been particularly prominent during this century.

One is the movement towards serving God through serving our fellow men. This is the route which has increasingly been taken by the World Council of Churches, founded nearly ninety years ago with a very different, and strongly missionary programme. It is deeply concerned with social justice, human rights, and movements of liberation throughout society.

A second is the worldwide movement of the Holy Spirit which began to make itself felt in the year 1900, first with the Pentecostal movement, but by the middle of the century in the neo-Pentecostal or charismatic surge which has swept through almost all denominations and is unquestionably the most influential Christian emphasis in our times, touching, as it does, more than a quarter of the Christians in the world. This movement lays great stress on the sovereign power of the Spirit to break into the lives of individuals and churches with supernatural grace and manifestations, which the old rationalism had almost persuaded the churches was a thing of the past. There is much froth in this movement: but what remains after the froth is discounted is a very substantial spirituality.

The third main movement in recent years has been towards the Catholic end of the spectrum. Not exclusively the Roman Catholics, though they are by far the largest church in Christendom. In the UK alone their advance has been meteoric. Little more than a century ago they were proscribed. Now they are the largest church in the land. What I mean is much more far-reaching, however, than the Roman Catholics. I mean the renewed interest in liturgy: alternative prayer books, the influence of Taizé, the rediscovery of the Eucharist as the central and main service on a Sunday, and the astonishing hunger for retreats. I mean, too, the steady move towards a Catholic form of spirituality among large numbers of Christians who began their pilgrimage as Evangelicals. There is, in fact, a crisis of spirituality among Evangelicals today. Its lynch pins of sabbath observance, family prayers, personal prayer and Bible reading each day, and a deliberate 'unworldliness' have collapsed; and in the absence of an alternative current and viable Evangelical spirituality, a great many from this wing of the church are looking more towards

Catholic practices and insights to give depth to their spiritual lives.

It was against this backcloth in the 1980s and ever since that Professor James Houston began teaching courses on spirituality at Regent College, the large Christian postgraduate institution in Vancouver. They have attracted an enormous following, clearly meeting needs that are widely felt, not least among the Evangelical community, of which Regent is largely made up. They take the student deep into the desert fathers, the mediaeval mystics, and the most helpful of modern saints and writers about God. But there remained a gap, which even Dr Houston has not addressed in print, and neither, so far as I know, has anyone else: New Testament spirituality. There are many books on worship or the sacraments in the New Testament, abiding in Christ, the prayers of St Paul, the ethics of St James, and the like. But there are few, if any, overviews of what made the early Christians so spiritually vibrant; what marked their spirituality above all. That is why my colleague, Dr Paul Stevens, and I offered a lecture course at Regent on New Testament spirituality. It was much appreciated, and was repeated, with variations. That is the *fons et origo* of this book.

We would not claim to have done more than scratch the surface of this great theme. And in the book we have necessarily been obliged substantially to curtail the content of a dozen lectures. Nevertheless we thought it right to accede to the encouragement of publishers on both sides of the Atlantic and attempt an outline of New Testament spirituality, accessible to the layman, and not only readable but spiritually enriching. Of course we have made many omissions. Of course our knowledge is not as great as we would like it to be. Of course much New Testament spirituality is built upon that of the Old Testament, which we have had little space to examine. We are aware of all this, and particularly of our own limited perspective and those failures in discipleship which blind us to the very spiritual truths we are writing about. Even so, it seemed a task worth attempting. We offer it, for what it is worth, in the hope that it may excite Christian readers to seek that depth in their walk with God which marked the first believers in Jesus. If that happens, we shall be well content.

We decided to write this book as we lectured: by joint teaching. Actually, the teaching was delivered in a three-hour session each week, with an introductory time of worship, and a lot of interplay between the two professors and the class, the third hour being given up entirely to an appropriate form of spiritual activity for the evening. Both of us were excited with the subject. Both were reckoned to be lively instructors. But our styles are as different as our backgrounds, and we make no attempt to iron out these dissimilarities in the book. Paul Stevens has had a most colourful spiritual history in Inter Varsity work, in the Brethren, in the Baptist ministry, in non-denominational church leadership, and he has been greatly influenced by Orthodox spirituality.

My background is much more prosaic: an Anglican clergyman with strong evangelical convictions and charismatic experience. Where we come together, apart from deep personal friendship, is that our careers have moved from academic to pastoral ministry and back again. And far from regarding this as a disadvantage (which from the point of view of academic minutiae it undoubtedly is) we both believe it has enormously enriched our academic understanding and our pastoral practice. It is too often forgotten that Jesus, Paul, Peter and the others were not academic figures, setting out the ground rules for others to write doctorates on in the succeeding centuries: they were men of action, men of passionate conviction and tireless ministry to others. Their theology arose from and in their work. For them there was no Enlightenment abstraction of knowledge from life. Faith and praxis went hand in hand. And so it has worked out for the authors of this book. Both have oscillated between the academic and the applied, with perhaps the accent most on the applied. But maybe when spirituality is the subject, that is not altogether a bad thing!

Michael Green

CHAPTER ONE

ABBA WORSHIPPERS

The Meaning of 'Worship'

The heart of spirituality, for the first Christians, lay in worship. For many of us in Western lands today, rediscovery of spirituality lies in a trip into our interior consciousness, attaining affinity with the earth goddess Gaia, or an attempt to maximise our human potential. But not for them. Spirituality meant worship, ascribing ultimate worth not to some fashionable idol, but to the Creator of the universe. He was the God of Abraham, Isaac and Jacob, the God who had invaded time and space and come to seek them in the person of Jesus the Messiah. He alone was worthy of worship.

But we must begin by looking more closely at this word which slips so glibly off the tongue. Christians today talk about holding a 'service of worship'. By that we mean either a liturgy, written by specialists and recited by the congregation – with or without hymns, sermon, or the full attention of the participants. Or else we mean a freewheeling event, with an opening invitation to 'worship', a few hymns or choruses, a choir item and an address. In either case, and on both sides of the Atlantic, it must be over within the hour.

That is a travesty of worship. It has nothing to bring us low before God, nothing to take us out of ourselves. When in such a service were you last 'lost in wonder love and praise'?

The Letter to Hebrews gives us a glimpse of what true worship means. 'Let us offer to God acceptable worship, with reverence and awe; for our God is a consuming fire ... Through him [i.e. Jesus] then let us continually offer up a sacrifice of praise to God, that is, the fruit of lips that acknowledge his name. Do not neglect to do good and to share what you have, for such sacrifices are pleasing to God' (Heb 12:28; 13:15–16). Here we are given five marks of 'acceptable worship'. It is offered in deep *awe and adoration*, a quality scarce today. It is *radiant with praise*. It is *the fruit of a life* and lips which consistently shine for God throughout the week: otherwise Sunday worship is a sham. It *does good*, in practical ways. It *touches our purse* in two challenging ways. We are to 'be content with what we have' (13:5) and to 'share what we have' – in strong contrast to the greed and selfishness which are two of the main characteristics of modern, as of ancient, society. Real worship changes all that. It leads to a simple and a generous lifestyle. Open to God, it is open to others. This may find its most obvious expression on Sundays, but it springs from seven-days-a-week living. Therein lies the truth of the old adage *laborare est orare* 'to work is to pray'. Worship and life cannot be divorced. They belong together. Worship without work is hollow. Work without worship is barren.

A good deal of light is shed on the nature of authentic worship by the two main words used for it in the Old Testament, which certainly influenced the outlook of the first Christians.

One is a word which means *bowing down in awe*. Both the Hebrew and the Greek word mean literally 'to prostrate yourself' before the Lord, to kiss his feet. That is what the Persians did in the presence of their 'divine' kings: it is a picture of total surrender and devotion, such as we find taken over into a Christian context in Revelation 5:9. That is what we are called to, as we come to worship. Contrast it with the casualness of our approach to worship: no preparation, no recognition of whom we are meeting, but a casual, hands-in-pockets attitude that treats God with familiarity, if not with contempt. But when real worship is carried out, when there is deep awe before the mystery and the majesty of God, men and women are drawn, as if by an unseen magnet, to join in that worship. It is profoundly attractive. It is, after all, what mankind was made for. 'O God you have made us for yourself. And our hearts are restless until they find their rest in you.' So spoke Augustine a millennium and a half ago. He was right.

There is another word for worship both in Hebrew and in Greek. It means *service*. The Hebrew *abodah* comes from the same root as *ebed*, meaning 'servant', supremely displayed by Jesus, the Servant of the Lord. It is worth noting that the Hebrew view of servanthood is very different from the Greek. It denoted privilege and honour, not abasement and bondage. To be a servant of God was seen to be a high privilege. When the seer gives us a picture of heaven, he can rise no higher than to say 'his servants will serve him' (Rev 22:3 NIV).

These two characteristics are vital in worship. If there is no sense of awe and wonder before God, allied to practical, joyful service of God, worship will fail to thrill, and worshippers will either continue to shop around, unsatisfied, among our earthbound, uncommitted congregations; or else they will drop out. Protestant and Evangelical Christians do themselves a disservice when they despise the emphasis, characteristic of the Orthodox and Roman Catholic communions, on beauty in buildings, reverence in gesture, and ornateness in ritual. They are equally far off the mark when they dismiss as 'liberal' any emphasis on social concern and striving for justice among their fellow-churchmen. Both are profoundly biblical strands in true worship of God; and the early Christians knew it.

The God we Worship

It is perhaps significant that the most common secular Greek word for worship is conspicuously absent from Christian terminology in the New Testament. It is *therapeuein*, which means literally 'to heal'. But its only occurrence meaning 'worship' is in Acts 17:25 where Paul *repudiates* it! The sublime Creator requires no 'therapy' from human hands. No, Christian worship springs from awe and glad surrender before the God who is utterly different from all idols, and whose worship must, accordingly, reflect that.

There are at least five characteristics of the God Christians worship which define the nature of that worship. They display what God has revealed of himself through the Scriptures of the Old Testament.

First, *he is alive*. He is the living God, the Creator and Sustainer of heaven and earth, from whom all life derives, and to whom all life must come. He is the absolute contrast to the dead and dumb idols against whom the Old Testament prophets so constantly inveighed. And that has a great message for our congregations. True worship will have expectancy, silence, waiting on God. We shall expect to meet with him each time we go to worship. The service should both embody his vitality and leave room for his intervention.

Second, *he is holy*. 'Holy, holy, holy is the Lord of hosts.' That holiness drove Abraham to confess he was just dust (Gen 18:27). It drove Job from self-justification to awe in the light of God's holy presence (Job 42:5–6). It drove Isaiah to a recognition of his utter unworthiness (Isa 6:5). And we find the same with Peter (Luke 5:8), Paul (Acts 9:3–4) or John (Rev 1:17). God is indeed, as Rudolf Otto saw, the *mysterium tremendum et fascinans*. He is utterly 'other' and transcendent. And this induces awe in us, but at the same time intrigues us and invites us to draw near.

Our services need to embody this element in worship, so that none are 'pally with the deity', but that all are brought low, and all are lifted up. The Eastern Orthodox Church is strong in this respect, with its *epiklesis*, inviting the awesome Spirit of God to come; and with its *anaphora*, lifting the whole congregation up to share in the worship of heaven.

Third, *he is unique*. He is to be worshipped to the exclusion of all else. He is a 'jealous God' (Exod 20:5; Isa 42:8). His glory he will not share with another. That would be *lèse-majesté*. Not that he is selfish; simply that he is true. Any divided worship, any split loyalty, contradicts reality. It is against the nature of things. He alone is Creator and Redeemer. He alone, therefore, merits the wholehearted worship of his people. Idolatry is both an insult and a lie.

We would be gravely mistaken to imagine that the day of idolatry had passed. The building in which we worship can become an idol. The minister can. Tradition can. So can denominational rules. But the God we worship cannot brook any rival to his sovereignty over his people's loyalties.

Fourth, *he is grace*. God is not just gracious, but grace itself: total self-giving for the utterly unworthy. He is 'the God of all grace' (1 Pet 5:10). He is the one who made us and all the world. He sustains it, and breathes life into it. He is the one who came to seek us out, when we would never have sought him. He is the one who died for us, rose for us, and comes to enter our hearts and direct our way. He is the one who will, at the end of the road, receive us into his glory. Amazing grace!

So our worship needs to declare his grace, admit our unworthiness, and yet have a deep confidence of access in the name of Jesus – which naturally leads to praise. The New Testament abounds in praise and adoration. *Eucharistein, eulogein,* and *ainein* are constantly in use; and the Book of Revelation gives a marvellous insight into the praises of the people of God, here as well as hereafter (cf. Rev 4:11; 5:9–10, 12–14). Praise and adoration are the only fitting response to grace. That is the answer to people who wonder why God wants to be praised!

In the Bible men and women praise God for a welter of things in their lives. He daily loads us with benefits (Ps 68:19). He gives us the fruits of the earth (Acts 14:17). He is the source of every good and perfect gift (James 1:17), including the money which so often becomes an idol (1 Tim 6:17). Yes, he 'gives us all things richly to enjoy'. But supremely Christians give praise to God for Christ, who brings us into God's family and makes new people of us (1 Pet 1:3; Eph 2:19). Jesus, therefore, needs to be central in our praises; and this the best hymn writers have perceived. Jesus incarnate, Jesus crucified, Jesus risen and exalted – these are the three themes of that 'new song' to be sung in heaven (Rev 5:9–14). Wisely, Professor Cranfield warns us that 'one of the worst forms of ingratitude is to be so occupied with thanking God for his innumerable lesser mercies that we have little time to thank him for his supreme gift'.

Fifth, *he is challenge*. Grace means 'all of him for me.' Faith means 'all of me for him'. That grace–faith reciprocal dominates worship from the time of Abraham until today. Grace is costly. So is faith. It calls for total surrender in practical, life-changing ways. It did for Abraham. It did for Jesus. It did for Paul. And so it does for us. Spiritual worship means not an hour on Sunday, but the responsive surrender of our bodies as a living sacrifice (Rom 12:1). It means the continual offering of a 'sacrifice of praise' in our daily lives, whatever the circumstances. That may mean hard times. It may mean prison. It did for Paul. But his response? 'Imprisonment and afflictions await me. But I do not account my life of any value, nor as precious to myself, if only I may accomplish my course and the ministry which I received from the Lord Jesus, to testify to the gospel of the grace of God' (Acts 20:24). That is worship. It offers every side of me as a love gift to the great Lover who has sought and redeemed my soul. Duty and privilege coalesce. It becomes not only our reasonable service but our highest joy to go up to the house of the Lord and to mingle in the courts of the holy place (Ps 84). Any worship which does not drive home the response of total self-giving, total servanthood to so kind a Lord, knows little of the cost and therefore little of the joy, of New Testament spirituality. 'Therefore let us be grateful for receiving a kingdom that cannot be shaken,' and in response let us offer to God 'acceptable worship, with reverence and awe; for our God is a consuming fire' (Heb 12:28–29).

The Dynamics of Worship

From all this it is not difficult to discern two of the main dynamics of Christian worship.

The *activating motive* is gratitude to God for all he is and all he has done for us. Our services must be marked by a strong note of praise and adoration, issuing in practical service of our fellow men out of love for God. If our worship brings us in touch with the God outlined above, we cannot emerge from our worship unchanged. We take on something of the God we worship.

The *controlling motive* of worship is reverence and awe. There is nothing drab about it: but something rather exciting as we wait for God to move. There is nothing clerical about it: every member is involved. There is nothing verbose about it: silence can be golden. 'There was silence in heaven for about half an hour' when the ascended Jesus disclosed himself (Rev 8:1). Time after time I have known a divine stillness fall upon a congregation when the Spirit of God has been active in it. Nobody moves. Nobody wants to go. Sometimes it is total silence. Sometimes it leads into informal praise. But everyone knows that the Lord has made his presence felt.

The Style of Worship

The style of worship is really immaterial. It is the inner reality that counts. The first Christians could worship in the temple – but also in prison or by the riverside. They were liberated from externals – and yet they used them as they were available. 'We have no priests' exulted the second-century writer Minucius Felix[1] – and yet we are told that the Apostle John wore the high priestly robe, the *petalos*.[2] 'We have no altars' they cried – and yet sacrificial language was used very early of the Eucharist: the second-century literature is full of the eucharistic application of Malachi 1:11. 'We have no temples,' they asserted; yet they were happy to keep the sabbath, the

Jewish feasts, even the ritual vows. Manifestly, the style of Christian worship was very flexible, but the essence was guarded with great care. It was nothing less than whole-hearted response to the God of all grace, who calls us all to be a people for his own possession. What a challenge to us!

Our worship is all too often spoiled. It is spoiled by the *tradition* in which we have been imprisoned. It is spoiled by the *externals* we venerate – while we often miss the inner reality. It is spoiled by the *mind*, which is fearful of mime and dance, colour and ceremony; fearful of emotion; above all, fearful of God breaking in. It is spoiled by *clericalism*, which ruins almost all the churches whatever their professed ecclesiology. It is spoiled by the *clock*, the plague of Western man. We have something to learn from 'African time'. It is spoiled by the *building*, which so often militates against real fellowship among Christ's people. It is spoiled by our *fear of the body*. Many Christians are suspicious of kneeling, or of arms raised in worship, of dance or of drama. We have no need to be fearful about physical gestures. After all, it is God who gave us our bodies!

The Characteristics of Worship

The style of worship among the first Christians was indeed flexible, but four strands are clearly discernible.

It was liturgical. There is, in the Christian worship preserved in the New Testament, a massive use of the Old Testament Scriptures to declare God's mighty deeds. It had a form with which ordinary worshippers could easily identify. Hence the words of institution, the Lord's Prayer, psalmody, and the gradual emergence of a creed prior to AD 150. The snatches of hymns or creeds reflected in Romans 1:3–5, Ephesians 5:14, 1 Timothy 3:16, Revelation 4:8, 11, 5:9–10, point in the same direction. Liturgy was not a form of words in these early days: but it was a recognisable sequence of elements.

It was charismatic. Prophecy, tongues, intervention by the Holy Spirit are common, and they could be introduced through any member who had been so gifted (Acts 11:27–30; 1 Cor chs. 12 and 14).

It was spontaneous. That is clear from Acts 4:24 among many other places: 'When they heard it, they lifted their voices together to God.'

It was corporate. Their worship was not dominated by any one person. Many people could, and did participate. This is clear from 1 Corinthians 14:26–33.

In a word, the special emphases which have differentiated the denominations in our day were all successfully held together in the churches of the New Testament era.

The Dimension of Worship

The dimension of worship in the earliest church was threefold.

It involved *the house meeting.* The Friday night *haburah* or gathering for worship in a Jewish home, led to the 'church in the home' of the first Christians (Rom 16:5 etc). This small home group facilitated love and mutual care among individual members.

It involved *the local assembly.* The Saturday synagogue was taken over into Christian worship. That is very clear from James 2:2, where the local church is still called 'the synagogue' (Gk). There needed to be a local gathering of Christian believers, like the Jewish synagogue, for purposes of identity, prayer, instruction, and worship. Incidentally, the 'presbyters' of the synagogue provided the prototype for the leadership of local Christian congregations.

It involved *the great festivals.* Jews were obligated to attend at least some of the great festivals of their nation – Pentecost, Yom Kippur, Tabernacles and the like. These were the times when God's people celebrated his mighty acts of deliverance. Participation cemented their belonging to a mighty enterprise. It is easy to recall Hebrews 12:23. 'You have come ... to the assembly of the first-born who are enrolled in heaven.' Christians followed their Jewish heritage by occasional such large celebrations.

In our worship today we need all three aspects of Jewish worship. The synagogue corresponds closely to our church worship, but we are woefully weak in the area of small groups and of major celebrations. We need them all if we are to be balanced in our worship.

The Wellspring of Worship

The wellspring, the bottom line of worship for the first Christians was that they could call God *Abba*, dear Father. It is an astonishing word, and its use was dangerous and courted misunderstanding. Yet it remains a fundamental insight if we are to think of God aright and worship him acceptably.

The Fatherhood of God

Some children idolise their fathers: some hate them. Some fathers spoil their children: some neglect them. If God is to be seen as Father, inevitably all human parenthood distorts to a greater or lesser degree what he is like. But God does intend our human parents to reflect his nature. That is why, I fancy, the command to honour father and mother comes where it does in the Ten Commandments: between the first four on our duty to God and the last five on our duty to men. It links the two strands in our relationships, the God strand and the human strand. But what distortion there has been of that image! People who have had strict fathers see God as out to punish them. Those whose father was rarely at home see God as absent. Those who experienced a father's love only with strings attached find the free grace of God almost impossible to appreciate, though they long for it with all their hearts. I am reminded of a doctor's question to a boy who had five sexual encounters a night, 'Why do you do it?'. The poignant reply was, 'I was looking for someone to love me.'

Despite all the attendant dangers, the Bible does dare to use this word 'Father' of God. It is rare in the Old Testament, occurring only some fourteen times. It points to

God as Creator (Deut 32:6; Mal 2:10), and as very merciful
(Ps 103:13–14). Long before the feminist reaction against
calling God 'Father', Professor Jeremias had observed
perceptively, 'For orientals, the word Father as applied
to God, encompasses, from earliest times, much of what
Mother signifies to us.' True, for we are created male and
female in the image of God who is both (Gen 1:27).

Most of the Old Testament references to God as Father
come in a context of human rebellion. We are all prodigals. With tenderness and weeping, like a heartbroken
mother, he calls on us to return home. 'With weeping
they shall come, and with consolations I will lead them
back ... for I am a father to Israel, and Ephraim is my
first-born' (Jer 31:9). The mercy of the divine parent
exceeds all human expectation. 'Is Ephraim my dear
son? Is he my darling child? ... Therefore my heart
yearns for him; I will surely have mercy on him, says
the Lord' (Jer 31:20). That is the Old Testament's last
word on divine Fatherhood. Its very nature impels him
to mercy and forgiveness. In those words, 'I must have
mercy', we see deep into the parent heart of God, and it
is the most wonderful sight imaginable.

Nevertheless, God is never called the Father of any
individual in the Old Testament. And never is God
addressed as *Abba*. It would be unthinkable. For *Abba*
is the most intimate form of family address. And how can
one be intimate with the Creator of heaven and earth?

The meaning of Abba
Jews, accordingly, never called God *Abba*. But Jesus
almost always did. We find him praying like this even at
the time of his greatest trial: 'Abba, Father, all things are
possible to you: remove this cup from me' (Mark 14:36).
More than 160 times in the Gospels Jesus is recorded as
calling God 'Father', and the survival of this Aramaic
word *abba* in the New Testament records shows that this
is the intimacy he claimed and this is how he habitually
addressed God – except in that terrible hour of bearing
the world's sin on the cross, when he was cut off from

that accustomed intimacy with his heavenly Father and called out, in the words of the psalmist, 'My God, my God, why have you forsaken me?' (Mark 15:34).

It is impossible to exaggerate the importance of this form of address. There is no example, in all literature, of any Jew ever calling God *Abba*. Yet here is Jesus doing it all the time. He, alone of all men, dared to call God 'Daddy'. And the unimaginable privilege of Christian worshippers is to call God 'Daddy' too. We find it in the Pauline congregations (Gal 4:6) and the non-Pauline congregations alike (Rom 8:15). Christians can call God *Abba*. We can enjoy the intimate personal relationship which Jesus had with God and which nobody before him ever enjoyed. We are not only allowed to address God thus: in the opening words of the Lord's Prayer we are bidden to do so. In the Greek the very first word is this staggering loan word from Aramaic, *Abba*. What an astounding privilege! We may come to God as sons and daughters alongside Jesus himself, and call the Creator of the universe *Abba*! The only difference is that Jesus has this position by right, we by grace. Jesus was the one and only Son of God by his essential nature; we, by contrast, are adopted children. It is significant that the New Testament writers take up this notion of adoption, unknown in their Jewish heritage but common in the secular world around them: it served their purpose precisely, to show that we have no inherent right to that status whatsoever, but it has been freely lavished on us by God the Father. It is a great word to express the intimacy and the permanence of the relationship into which we have been introduced through his inexpressible generosity.

This word *Abba* takes us to the heart of the gospel, as Joachim Jeremias so clearly saw in his short (but mighty) book *The Central Message of the New Testament*.[3] It denotes three things, all unique.

First, a *unique relationship*. The Jews said in the Talmud, 'When a child is weaned it learns to say *abba* and *imma*.' *Abba* is one of the first words a baby utters.

An intimate word. A family word. Jesus enjoyed that relationship with God, and he allows his followers to share it. The New Testament does not teach that all people are children of God. Jesus went to considerable pains in his teaching to differentiate between the relationship he had with God and that which his followers had. He spoke of 'My God and your God, My Father and your Father' but *never* of 'Our Father' embracing himself and them. There is indeed a great difference. 'He came to his own, and his own did not receive him.' That remains the sad truth about so many in our world, a settled rejection both of God and of his Jesus. Their names have become mere swear words, their love despised, their very existence denied. 'But to all who received him, who believed in his name, he gave power to become children of God' (John 1:12). They become it, please note: they were not always 'sons', except in the very general sense of being his creatures. And the evangelist drives the wonder of this adoption home in his next words. They were 'born not of blood nor of the will of the flesh nor of the will of man, but of God' (v13). What human parentage, human effort, and human mediation could never achieve, God has done. He has taken us into his family. We can cry, *Abba*! You will never in all the world's religions find hopes of any such intimacy held out to the worshippers, a childlike relationship with God as warm and trusting as a baby at its mother's breast or on its father's knee. It is utterly without parallel.

Second, *a unique revelation*. Most dads love to teach their kids. But with the Jews it was much more. It was the sacred duty of the father to teach his son the Law. And Jesus claims that God his Father has done just that for him. 'All things have been delivered to me by my Father; and no one knows the Son except the Father, and no one knows the Father except the Son and anyone to whom the Son chooses to reveal him.' Such is the claim in Matthew 11:27. He is saying that nobody but he knows God in this intimate, family way – an interesting sidelight on John 14:6, 'No one comes to the Father but by me.' He is also saying that just as the Father has transmitted to him the true disclosure of himself, so he can pass it on to those who trust and obey him. In that word *Abba* we see Jesus making a claim to ultimate, reliable revelation of who and what the Father is.

Third, *a unique authority*. We are not finished with *Abba* yet, for Jesus taught his disciples a prayer, the Lord's Prayer. And with breathtaking boldness he says to them, in effect, 'I am giving you, too, the privilege of addressing God as nobody before me has ever addressed him. I give you the right to call him *Abba* when you pray.'

And they did! The foreign Aramaic word stuck firmly in the prayer language of the Greek-speaking communities of the early church. They exulted in it. For this God whom Christians worship is not unreal, not absent, not too busy to bother, not deaf to our requests, not someone to be in fear of. He is our dear *Abba*. No wonder many eucharistic liturgies exult 'Therefore *we are bold* to say "Our Father . . ."'. No wonder the Lord's Prayer lies at the heart of many liturgies, next to the act of reception. The family meal and the family prayer go together.

Yes, this little word *Abba* does indeed take us to the heart of the gospel. It shows us Jesus' unique filial relationship with God. It shows his unparalleled intimacy with God. And it reveals his authority to draw those who follow him into the same relationship.

For you and I have not received some spirit of slavery to drag us back into fear and moral bondage. No, we have received the Spirit of Jesus, the Spirit who made us children of God. That same Spirit within us prompts the first cry of the baby in the family, '*Abba*, Daddy!' And when he does so, that is his witness with our spirit that we are indeed children of God. And if children, then heirs, heirs of God and fellow heirs with Christ. Of course we shall suffer with him. But equally certainly we shall also reign with him. We will share his glory. That is the thrust of one of St Paul's most passionate and heartfelt outcries in Romans 8:15ff. That is our position if we are Christians – children in the Father's very own family. That is our

confident cry, *Abba*. It speaks of his past adoption of us.
It speaks of his present intimacy with us. It speaks of his
future destiny for us.

Praise God for the privilege of being Abba worshippers!
That assurance underlies all our worship, all our prayer
and confession, our adoration and service. Nothing in all
creation can rob us of that precious standing. 'For I am
sure,' continues St Paul in that same eighth chapter of
Romans, 'that neither death, nor life, nor angels, nor
principalities, nor things present, nor things to come,
nor powers, nor height, nor depth, nor anything else in
all creation, will be able to separate us from the love of
God in Christ Jesus our Lord' (vv38–39).

CHAPTER TWO

DISCIPLES OF JESUS

Either we will receive into our hearts the Spirit of Jesus and become, as never before, men and women of prayer, mercy and peace, real followers of Jesus: or else, everything will disappear in chaos. Today is the moment of Jesus.
Jean Vanier

Christianity has not been tried and found wanting; it has been found difficult and not tried.
G.K. Chesterton

In the context of teaching the Bible to street-people in Boulder, Colorado, I stumbled on the connection between knowing the Father and being disciples of Jesus. Some friends had organised food and accommodation for dozens of homeless young people struggling with drug addiction and meaninglessness. In addition to feeding the body they offered some nurture for the soul. In the evening there was an optional teaching session from the Bible. Most of the young people decided to stay for the 'soul food'.

One of them, Eddie, had begun to follow Jesus. He was raised on the streets of Detroit. He did not know who his parents were – he had no family, no identity and no home.

During the teaching session, Eddie started to fight with the men sitting beside him. He had a violent past and was only beginning to experience the touch of Christ. Rather than interrupt the teaching they took him out of the room to the porch outside where, as he struggled with them physically, they pressed him to the ground and three men sat on him. As I continued unabated in my teaching I could hear them 'counselling' Eddie just outside the patio door.

Eddie responded, 'I would like to pray.' And this man, devoid of identity and family, prayed: 'God! I have wanted to call you Daddy for a long, long time. Do you think I could call you Daddy tonight?'

James Packer says that the simplest definition of a Christian is someone who has come to know God as Father. Since Jesus reveals the heart of the Father and leads his followers into his own relationship with the Father, the way to the Father is by discipleship to Jesus. There are good reasons for this.

Jesus is a truly superlative person worthy of following even as a man. But his claims demand his being considered as more than a man. He claimed to have a unity with God that is essential and absolute: 'I and the Father are one' (John 10:30). He claimed that our relationship with him settles our eternal destiny one way or the other (Matt 10:32–33). He claimed to be able to satisfy our deepest needs, including our need for affection and meaning (Matt 11:25–30). In so speaking of himself Jesus revealed that he is either mad (a megalomaniac), bad (an imposter), or God. Yet his quality of life shows him to have been the sanest person to have walked across the stage of history. His claims are not only vindicated by his words and his life but also by his works, supremely his deeds of personal liberation and his ultimate act in the crucifixion and resurrection. Who would not want to follow such a person?

Why Discipleship?

Churches in the developing world, or the newly industrialised world, churches that are growing like a forest fire have much to teach the West on this matter. Dallas Willard observes:

Multitudes are now turning to Christ in all parts of the world. How unbearably tragic it would be,

though, if the millions in Asia, South America and
Africa were led to believe that the best we can hope
for from the Way of Christ is the level of Christianity
visible in Europe and America today . . . The greatest danger to the Christian church today is that of
pitching its message too low.[1]

Confronted as I am with that beneficent forest fire
when I travel to countries where the Christian way is
attractive and winsome, I keep asking, Why have we in
the post-Christian West settled for Christianity without
discipleship?

Being a 'Christian' today is a complicated matter. The
term can be used to describe those who go to church,
or those who prefer not to be counted with Muslims
and atheists. Many Christians use the wretched term
'non-Christian' to distinguish themselves from those who
do not believe as they do. A radical but intriguing proposal
is to accept a moratorium on the term 'Christian' for a
year and to substitute the more biblical term 'disciple'.
Let me suggest some reasons why.

Disciples and the Way

It is seldom noticed that the first Christians in the Acts of
the Apostles were called Christians by not-yet-Christians
who observed the total orientation of their lives around
Jesus Christ. When observers could not regard the Jesus-
followers as members of a sect of Judaism (Acts 11:26)
they coined the word 'Christian' to describe the Christ-
people. Apparently believers did not describe *themselves*
this way when asked about their belief and their pattern
of life. Rather than using terms which would imply that
they were 'in' while others were 'out', they directed
people to their Lord by describing themselves as 'disciples' (Acts 6:1; 9:1; 13:52) and 'followers of the Way'
(Acts 9:2; 19:9, 23; 22:4; 24:14). Taken together the
terms invite the questions, 'Disciples of whom?' and
'The way to what destination?' One can be a close or

distant follower of Jesus and still direct onlookers to
one's Lord. One can be 'on the way' heading in the right
direction without boasting about being 'almost there' or
despairing about 'just having begun'. The Greek word
for 'disciple' communicates the same truth. It means
'learner', 'pupil', 'apprentice', or 'adherent'. What if,
during the year of my proposed moratorium on the term
'Christian', those of us who wish to express our Christian
allegiance simply answered the question 'What are you?'
with the simple statement, 'I am an adherent of Jesus'?
The fact that the term Christian is used only three times
in the New Testament while disciple is used 269 times is
reason enough to address the topic of discipleship. But
there is an even better reason.

The essence of the Christian Way is the all-embracing
and life-giving relationship of normal human beings
with the living Christ who, following his death and
resurrection, is as alive today as when he touched the
lepers long ago. Jesus is our contemporary. So being a
disciple means much more than going to church, having
correct beliefs or observing the Christian liturgy. Being
a Christian involves something more than following the
teachings of a once-vital but now entombed guru, or
living by Christian principles. Discipleship is essentially
a transforming relationship with someone who is as
influential today – even more so – than he was when the
first Christian disciples turned the world upside down.
Christianity is Christ, and to be a Christian is simply to
be a disciple of Jesus Christ. Discipleship implies growth,
nurture, education, deepening intimacy, shared goals and
life-direction, all facets of relationship with a person.

Joining God
Unfortunately, most people associate following Jesus
with joining the church. Though, as we will suggest
later in this book, joining the church is part of loving
the people Jesus loves, the first step is quite different.
The essential and primary invitation is to join God. We
do this through adherence to Jesus who includes us in

his own relationship with the Father. This is much more than joining the church, and indeed we are on the wrong track when we invite people to do so before they have joined God. Why? Because becoming an adherent of the church without becoming an adherent of Jesus can lead to following followers of Jesus instead of following Jesus himself.

Following followers is almost always a disappointing experience. Inevitably these 'models' prove to have clay feet when they reveal a discrepancy between profession of their faith and life or when they succumb to one of the triple terrors of Christian leaders – sex, money or power. When the 'model' falls, their followers fall with them. The pain of this disillusionment is excruciating and some never recover. Because Jesus has chosen to associate himself with people such as us how much healthier to associate with him, and then to embrace the people he loves, no matter how well or how poorly they are following.

So relationship with Jesus is not the means to the end of our spirituality. Relationship with Jesus *is* Christian spirituality. By adhering to Jesus we enter the life Jesus has with the Father through the Spirit. Since the ambition of Jesus was to reveal the Father and to do the Father's will, the person who is learning from Jesus, adhering to him, and being educated by him, will, like Eddie, make the greatest of all confessions: the confession that he or she has come to know and be known by Abba-Father and belongs eternally in the family of God himself. That is the vital centre of the invitation of Jesus to follow him. But the invitation turns out to be a compelling summons.

The Call to Discipleship

The Gospels reveal concentric circles around this most amazing person, each circle representing a progressively deeper response to his call. The largest circle was represented by the crowd who loved to hear him teach and to observe his miraculous signs and wonders. Many of them carried on life afterwards with little or no change. The next, smaller, circle was occupied by the seventy disciples, who engaged in short-term missions on his behalf. Then there were the Twelve. Of these Mark records that, 'Jesus went up on a mountainside and called to him those he wanted, and they came to him. He appointed twelve – designating them apostles – that they might be with him and that he might send them out to preach and to have authority to drive out demons' (3:13–15).

Within the Twelve there was a special 'inner circle' – composed of Peter, James and John – who were with Jesus at the healing of Jairus' daughter, on the Mount of Transfiguration and in the Garden of Gethsemane. These concentric circles suggest that we can be as close to Jesus as we want. But there is more to discipleship than volunteering to be close to the most important person ever to have walked across the stage of human history. There is the call.

Mark's crisp summary is helpful. Disciples are people who know themselves to be called 'to be with' Jesus and to be sent out *by and with Jesus* to participate in his continuing work of liberating and empowering people. To be with Jesus in mission and friendship is the essence of Christian discipleship – the outstroke of action and the backstroke of reflection and relational rest. Both are dimensions of discipleship to Jesus. But both dimensions – to be with him and to be sent out – are dependent on the initiative of Jesus.

Disciples are neither volunteers for intimacy with the Son of God nor volunteers for an exciting and dangerous adventure. In the first century Jesus turned down some volunteers who did not know what they were getting into, and he did so for their own good! What enables us to continue the life of discipleship is the call of Jesus not our good intentions. So the call of the Twelve in the Gospels becomes a model for disciples in every century.

Everyone is called

Nineteen centuries of clericalism makes it hard for us to understand the call to everybody because the clergy–lay distinction has been institutionalised in the church. The standard argument goes like this: The call of the Twelve, as evidenced in Mark 3:13–15, is a special, once-for-all call issued to twelve special people in the first century and a few people in every succeeding generation. Most people in the first century did not leave job and family to follow Jesus but just carried on, grateful for the influence of this remarkable rabbi. In the same way, it is argued, most people today are not called to the same degree of commitment as the first disciples, but are merely called to observe the teachings of Jesus as best they can in the context of normal experiences of home and business life. But people who are *really* called like the Twelve, should go into the ministry, become monks or nuns, or volunteer to serve sacrificially on the mission field.

John Calvin, the great Reformer, unfortunately popularised the idea of a 'secret' call which some special Christians receive and which is a prerequisite for going into 'the' ministry. Most denominations still require evidence of such a call before ordination. Arguing from the Old Testament model of priesthood of which it was said that 'No one takes this honour upon himself; he must be called by God' (Heb 5:4), Calvin spoke of 'that secret call, of which each minister is conscious before God, and which does not have the church as witness'.[2] Without this special call, Calvin maintained, our ministry would not be approved by God. Even the radical reformation leaders who championed the priesthood of all believers, inadvertently promoted a two-level Christianity. Level one is for ordinary people who choose to follow Christ in the ordinary way. Level two is for superior Christians who are called into ordained service in the church or mission field. But there is no two-level spirituality in the New Testament. Over and again, the letters of Paul use 'call' language to describe the summons of the living God to all people to live for the praise of God's glory in the totality

of their lives. All are called and all are exhorted to walk
in the way worthy of the calling they have received (Eph
4:1). The question is not whether they have been called
but whether they have ears to hear!

Within this general and universal call to discipleship
each person is led by Jesus to serve God in a special
way appropriate to their gifts. So it is fitting to speak
of being called to pastoral ministry. But it is equally
fitting to speak of being called to home-making. Martin
Luther understood this matter with penetrating clarity.
Even though his teaching was frequently marked with an
overreaction to mediaeval monasticism, Luther grasped
there is no two-level system of call in the New Testament.
He said:

> Monastic vows rest on the false assumption that
> there is a special calling, a vocation, to which superior
> Christians are invited to observe the counsels of
> perfection while ordinary Christians fulfil only the
> commands; but there simply is no special religious
> vocation since the call of God comes to each at the
> common tasks.[3]

Subsequent generations chose to follow Calvin who for-
mulated the doctrine of an immediate and special call
believing the call of the Twelve in the Gospels to be
the obvious precedent. Speaking of their call, Calvin
said 'The ministers of the Word ought, in a particular
manner, to be directed by this example, to lay aside all
other occupations, and to devote themselves unreservedly
to the Church, to which they are appointed.'[4] Unfortunately Calvin and his followers misunderstood *why* the
call of the Twelve was placed in the record in the first
place.

The Gospels record the calling of the original disciples
in order to expound what following Jesus means for all
disciples both then and today, not to legitimise the special
calling of church leaders and monks. Disciples then and
today discover that following Jesus involves complete

abandonment of all that holds us, at his initiative. To put it simply, to be saved involves becoming a disciple. The experience of the first twelve disciples is the normal Christian experience. Dietrich Bonhoeffer is one of the few modern authors who refuses to let us interpret the hard words of Jesus as applying to a special category of disciple.

> When Christ calls a man, he bids him come and die. It might be a death like that of the first disciples who had to leave home and work to follow him, or it may be a death like Luther's, who had to leave the monastery and go into the world. But it is the same death every time – death in Jesus Christ, the death of the old man at his call ... But we do not want to die, and therefore Jesus Christ and his call are necessarily our death as well as our life.[5]

In the same way, the apostle Paul describes the universal call of people to be followers of Jesus. He says to his friends 'And you also are among those who are called to belong to Jesus Christ' (Rom 1:6). The call here and elsewhere in Paul's writings is equivalent to salvation. When Paul describes his own unique call to be an apostle to the Gentiles, as he does in Romans 1:1–7, he is careful to distinguish the call by which he became a servant of Jesus Christ (which is the normal experience of all true disciples), from the call by which Paul himself was commissioned to a unique once-for-all apostleship. Of crucial importance is the fact that Paul never uses his own call to apostleship as a model for the secret, immediate and special call of church leaders.

The vocation of vocations
Simply put, this means there are no second-class disciples. We do not have two options set before us: full-timers (the clergy who are called to the ministry) and part-timers (the laity who receive the ministry of the 'called' people). All are called to be with Jesus and to be sent out with

him. All within hearing range of Jesus of Nazareth are summoned to complete abandonment at the initiative of Jesus and therefore to a life of overflowing fullness. Since the English word *vocation* comes from the Latin word for 'call' we are entirely correct in stating that discipleship is the vocation of vocations.

A young PhD student at the University of British Columbia knelt beside his bed to yield his life to Christ. He was brilliant and was destined to a stunning career in India. When I noticed that he had finished his prayer I turned to him and said words which I had not premeditated. 'You now have a vocation greater than becoming the Prime Minister of India.'

'How did you know?' he responded.

'Know what?'

'That my life ambition was to become the Prime Minister of India.'

'Whether you do this or not,' I continued, 'you now have a greater vocation that embraces everything from politics to family life. You are called to be a disciple of Jesus.'

Unpacking what that meant took several weeks of meeting together over the Scriptures. This sort of follow-through is crucial because there is misunderstanding not only on the subject of who is called, but on what it means *on the inside* to live as a called person.

Inside Discipleship

What is it like to be a disciple of Jesus? I was once asked by a student for permission to be followed for several days in order, in his words, 'to find out what it is like on the inside'. But this question is related to the one most commonly asked, 'How does one become a disciple of Jesus?' Many answers are given to this but some of them, whilst attractive, are a dangerous diversion.

Imitating Jesus
One such answer is the idea that one becomes a disciple of Jesus by copying him. Thomas à Kempis' classic, *The*

Imitation of Christ seems to recommend this way. Kempis says, 'Wherefore let our sovereign study be – in the life of Jesu Christ . . . For whoever will understand the words of Christ plainly and in their savour must study to conform all his life to his life.'[6]

A popular book invites us to ask in every situation, 'What would Jesus do now?' It is a good question. But it is also depressing.

On one hand the idea of imitation is implicit in discipleship. It is literally true that we become like the person we follow. As Jesus said: 'A student is not above his teacher but everyone who is fully trained will be *like* his teacher' (Luke 6:40 italics mine). Children inevitably copy their parents in ways that become an embarrassing self-revelation to the parents themselves. Like discipling, parenting is literally an imitation process. The learner does not usually get to know what the teacher knows. More important, the learner becomes *like* the teacher. But to imitate the only flawless person who has graced human history is an impossible ideal. The characteristic summons of Jesus to disciples was not 'Copy me', but 'Follow me.'

At no point can we turn, as Jesus did to those scrutinising his life, and say, 'Which of you convicts me of sin?' The struggle to imitate the perfect life of Jesus can even become a form of 'works' or achievement-righteousness as we strive towards an impossible ideal which becomes a supremely intolerable burden. The theologian P. T. Forsyth was right when he said that Jesus is either our supreme deliverer or our supreme burden. As exemplar he would be the latter if he demanded that we copy him. Our only hope would be the possibility that he is willing to live his own life through us. But before we explore this, we must look at one more misunderstanding.

Obeying Jesus
Some think that the disciple is not one who copies the master but rather does what the master requires.

There is profound truth in this. Following Jesus is both an experience *and an ethic*. But one wonders whether those who promote this as the essence of discipleship have understood the Gospels. The Sermon on the Mount (Matt 5–7) calls disciples to live with,

(1) extraordinary righteousness (exceeding that of the scribes and pharisees – 5:20);

(2) extraordinary respect for people (renouncing hatred – 5:21–26);

(3) extraordinary sexual fidelity (allowing no lust to enter our hearts – 5:27–30);

(4) extraordinary covenant loyalty (no divorce – 5:31–32);

(5) extraordinary integrity (being utterly reliable in our words, not needing oaths – 5:33–37);

(6) extraordinary generosity (through doing more than your duty and practising non-retaliation – 5:38–42);

(7) extraordinary hospitality (welcoming and loving our enemies and persecutors – 5:43–48);

(8) extraordinary generosity (giving generously *in secret* – 6:1–4).

After reading this, one not-yet-Christian concluded: 'As society is presently constituted, literal obedience to the commands of Jesus would mean instant death. The meek do not inherit the earth, at least not our kind of earth.' That is an overstatement, but one which is closer to the truth than pious comments about 'simply living by the Sermon on the Mount'.

There is no escape from the radical ethics of Jesus by taking refuge in the view that the teachings of Jesus are meant for some ideal Kingdom age in the future. Jesus concludes the Sermon on the Mount with these searching words: 'Everyone who hears these words of mine and does not do put them into practice is like a foolish man who built his house on sand. The rain came down, the streams rose, and the winds blew and beat against that house, and it fell with a great crash' (Matt 7:26–27). The ethics of Jesus demand a complete transformation. While perfection is never complete in this life, we must at least *start* being perfect because we are children of God (5:48). Indeed unless we become children of God by entering into a transforming relationship with Jesus, we cannot start. But this is the point: without relationship with Jesus the commands of Jesus are simply an impossible burden.

One could zealously imitate Jesus and attempt to obey his commands without being a disciple. Like the elder brother in the parable of the two prodigals, one could say self-righteously to the Father, 'Look! All these years I've been slaving for you and never disobeyed your orders' (Luke 15:29). The supreme tragedy of that 'good' man was that he worked hard and lived by the commands of the father, *but did not know the Father*. As an example of an 'almost Christian' the older brother shows us there is more to discipleship than imitating and obeying. There is knowing and being known in a relationship of belonging. I cannot think of any worse tragedy than to come to the end of one's life and be confronted with these devastating words of the God of the universe: 'I never knew you' (Matt 7:23).

Experiencing Jesus

We are now at the heart of the matter. Discipleship is a relationship with Jesus in which we taste some of his experiences and allow him to share ours. His life shapes ours. We live because he lives in us. For the disciple this involves tasting incarnation, transfiguration, crucifixion and resurrection.

In the Incarnation God became a human being, the Word became flesh and dwelt among us. God in Jesus went through a complete human experience from conception to resurrection. So Jesus meets us in the realities of our bodily life – work, leisure, family, and even our sleep. Christian spirituality discerns a transparency in the world and refuses a sacred–secular segmentation of life. We live for Jesus and he lives in us, at the very centre rather than at the religious perimeter of our lives. Jesus has placed himself irrevocably at our disposal, so much so that we actually minister *to him* when we open our hearts to the poor, the stranger and the imprisoned (Matt 25:31–46).

'As the Father has sent me, I am sending you' (John 20:21). This is the interior spirituality of the outgoing dimension of discipleship. Disciples are called to be 'with him' and 'to be sent out'. But the sending out is shaped by the Incarnation. Just as Jesus went out with all the resources of the Trinity to become enfleshed, embodied, and earthed, so he sends us out *with him* to present our whole lives as a living and spiritual sacrifice (Rom 12:1–2). Just as Jesus emptied himself of power and privilege to identify with the least, the last and the lost, so the Christian disciple will experience self-emptying as he or she lives in Christ (Phil 2:1–11). But there are some important differences.

When Jesus identified with us, he went down. He, as a divine, sinless being identified with humankind and with sinners. But when we identify with others, there is nowhere farther down to go. We are already human beings and sinners. While working with a friend in the inner city of Montreal where we tried to 'identify' with the poor, my friend expressed the difference eloquently.

> Identification for us is not so much a matter of going up or down to the level of another, but rather *conformity to the mind of Christ*. We are to seek identity not with men but with Christ ... Gazing into his face the Christian is changed into his likeness (2 Cor 3.18) ... While we talk about identifying with a class of people, we flee the yoke of Christ. Our identification with man is less of identification and more of condescension and self-congratulation. The problem then is not identification but humility ... Through the power of the love of Christ working in and through us, our pride can be transformed into his humility.

Incarnation is the first pattern of discipleship. The second is transfiguration. In his transfiguration (Luke 9:28–36),

Jesus communed with the Father in such a way than his very being glowed with beauty. This too is a pattern of our relational harmony with Jesus. As we follow Jesus we experience the transformation (Rom 12:1–2; 2 Cor 3:18) of our persons from inside out, often without our knowing this is happening. This comes as we behold his glory; others then behold his glory *through* us, like light passing through a Kodachrome transparency. When people look at us they may see little more than what is seen when someone looks at a coloured transparency. But when we live without mask or pretence and are held to the light of Christ, people can look through us to see something of the image of Christ. Paul referred to this in 2 Corinthians 3:18. 'And we, who with unveiled faces all reflect the Lord's glory, are being transformed into his likeness with ever-increasing glory, which comes from the Lord, who is the Spirit.' The disciple of Jesus is more like Jesus on the Mount of Transfiguration than he or she is like Moses on Mount Sinai, his face glowing temporarily with the presence of God (Exod 34:29–35). Incarnation – the first pattern – is followed by transfiguration – the second. But these led in our Lord's life to crucifixion – the third pattern.

In the crucifixion, Jesus gave up his life for others, bearing in his own person the sins of us all. As we follow Jesus we identify with his suffering for the sake of his body, even 'filling up that which remains of his suffering' (Col 1:24). Cross-bearing (Matt 16:24) is the Christian experience of life through death. It is neither martyrdom nor suicide. Rather it is discovering, through identification with Jesus and his interests, that reality of divine strength through weakness: 'For to be sure, he was crucified in weakness, yet he lives by God's power. Likewise, we are weak in him, yet by God's power we will live with him to serve you' (2 Cor 13:4; see also 12:9–10). By 'living on a personal cross' the disciple inverts the world's definition of success (Phil 3:10).

Thomas à Kempis reflects deeply on the place of the cross in the disciple's life.

Jesu hath many lovers of the kingdom of heaven but few bearers of the cross; he hath many who desire consolations and few desiring tribulations: he findeth many fellows of the table and few of abstinence.

All desire to joy in him; but few will suffer any pain for him.

Many follow Jesu unto the breaking of bread, but few unto the drinking of the cup of his passion.

Many worship his miracles but few follow the reproof of the Cross.[7]

Crucifixion is followed by resurrection, ascension and enthronement. As we follow Jesus we experience his lordship and permit his power to work in and through us (Eph 1:19–21), demonstrating that the new age has begun and anticipating our own resurrection, and the renewal of all things in Jesus in the age to come. The glorified scars on the resurrection body of Jesus are powerful symbols of what Christ will do to our own personal and emotional scars by his resurrection power as he makes all things new. This vision of the exalted Christ (and *not* the need of the world) is the primary source of Christian ministry and mission (Isa 6; Acts 7:56; 26:19).

What a revolutionary life the disciple is summoned to embrace! Dr Hocking was once professor of philosophy at Harvard University. He tells how, when he was an aspiring teacher of ethics, a student reminded him 'You cannot prove that a man ought to love his neighbour and if you could prove it, that would not in the least help him to do so'. The question that followed was an even keener thrust, Dr Hocking admits. 'I can understand,' the student went on to say, 'how Jesus or a Nietzsche could turn the world upside down. But I cannot understand how a college professor could turn the world upside down.' Dr Hocking agreed that the student was essentially right. It is precisely the business of Christianity to turn the world upside down by making revolutionary demands on motivation. What we have learned in this chapter is that the revolutionary demands are not made by standards, example or commands, but by the expulsive power of a new affection, by the inundation of our ordinary existence with the presence of the living Jesus. Only when I am certain that I am a disciple of Jesus and not a follower of followers, or an adherent to Christian principles, is it safe for me to hear the challenge of Thomas à Kempis' words – to become an imitator of Jesus.

With incredible courtesy Jesus stands at the door of the last sanctuary of our lives, the will. He gives us an invitation rather than a demand. Within certain limits we can do what we want with our lives. We are free to be engaged in a vocation that transcends all other vocations and makes revolutionary demands on our mind, our heart and our will. To neglect this gentleman at the door is also to make a decision. And as a perfect gentleman Jesus warns us that the life out of harmony with the Creator of the universe will be as costly, indeed even more costly than the invitation to take up our cross and follow. Kierkegaard once said that 'It costs a man just as much or even more to go to hell than to come to heaven. Narrow, exceedingly narrow is the way to perdition!'[8]

So what do we get out of following Jesus? The primary gain for the disciple is simply to be with Jesus and to be sent out with him! All the references to exchanging a lower life for a higher one (Matt 16:25), gaining treasure in heaven (19:21), gaining shared leadership with Jesus (19:27–30) and eternal life (Mark 10:28–31) are ways of expressing the benefit of being with Jesus. The disciple has his or her wish: to know Christ and to make him known.

Bonhoeffer calls this costly grace and compares it with the cheap grace of easy Christianity.

Cheap grace is grace without discipleship, grace without the cross, grace without Jesus Christ, living and incarnate.

Costly grace is the treasure hidden in the field; for the sake of it a man will gladly go and sell all that he has. It is the pearl of great price to buy for which the merchant will sell all his goods. It is the kingly rule of Christ, for whose sake a man will pluck out the eye which causes him to stumble, it is the call of Jesus Christ at which the disciple leaves his nets and follows him.

Such grace is *costly* because it calls us to follow, and it is *grace* because it calls us to follow *Jesus Christ* (italics mine). It is costly because it costs a man his life, and it is grace because it gives a man the only true life.[9]

CHAPTER THREE

TEMPLES OF THE HOLY SPIRIT

The date is probably AD 49. The Apostle Paul is writing what may well have been the first New Testament letter. And he asks the Galatians, a mix of Jews and Gentiles who have become believers in Jesus, a most arresting question. 'Let me ask you only this: Did you receive the Spirit?' (Gal 3:2).

He is clearly talking about the essence of being a Christian. Did you receive the Spirit? Are you sure of it? Many moderns are not at all sure of it, and they would regard the question itself as impertinent. For their part, the Galatians had been bewitched. They apparently thought they could live the Christian life by *doing* something, what Paul calls 'the works of the law'. They were regular in worship, orthodox in belief, moral in behaviour. Surely that will do? No doubt that is what they felt, along with many a modern churchman. And Paul bursts in, 'No, it will not do. You foolish Galatians. To be a Christian is not primarily to *do anything*. It is to *receive someone*, the 'lifegiving Spirit of God'. He is the indispensable gift that nobody can earn, yet all true Christians must possess.'

Paul is unambiguous on the matter. The indwelling Spirit of God is the hallmark both of the individual Christian and of the Christian assembly. In 1 Corinthians 6:19 he tells these converts from a very murky past that their bodies are the temples where the Spirit lives; while in 3:16 it is the church which he describes as the dwelling place of the Spirit. If anyone does not have the Spirit of God he is not a Christian, according to Romans 8:9. Thus the individual is the place where the Spirit dwells. But equally 'the whole structure [*sc.* of the Ephesian church] . . . grows into a holy temple in the Lord; in whom you also are built into it for a dwelling place of God in the Spirit' (Eph 2:21–22). The indwelling of the Spirit is the one indispensable essential both for the Christian and his church.

That claim was mind-boggling to Greeks and Hebrews alike. The Greeks could hardly imagine what was meant by the Spirit of God. For the Jew, it was beyond his wildest imaginings. Yet to the Christian it has become, thus early, the bottom line. How could that be? Let us start at the beginning.

The Spirit in the Old Testament

The word used for the Spirit in the Bible is significant, both in Hebrew and Greek. The same word does duty for wind, breath and Spirit. The Spirit is God's lifegiving breath without which man is inert. It is his mighty, mysterious wind which you and I, like Nicodemus, cannot understand let alone harness or organise. But we can feel and recognise its impact.

We can sharpen our picture of the Spirit in the Old Testament when we see what it is not.

It is not the same as the human spirit. There is a perfectly good word in Hebrew for that: *nephesh*, the 'spirit' that differentiates a live person from a corpse. But the 'Spirit of God', the *ruach Adonai*, is quite different from that.

Nor is it to be found in other religions. Attractive though that hypothesis is to many, it is nowhere taught in the Scriptures. They do not deny that there is some light in other faiths. But they never call that light 'the Spirit'.

No, we have to do with nothing less than the Spirit of the living God, Yahweh himself. There are a very few places where the Spirit may be associated with Yahweh in creation, such as Genesis 1:2 and Psalm 104:30; but these are all questionable. The main emphases about the Spirit in the Old Testament are as follows.

The Spirit is always God's gift. It is never an inherent quality in man himself. It comes on him from *outside*, from beyond.

Accordingly, it is often used of *empowering*. Gideon was a very ordinary man until the Spirit of the Lord came upon him (Judg 6:34). Samson's strength was nothing out of the ordinary until the Spirit of the Lord came upon him (Judg 14:6). Bezaleel was nothing to write home about until the Spirit came upon him, and he then became a fantastic craftsman (Exod 31:3).

But it was not just in power but in *revelation* that the Spirit was active. The word of the Lord (*dabar*) and the Spirit of the Lord (*ruach*) work together. God's Spirit is in the communication business. Thus 'The Spirit of the Lord speaks by me, his word is upon my tongue' (2 Sam 23:2). It is because of this essential link between the word and the Spirit of the Lord that the prophets claimed inspiration by God's Spirit as they spoke God's word (Isa 48:16; Mic 3:8; Zech 7:12).

There were three aspects of the Spirit's activity in the Old Testament which concern us particularly, since they anticipate both Jesus and the church.

The first is *servanthood*. The Spirit of the Lord was especially promised to the Servant of the Lord in those four great Servant Songs in Isaiah. 'Behold my servant, whom I uphold, my chosen in whom my soul delights; I have put my Spirit upon him' (Isa 42:1), or a similar passage outside the Servant Songs, 'The Spirit of the Lord God is upon me, because the Lord has anointed me to bring good tidings to the afflicted . . .' (Isa 61:1). Jesus claimed to fulfil both those passages in his ministry. He, the supreme Servant of the Lord, was uniquely equipped by God's Spirit.

The second is *kingship*. The king of Israel might expect to have God's Spirit (1 Sam 10:1, 6; 16:13), and although some kings were notably deficient in this area, the hope of Israel was that her coming great king would be equipped with his Spirit to a remarkable degree. This hope had been there a thousand years before Christ (2

Sam 7:14–16 was a much treasured text) and it persisted,
not only through the prophets (cf. Isa 11:1) but into the
intertestamental period. 'God will make the Messiah
mighty in the Holy Spirit' sang the *Psalms of Solomon*[1]
in the first century BC. The kings of Israel had often
disappointed. This king would not.

The third is *people*. In Old Testament days you had
to be rather special to have the Holy Spirit given you.
A prophet, a king, a very wise man, perhaps. But the
Spirit was not for the common man. Yet there was a
hunger for the gift of the Spirit to be poured out on all
God's people. Many a Jew must have felt how great it
would be if Moses' hope could be fulfilled: 'Would that all
the Lord's people were prophets, that the Lord would put
his spirit upon them!' (Num 11:29). And that is precisely
what some of the prophets foresaw for 'the last days'.
Thus Joel's prophecy (2:28) about the universality of
the gift of the Spirit came strikingly true on the Day of
Pentecost, and those present were well aware of it (Acts
2:17–18). Jeremiah cherished much the same hope, as did
Ezekiel. God's covenant with Israel kept getting spoiled
because Israel kept breaking it. So Jeremiah and Ezekiel
looked for the day when God would not only keep his side
of the covenant but empower Israel to keep hers. It would
be a day when they all knew God personally, when they
were aware that sins had really been forgiven, and when
they received the gift of the Spirit to internalise God's law
on their hearts so that obeying him would become like
second nature (Jer 31:31ff.; Ezek 36:25ff.). That was what
was wanted. A new covenant, where a new experience of
God's Spirit within man would warm his heart to want
to go God's way, and empower his will to do it. In due
course, all that came true.

But in the meantime there were three great disadvantages in human experience of the Spirit in the Old
Testament.

First, the Spirit was sub-personal. It was naked power,
wild, untamed, like the winds that roared down the desert
wadis.

Second, the Spirit was impermanent. It could be not only bestowed but removed, as both Samsom and Saul discovered (Judg 16:21; 1 Sam 15:26; 16:14).

Third, the Spirit was restricted. It was a gift for some of God's people, not all. The hope was, that on God's great day of deliverance for his people, the Spirit would be universalised.

The Spirit and Jesus

Jesus fulfilled all the Old Testament expectations and longings for the Spirit.

Jesus was *the unique man of the Spirit*. The Spirit 'rested' upon him at his baptism and stayed with him all his life (cf. John 1:32). In his baptism Jesus received the calling to be both the Son and the Servant of God, and for those dual roles he was mightily equipped by the gift of the Spirit coming upon him like a dove. The Spirit did not rest upon him in any limited way: he was filled with the Holy Spirit (Luke 4:1). No wonder this was unprecedented, for he was the messianic king. He was the suffering Servant. He was the prophet like Moses. All three strands of Old Testament prediction came to a head in him. In his own person he embodied the prophet, priest and king who had been most commonly recipients of the Spirit under the old dispensation.

Jesus was also *the unique dispenser of the Spirit*. John the Baptist saw this. He realised that Jesus would baptise people with the Holy Spirit (Mark 1:8 and parallels). 'Receive the Spirit,' Jesus says to his disciples in John 20:22. The Spirit which had so notably filled him is now to be given also to his disciples. The mission committed to him by the Father becomes their mission now – and they are going to need the Spirit without whom it cannot be attempted. For the mission and the Spirit belong together. And that is what John 20 and Acts 2 stress in their very different ways. If the Spirit is not in us, we cannot evangelise. If he is, we must.

The Spirit and the Church

When the Spirit came upon the earliest church on the Day of Pentecost, it became clear that the restrictions and disadvantages under the old covenant were gone.

The Spirit which in the Old Testament days had appeared subpersonal, almost naked power, was now seen to be clothed in the person of Jesus of Nazareth. The Spirit was 'the Spirit of Jesus'.

The Spirit which in the Old Testament days had been reserved for special people was now made universally available: the wide variety of people from across the world who were present at Pentecost is a notable feature of the account. The days of restriction are over.

The Spirit which in Old Testament days would come and go, dependent upon the recipient's spiritual state, was now a permanent resident in the lives opened up to him. He would never be withdrawn.

It is this Spirit – divine, personal, unwithdrawn and universally available – which was the parting gift of the ascended Jesus. The giving of the Spirit to his followers was the fruit of his death, resurrection and ascension. In the days of his flesh, 'the Spirit had not been given [to believers], because Jesus was not yet glorified' (John 7:39). But after his passion and Pentecost, the gift of the Spirit came to indwell the hearts and lives of all believers, as Jeremiah, Ezekiel and Joel had predicted so long ago.

Think of what that implies.

1. It means that your body is the shrine which God inhabits. The *skekinah* glory which was absent from the second temple, was wonderfully present in Jesus (John 1:14) and shines progressively in you (2 Cor 3:18).
2. It means that the Christian church at worship is the place where the Holy Spirit is longing to make himself known (Eph 2:22).
3. It means that God's new and everlasting covenant

with men and women is in operation and the hopes of the prophets of old have been fulfilled (Jer 31:31–34). Sins forgiven, God known personally, and his *torah* interiorised. Our Teacher dwells within!

4. It means that the Holy Spirit makes Jesus our contemporary – as real as he was to those first disciples. Jesus is God's last Word to man. What more could God add to personal self-disclosure through incarnation? And the function of the Spirit is not to give some new revelation of his own (we should distrust such pretended revelations) but to bear witness to Jesus, to make him real to us, and to draw out the implications of God's last Word. So the Spirit does for disciples all that Jesus did. He remains with them and guides them (John 14:16–18), leads them into all the truth (John 14:6,17) and continues to teach them (John 15:26; 16:13). What is more, the Spirit continues not only to comfort the disciples but to challenge the world, just as Jesus did. As Jesus predicted, the Spirit does show men and women they are in the wrong. Wrong with their moralistic ideas about *sin* (which is not so much infringement of God's rules as rejection of God's Son). Wrong with their ideas of *righteousness* – Jesus has been shown to be in a class of his own by his resurrection to the Father's side. And wrong, too, in supposing that *judgment* is either unreal or exclusively future: the decisive battle has been fought, and Satan is a defeated foe (John 16:7–11). In a word, what Jesus did and was, so the Spirit now is and does.

5. It means, too, that we are not worse off than the first disciples, but better off. Jesus was with them for a limited period of time. But the Spirit remains with us all the time (John 14:17–18). And to this extent we need never bewail our lot at not having been contemporaries with Jesus: the Spirit makes him our contemporary.

6. What is more, it means that we have a foretaste of heaven. The Holy Spirit is that part of God's future

who is already present: he is a first instalment of
all God has in store for us (Eph 1:13–14). He is
the seal and guarantee of our inheritance until we
acquire full possession of it. So we need never wait
unimaginatively for the parousia. We should rather
rejoice in the gift of the Spirit, the pledge that the last
days, inaugurated by the first advent of Jesus, will be
consummated at his return.

The Work of the Holy Spirit

Why has God chosen the amazing step of indwelling his
followers through the Holy Spirit? There are at least
seven answers to that question.

1. *To make us like Jesus*
That is the ultimate goal. He longs for us to be so
changed that we reflect his face. The Lord who is the
Spirit transforms us into the likeness of God's Son, full
of his life and power, his love and joy.

But where is the Spirit to start on this daunting task?

2. *To baptise us into Christ*
That is his stated purpose in 1 Corinthians 12:13. Baptism is always an initiatory rite in the New Testament.
And baptism 'in' or 'with' the Holy Spirit (the same
Greek preposition has both meanings) is the initiatory
Christian experience, not some high octane spirituality
into which some are initiated. There are just seven
references to being 'baptised in the Holy Spirit' to be
found in the New Testament, and they all speak clearly of
initiation. Matthew 3:11, Mark 1:8, Luke 3:16, and John
1:33 all contrast John's baptism in water with Jesus'
forthcoming baptism in the Spirit. Acts 1:5 is explicit in
its allusion to Pentecost, when they would for the first
time be plunged into the realm of the Holy Spirit. And
that was fulfilled a few days later when the Spirit which
had 'rested' on Jesus 'rested' on them too. It was the
beginning of a new life, life in the Spirit. Acts 11:16, the

sixth reference, is just as initiatory. The Gentiles receive
the same gift as Jewish believers had, all in fulfilment
of John the Baptist's prediction. Jesus is baptising them
with his Spirit. And it is just the same in 1 Corinthians
12:13. He, he alone, baptises us into Christ. That is why
the new birth is described, in John 3:3, 5, as brought
about through 'water and the Spirit'. Baptism is the
initiatory Christian action which we receive outwardly
on our bodies, just as the Spirit of Jesus is the initiatory
bearer of God's life to our souls. Baptism in the Spirit,
then, is never in the New Testament portrayed as a
sort of 'part two' initiation for some Christians. It is
the indispensable prerequisite for being a Christian at
all. God takes sinners and plunges them into the river of
his Spirit, irrigating the parched earth of our lives with
his living water.

3.   *To produce fruit of character in us*

That, of course, is the thrust of Galatians 5:22–23, the
famous passage about the quality of fruit the Spirit
produces. Notice that these are not individual fruits:
they are 'fruit', or 'a crop'. The singular is important.
For this is the crop that the Spirit will always produce in
us if we allow him, and do not quench him by disobedience
or neglect. Have you ever seen one of those apple trees
with four or five different varieties of apples on it? The
branches are grafted into the stock, but then the same
sap brings them all to fruitfulness. That is the variegated
crop of virtues which the Spirit wants to grow in us by
his sap.

4.   *To enable worship*

Worship is foreign to us sinful people. And part of the
function of the Holy Spirit is to enable us to enter into that
eternal self-giving, or ascribing of 'worth' which marks
the heart of the Trinity. The supreme quality of worship is
that it should be inspired by the Spirit (John 4:24). Then
worshippers become in truth 'a temple of the Spirit' and
'a place where God dwells by his Spirit'. That is one of

the reasons why prayer is so vital: it opens the way for the
Spirit to come into his own home and lead us in worship.
That is why openness to change is so important – it leaves
room for the Spirit to mould us and our worship. That is
why expectancy is so important as we come to worship:
it invites the Spirit to come and enliven us. Alas, there
is little prayerfulness, little flexibility, little expectancy
in many a church. The result? There is little evidence of
the Spirit.

5. *To inspire mission*

Mission and the Holy Spirit are inextricably linked. The
Lord knows it is so against our nature to reach out
to others that he offers his own love and power, his
own Spirit, to enable us to do so. Passages such as
Mark 13:9–13, John 15:26–27, and Acts 1:8 make that
very plain. So does Acts 10:38. 'God anointed Jesus of
Nazareth with the Holy Spirit and with power' for his
mission in the world. That takes us back to Isaiah 61:1
which Jesus claimed he was fulfilling. 'He has anointed
me to preach [the] good news' (Luke 4:18). In and through
Jesus, the Spirit, designed for Messianic days, the days of
salvation, had come to stay. He equips the disciples for
their mission, as he had Jesus for his.

Thus we find it is the Spirit who initiates the Christian mission constantly in Acts. Sometimes through a
committee (15:28), sometimes through a prophet (11:28),
sometimes through a trance (10:19), sometimes through
a community at worship (13:2), he inspires the mission of
the church. He is central throughout. He alone convicts
of sin. He alone makes Jesus glorious (John 16:8,14). It
is he who enables people to confess Jesus as Lord (1 Cor
12:3). He baptises people into Christ (1 Cor 12:13). He
brings about the new birth (John 3:8). It is he who gives
assurance to the infant Christian that he belongs in God's
family (Rom 8:15). He helps our weaknesses and aids our
prayers (Rom 8:26–27). From first to last it is all the work
of the Spirit.

Very well, then. Given the powerful link between the

Holy Spirit and outreach, mission and evangelism, two painful results flow. The modern church in the West knows so little about evangelism because it is so closed to the Spirit. And conversely, because it knows so little of the Spirit it knows so little of evangelism, for the Spirit is essentially given for that purpose. No evangelism – no Holy Spirit. No Holy Spirit – no evangelism. That is the brutal truth.

6. *To proffer gifts*

The Holy Spirit is the Giving Gift. It is he who gives us the equipment we need if we are to engage in the spiritual battle incumbent upon all followers of Jesus. The New Testament affords us many examples of these gifts. They are outlined for us (1 Cor 12:7–11, 28–30; Rom 12:4–13; Eph 4:10–12; 1 Pet 4:7–11) and we see them operating in the Acts as the early Christians work on their calling: tongues, healings, exorcisms, discernment, administrative gifts, leadership gifts, preaching and practical goodness of various kinds. No wonder Peter rejoices in the 'variegated love gifts of God' (1 Pet 4:10).

The whole subject of the gifts of the Spirit has been bedevilled in recent decades by the use of the word 'charismatic'. It has not made for lucid thinking. Three things need to be made clear.

First, nowhere does the New Testament differentiate between 'charismatic' and 'non-charismatic' gifts. To do so is to open a Pandora's box of jealousy, pride, divisiveness and seeking to gain certain gifts rather than seeking to live closer to the Giver.

Second, insufficient notice has been taken of the fact that the Greek word *charisma* is used only by Paul except for the single occurrence in 1 Peter 4:10. It is not even used anywhere in the Acts where you might well expect it to be.

Third, the word *charisma* is used by Paul of marriage and celibacy (1 Cor 7:7). These estates, one of which we all share, are designated 'gracious gifts of God' to us. Even more impressive is Romans 6:23 where, in contrast to the wages of sin, death, we are told that the free gift, *charisma*, of God is eternal life; and that is something in which all Christians share. So 'charismatic' is the last word that should ever have become the watchword of a movement!

But let us not argue about the word. Let us concentrate rather on the power, the vitality when the Spirit came. Acts 2 is as good a place to look as any.

- When the Spirit came, disciples received a new power to praise God and pray to him with confidence (2:11, 42, 47).
- When the Spirit came, disciples gained a new power over selfishness (2:44, 45). This took two notable forms. Instead of doing their own thing they were knit together in unity. And instead of holding on to their own possessions we find them sharing with one another in an unparalelled way.
- When the Spirit came, they had a new insight into the coherence and relevance of the Scriptures. A whole variety of Old Testament passages are quoted in that address of Peter's, and its major thrust is one of fulfilment: 'this is what was spoken by the prophet . . .' (2:16).
- When the Spirit came, the gift of tongues was given (2:4). That gift continued in the church, and still does.
- When the Spirit came, the disciples gained power to heal, at all events on occasion (3:7). Though Paul's 'thorn in the flesh' was not healed, and he had to leave Trophimus at Miletus sick, yet there are many examples of the healing power of God flowing through the early Christians. This too continues, and has had a remarkable flowering in our day.
- When the Spirit came, he opened up afresh the gift of prophecy which he had inspired in the prophets centuries ago. This gift is much in evidence in Acts (e.g. 11:27ff) but its prevalence is nowhere better shown than in 2:17ff. Peter is quoting Joel, but

the words 'and they shall prophesy' do not occur in that Old Testament passage. Yet they are seen by Peter to be such an inherent part of the new age which has dawned that with great naturalness he includes them!

- When the Spirit came there was a new joy and confidence in belonging to the company of Jesus' disciples. That shines out of every verse of Acts 2.
- When the Spirit came, ordinary fishermen and the like had the courage to get out on the streets and bear bold and confident witness to Jesus – something most churchmen find terrifyingly difficult. The first disciples faced fierce opposition cheerfully.

Further chapters in Acts reveal other gifts in operation. The gift of wisdom is very plain in the Apostolic Decree, and it is specifically attributed to the Holy Spirit (15:28). The gift of exorcism is powerfully at work in 16:18; 19:18ff. The gift of divine guidance through the Spirit is very plain in 16:6–10. The gift of knowledge through a dream or a vision comes from time to time, notably in 10:1–23.

We have here a mix of what today we would call 'charismatic' and 'non-charismatic' empowerings by the Spirit. It all goes to show how unwise it is to suppose there are nine spiritual gifts, no more and no less, and that they are defined exhaustively in 1 Corinthians 12! To that extent the Pentecostal emphasis is misplaced. But on the matter of the vital presence of the Spirit in the church, and our need to be daily filled with him, they have put the whole of Christendom in their debt.

7. *To fill us to the full*

If our body is the temple of the Holy Spirit, it is only natural for him to want to own it completely. If we are the field of the Spirit, naturally he wants to irrigate us so that we may be fertile. If we are, as some of the second-century writers put it, 'the lyre of the Spirit', he wants to play all manner of beautiful tunes on us. We are meant to be filled with the Spirit, no less. Indeed, we are so commanded

(Eph 5:18). And the Greek rubs the point home: it is a present imperative, and means that we must *go on being filled* with the Spirit. It is not so much a one-off crisis as a continual dependence.

What might it look like?

The context in Ephesians is very suggestive. A person full of the Spirit is a joyful person – someone it does you good to meet (5:19), a person with deep and radiant contentment. Such a person is full of praise and thankfulness both to God and to other people (v20). He or she is a humble person, always putting others first, particularly one's nearest and dearest, though that is often the hardest place of all (vv21ff). A person full of the Spirit will always be on the lookout to introduce others to the Lord (v16). And those full of the Spirit will be careful to allow no hint of moral darkness to cloud their living in the light of Jesus (v14). That is what it might look like.

Another approach is to glance at the five places in Acts where people are said to be filled with the Holy Spirit. They are illuminating.

The first is Pentecost (2:1ff) where profound praise and the gift of tongues are among the major characteristics.

The second concerns Peter (4:8). He needs, and receives, a new infilling with the Holy Spirit when he has to face perilous circumstances and give a bold witness.

The third occasion concerns the infant church (4:31). After intensive prayer they are filled anew with the Spirit so that they may bear bold testimony in dark days.

The fourth example is Saul of Tarsus (9:17). His blind eyes were opened by the Spirit and his empty life was filled.

The fifth occasion is the Elymas incident (13:9). As Paul bears witness against this powerful exponent of the occult arts, he is filled with the power of God and brings judgment on the sorcerer.

It is clear from all this that being filled with the Spirit is not a once-for-all and unrepeatable experience. We may – and should – be filled with the Spirit often in our Christian lives. Christians should always be full of the Spirit, as Jesus was (Luke 4:1), as Stephen was (Acts 6:5), as Barnabas was (Acts 11:24), as the Seven were (Acts 6:3). There is no way that we can be sinlessly perfect in this life, but being full of the Spirit should be our normal, settled condition. Alas, it is not. We sin. We get dry. We are often blind to his offer of grace.

And the marvel of it is that the Lord invites us to come back to him and be refilled with his gracious Holy Spirit. As we have seen, he will never leave us. But he may be like a visitor politely confined to the front room in the house of our lives. When we ask him to fill us, we offer him the bunch of keys which will open every room in the house, however embarrassing its contents. Think of a fountain pen: it runs dry, and then it can no longer write. I am often like that, and the trouble is I am so blind that I do not even realise I have run out of ink. That pen does not need an entirely new start. It is not utterly useless. It simply needs to be filled anew. And so do we. Or think of a boat with flapping sails, becalmed. They need to be filled with the wind. And we need to be filled daily, hourly with the wind of God, his gracious Spirit. Surely the whole heartbeat of New Testament spirituality is that each of us is the temple where the Holy Spirit lives. Come, let us allow him to possess his inheritance, and fill the temples he has deigned to inhabit!

CHAPTER FOUR

PEOPLE OF PRAYER

Bible searching and searching prayer go hand in hand. What we receive in the Book's message we return to Him with interest in prayer.
Prayer is, for us, paradoxically, both a gift and a conquest, a grace and a duty.
P.T. Forsyth

Prayer is difficult. A few giants of the faith say that prayer is as normal to them as breathing. But most of us find that prayer is like any other form of relational communion — it takes constant effort. One never feels that graduation from kindergarten has taken place. Prayer is not only difficult but, not surprisingly, it is largely unpractised even today. The growing interest in spirituality seems focused on spiritual enhancement and personal development rather than the conquest of God in prayer. We are a prayerless generation. Even preachers, whose business it is to pray, on the average pray only a few minutes each day. Some have given up praying completely. What relief can be brought to this famine of the soul?

In this chapter we will look for answers in the prayer life of Jesus, of the first disciples, of the Apostle Paul and John, the author of Revelation. What we need in order to counter prayerlessness is not burdensome exhortations or prayer patterns but a rediscovery of the source of Christian prayer. Prayer is communion, conversation and spiritual conquest. This must be voluntary and mutual, just as satisfying lovemaking between a husband

and wife cannot be compelled or reduced to a technique described in a manual. As we examine the prayers of Jesus, Paul and John we will discover that the source of our prayerlessness is not to be found in our lack of method or time but our inadequate grasp of the God with whom we commune. True prayer is not taught but evoked by the God who is Lover, Shepherd, Husband, Friend, Judge, Saviour, Visitor and Counsellor. We are drawn to prayer by the seeking Father and driven to prayer by our hunger for first-hand encounter with God. So we begin our enquiry by trying to 'get inside' the spontaneous prayers of Jesus to discover the possible sources of our own liberation in personal prayer.

Praying Spontaneously

The most revealing statement by Jesus about his life of prayer is simply, 'I and the Father are one' (John 10:30). Prayer for Jesus was not primarily a 'discipline' but the daily meat and drink of fellowship with the Father. Prayer is like friendship. As in friendship, prayer is not *for* anything at all, not even for 'answers'. It is for the relationship. It is for communion. What we are speaking about is not the natural or instinctive turning to God in a crisis – good as this is – but turning in faith to God moment by moment with the actual details of our life, and so praying without ceasing. To do this we must know the character of the one to whom we pray. The primary contribution of Jesus to the life of personal prayer is just this: he reveals the Father. As Forsyth says, 'God draws us out by breathing Himself in.'[1]

Jesus reveals a Father-God who is more willing to give than we are to ask, a God who invites us to come boldly, persistently and honestly (Luke 11:1–13). Equally importantly Jesus reveals that what God wants from our prayers is not the substance *but the relationship* implied in our praying. So there are probably no 'bad' prayers, and if there are, praying them is probably better than not praying at all. It is my hunch that praying even inadequate prayers places us in a spiritual position where God can teach us more about prayer. We learn to pray by praying. Were we to wait to be proficient we might never start. So we have every reason to be spontaneous when we pray and not to worry what God or anyone else thinks about the form of our prayers. God looks at the heart not the words of our prayers.

From the record in the Gospels one is hard-pressed to find Jesus 'organising' his prayer life. We are introduced to a person who continuously enjoyed spontaneity in the Father's presence. What apparently makes prayer to the Father spontaneous both for Jesus and for us, is not merely permission to come to him with an unplanned and personally composed speech. Even that could be a mere monologue delivered without reference to the audience. Rather, it is the Father's willing engagement of our whole person when we draw near him in prayer that liberates us from trust in the prayer's design, from guile, and from commercialism that would use prayer to strike a bargain with God. God not only permits the free expression of our inmost being but he evokes it. It matters not whether the vehicle of this expression is a time-tested liturgical prayer or something of our immediate composing. The substance is this: deep speaks to deep, and deep answers deep. P. T. Forsyth expressed this admirably: 'He who speaks to us also hears in us, because He opens our inward ear (Rom 8:15; Gal 4:6). And yet He is Another, who so fully lives in us as *to give us but the more fully to ourselves*. So our prayer is a soliloquy with God, a monologue *à deux*.'[2]

This deeper principle of spontaneity, involving the liberation of the person to relate authentically with God, is illustrated by the windows given to us in the Gospels on the spontaneous prayers of Jesus.

Enjoying God

There is the prayer of spontaneous joy. Jesus worshipped the Father in the Spirit at the return of the seventy disciples from a successful mission.

> At that time Jesus, full of joy through the Holy Spirit, said, 'I praise you, Father, Lord of heaven and earth, because you have hidden these things from the wise and learned, and revealed them to little children. Yes, Father, for this was your good pleasure. (Luke 10:21)

Recognising that the Father had not signalled the presence of his Kingdom by employing the theologians and established religious leaders but, rather, a motley collection of disciples, Jesus exulted in the wonder of God's ways. The text suggests, though it does not clearly say so, that Jesus may have spoken in a prayer language or in tongues on this occasion. He enjoyed the Father not in a mere hedonistic way but in the depths of his spirit. It was a joy that needed to be expressed.

In the Gospels Jesus is presented as nurturing his relationship with the Father by frequent, extended times of prayer alone on a mountain (Luke 6:12), in a solitary place (Mark 1:35), or in a private garden. On one such occasion he invited his 'inner circle' of disciples to be present. On the occasion of the transfiguration, Peter, James and John witnessed Jesus' majesty and joy in the Father as he prayed. We could speak of this as the *prayer of divine affirmation*.

Christians of the Orthodox persuasion especially prize icons of the transfiguration as this prayer-event forms an essential paradigm of the spiritual life. As we commune with God we are transfigured (2 Cor 3:18) just as Jesus was. Then, like the disciples we are inspired to become, in a limited way, 'eye-witnesses of his majesty' (2 Pet 1:16), so ministering out of who we are becoming in Christ and not merely delivering words we have heard.

The liturgy for the Feast of the Transfiguration contains some insightful words about the connection of the disciples' experience of Jesus and their own future ministry. Reflecting on the presence of Moses and Elijah who spoke with Jesus about the 'departure [*exodus*], which he was about to bring to fulfilment in Jerusalem' (Luke 9:31) we are invited to pray:

> Having uncovered, O Saviour, a little of the light of Thy divinity to those who went up with Thee into the mountain, *Thou has made them lovers of Thy heavenly glory*. Therefore they cried in awe, 'It is good for us to be here.' ... Thy disciples beheld Thy glory, O Christ our God, as far as they were able to do so that when they saw Thee crucified, *they might know Thy suffering was voluntary*, and might proclaim unto the world that Thou art truly the Brightness of the Father.[3] [italics mine]

Trusting submission

Transfiguration and crucifixion are closely linked. After Jesus completed the Last Supper he went with his disciples to the Garden of Gethsemane to pray before his arrest, trial and crucifixion (Matt 26:36–46). This prayer, in the presence of the disciples, illustrates perfectly that the relationship of the Son to the Father was one of voluntary submission and not involuntary obedience or compliance. Firstly Jesus addresses God each time as 'My Father'. The Aramaic *Abba* also includes the idea of a child's familiar access to a father, though it expresses a deeper respect and loyalty than is normally communicated by our use of 'Daddy'. The biblical basis of seeking God's will is the supremacy of our heavenly Father who knows better than we do what we need. So to pray, 'thy will be done', as Jesus does here, is to decide not to ask God to embrace our will. Forsyth suggests, 'Nothing would do more to cure us of a belief in our own wisdom than the granting of our eager prayers.'[4]

Further, to desire to do God's will is not the same as blindly submitting to the inexorable will of God.

In this matter Jesus models humility and true meekness, which is more God-honouring than it is self-depreciating. In the garden prayer Jesus freely expresses all that is on his heart to the Father, always affirming that his central desire is that the Father's will be done. He explores with the Father what drinking the cup of suffering might mean and asks if there is any way for the cup to be taken from him. There is struggle in this prayer and only a misdirected reverence for the divinity of Jesus can ignore it. As Jacob discovered long before (Gen 32:22–30), those who fight with God receive blessing while those – like Esau – who do not care enough for the blessing of God to fight for it never know communion with him. Therefore the anonymous author of Hebrews later reflects that Jesus was superbly equipped to be our human and divine high priest because he was tempted at all points as we are in moments like this (Heb 5:7–10; 4:15). As Jesus prays he freely agrees with the Father's will. But he does so as a matter of submission rather than compliance. Compliance in marriage and in prayer is a psychological adaptation to avoid pain. But there is always a sliver of resentment in the compliant person; there is no such sliver in the heart of Jesus. One reason is the remarkable candidness with which he explored the options of his own heart with the Father. Behind this deep spontaneity is the trustworthy Father who invites such a conversation around a will (his) that *could* be imposed, but is not.

Father, forgive them

The same freedom is revealed on the cross. 'Jesus said, "Father, forgive them, for they do not know what they are doing"' (Luke 23:34). This prayer reveals his mediatorial, saving work even for those who were instruments of his crucifixion. It also reveals his unsullied integrity. He had earlier taught that we should 'pray for those who ill-treat [us]' (Luke 6:28). It is hard to believe this prayer was premeditated. But Jesus had been prepared to pray this by living a life of prayer. Taken with his spontaneous ministry to the repentant thief at his side (23:43), Jesus' prayerful responses to the violence of crucifixion are profoundly significant, especially as the prayer from the cross indicates.

The cry of dereliction on the cross (Matt 27:46) is also a window onto the interior life of Jesus, now darkened by the full weight of our sin, and therefore alienation from the Father. He became 'sin' for us that we might become in him the righteousness of God (2 Cor 5:21). 'My God, my God, why have you forsaken me?' is an obvious quotation from Psalm 22, the paradigmatic prayer of the innocent sufferer who finds his vindication and deliverance in God, even in face of death. Jesus turns to God in his darkest moment, speaking God's own word as a prayer, and, in Luke's account, commits his spirit to Father as a final act of prayerful trust (Luke 23:46), a prayer that is echoed in the prayer of Stephen the first Christian martyr (Acts 7:59). As with all true prayer there is paradox here as well. Luther is said to have exclaimed, 'God forsaken by God! Who can understand this?'

These glimpses into the prayer life of Jesus are highly evocative. The God and Father of Jesus Christ is one to whom we can pour out all our thoughts and concerns, our joys and our sorrows, our ecstasy and our anger, knowing that a faithful God will sift out the wheat and, with a breath of kindness, blow the chaff away. God is Father, Shepherd, Lover, Judge and Saviour waiting to vindicate us (Luke 18:14). A wise answer was once given to the age-old question, 'If God is as good as you say, and knows what we need before we ask, then why should we need to ask?' The answer is deep. What if God knows that what we need more than anything is himself? And what if asking for things and pouring out our hearts about our needs and decisions is God's chosen vehicle for giving us what we most deeply need – though we may not know it at first?

Praying Corporately

Most of the prayers of Jesus recorded for us are solitary prayers. But solitary prayer is not really an individual activity. We are never alone when we pray *to* the Father *in the name* of Jesus *through* the Spirit. Solitude invites communion with God, in contrast to loneliness, even loneliness in prayer, which is the excruciating experience of personal isolation. Ironically, among the prayers of Jesus only the prayer of dereliction from the cross seems to be a lonely prayer. But even in this prayer – wrung from his priestly heart on our behalf as he takes our sin upon himself – Jesus had the joy of restored fellowship with the Father in view (Heb 12:2). In contrast, Jesus warns against real loneliness in prayer for those who 'parade' their prayers to impress their human listeners. These get their reward *now*, in contrast to those who pray 'in the closet' (seemingly alone) but who get the implied greater reward, the presence and affirmation of God himself (Matt 6:5–8). The first, like the Pharisee in the parable, may turn out to be praying either 'with' himself or 'to' himself (Luke 18:11) even though onlookers may be duly impressed. But corporate prayer includes both the Lord and other believers. True corporate prayer is encouraged by Jesus when he gave us the 'Our Father' prayer (Matt 6:9–13; Luke 11:1–13). While it is often called 'the Lord's Prayer' it is more accurately described as 'the Disciples' Prayer'.

The Disciples' Prayer

There are at least two remarkable features of the origin of this perfect prayer. One is that it originates in the disciples observing Jesus at prayer himself (Luke 11:1). The second is the fact that this prayer arose as a response to the request of his disciples to be taught to pray as John the Baptist taught his disciples. Luke's Gospel – written for a Gentile constituency – views the prayer as offered to teach them to pray. Matthew's Gospel – written for a Jewish constituency – sees the prayer as teaching the disciples to pray aright. In both cases Jesus responds to the request, 'Teach us to pray' by saying, in effect, 'Let us pray!' We learn to pray by praying, by *praying* like this, not merely by praying *this*.

In A. B. Bruce's classic examination of the Lord's training the disciples in prayer, Bruce notes that Jesus dealt with the three 'wants' that shut down our prayers: a lack of ideas, of words or of faith. The Lord's Prayer, he says, forms 'the alphabet of all possible prayer. It embraces the elements of all spiritual desire, summed up in a few choice sentences, for the benefit of those who may not be able to bring their struggling aspirations to birth in articulate language.'[5] If the Disciples' Prayer teaches us how to pray, the true Lord's Prayer teaches us why.

In John chapter seventeen we are permitted to overhear the actual prayer of Jesus. This is actually 'the Lord's Prayer', though the Lutheran theologian David Chytraus (1531–1600) gave this prayer the title, 'the high priestly prayer'. The title 'stuck' for good reasons.

The Lord's Prayer
Speaking of this magnificent prayer, Milligan and Moulton describe some of the qualities: 'No attempt to describe the prayer can give a just idea of its sublimity, its pathos, its touching yet exalted character, its tone at once of tenderness and triumphant expectation.'[6]

In passing we notice that, unlike the incident in John 11:41–42 where Jesus prays out loud for the edification of his disciples, the high priestly prayer was prayed not to give an example to his disciples but because *Jesus wanted and needed to pray*. This is all the more remarkable when one believes, as the authors of this book believe, that Jesus was both man and God. God praying to God! But if God is Father, Son and Holy Spirit, dwelling in a family of covenant love, and if prayer is the way that one person communes with another person, then for Jesus to pray is divinely reasonable. Further, the Lord's Prayer shows us the social and relational nature of prayer. This prayer more than any other demonstrates that we are least alone when we pray.

In each of the sections of this prayer in John 17 Jesus begins with a statement (he speaks about someone) and then moves into a petition (he speaks on behalf of someone). This structure is significant. The Christian life moves from the indicative to the imperative, from what *is* to what *should* be. In communion with God we should move from certainties to concerns, from worship to petition.

In the first section (17:1–5) Jesus prays for himself. 'Father, the time has come. Glorify your Son, that your Son may glorify you.' Among the many remarkable dimensions of this prayer is the fact that Jesus prayed for himself *without a shred of selfishness*. Here is petition without self-centredness.

In the second section (17:6–19) Jesus prays for the disciples. The disciples *belong* to God. 'They were yours; you gave them to me' (17:6). In response to the statement of Jesus, 'all you have is mine' (17:10), Luther is reported to have said, 'This no creature can say with reference to God'. As high priest Jesus prays not that they will be taken *out* of the world (17:15) but that they will be protected from the evil one, while they are *in* the world.

In the final section (17:20–26) Jesus prays for all future disciples. Others will believe in Jesus through the message of the first disciples. Of all the things he could have prayed for the believers who would follow, it is remarkable that his petition focuses on unity: 'that all of them may be one, Father, just as you are in me and I am in you. May they also be in us so that the world may believe that you have sent me' (17:21). The deepest prayer of Jesus on the way to the cross, when his hour had come (12:23; 17:1), is that his disciples will experience Trinitarian unity (17:21, 23). This was his priestly passion in prayer; it could well become our passion, especially in corporate prayer.

Trinitarian unity is not 'mashed potato' unity, as someone tried to describe it, in which the individual identities of believers are lost in a great social merger. Not so. Each is more himself by being in unity. God the Father, Son and Holy Spirit who invite us to join *their unity* dwell in a complex fellowship in which each is for the other but all are for the One. The Orthodox theologian Tomas Spidlik notes that within Orthodox spirituality 'the divine Trinity is the fundamental mystery of the Christian faith'. Spidlik says that 'only the Christian revelation teaches the highest and most intense union as embracing that which in the finite realm divides and is a principle of division: personality.'[7] In other words, God is one, not in spite of being three, but *because* he is three. Christian experience means being included in the unity of the Trinity, participating in the mutual love, order and interdependence of the three Persons of the Trinity. Speaking of this, James Houston says, 'to know the triune God is to act like Him, in self-giving, in interdependence and in boundless love.'[8] In this way John allows us to view discipleship to Jesus as a transcendent experience in prayer.

In the Synoptic Gospels (Matthew, Mark and Luke), disciples of Jesus are presented as being with him and being sent out by him. In those days of his earthly ministry this involved having physical proximity with him, joining his company, observing his lifestyle, hearing his words, and sharing in the healings and controversies that surrounded him. But John presents discipleship as the privilege of being included in the life of the Father, the Son and the Holy Spirit, not merely doing what Jesus asks or hearing what he says. To be *with* Jesus means to be drawn into the mystery of God, and to be sent out in mission with all the resources of the Holy Trinity (John 20:21). Far from being alone when we pray together, it, perhaps more than any other, shows us the true nature of corporate prayer. It is not merely speaking a prayer out loud in the presence of other believers, or even saying the same words of a prayer in unison. Corporate prayer is prayer that takes us into the corporate life of God and, through the Lord's continuing high priestly intercession, invites us to discover our common life as disciples in him. Corporate prayer has as its goal knowing God (17:3), and therefore results in embracing God's goal for us – unity.

This brings new meaning to the phrase 'the love of God'. To confess 'God is love' (1 John 4:16) is not merely to describe an attribute of God but to confess the affectionate loyalty that exists within God himself, a love which Jesus enjoyed even before the world was created (John 17:24). The world was created through that love and literally runs on love. *Agape*-love cannot mean simply 'love for the unlovely' because God's love is expressed first of all to God. The overflow and fruit of that love produced the world and us! As we continue to allow this love to inundate our lives – for this must surely be one of the main fruits of prayer – we can realistically experience Christian unity on the micro-level by valuing and respecting every believer, no matter what his or her station in life, personal gifting, or personality. On the macro-level Jesus' prayer invites believers to seek visible and heart unity with believers in all parts of the church. They do this in order that the world might believe in the divinity of Jesus (17:21,23). As A. B. Bruce notes, 'nothing but a divine influence could thus subdue the centrifugal forces that tend to separate men from each other'.[9] What has become of Jesus', and our own, prayer for unity?

The church's prayers
As we turn briefly to the rest of the New Testament, we note both the communal *practice* of the first generation of disciples, and the communal *content* of the prayers which were meant to be shared as communal prayer. On the first, it appears that the Lord prayed in the Temple. We can assume this from Luke 18:10 and from his presence at festivals like the Passover where he would sing the Hallel (Mark 14:26). In the Acts of the Apostles the first disciples continued the Lord's practice by daily attending the Temple for prayer (Acts 2:46). More remarkable still is the extended prayer meeting in the Upper Room following the Lord's ascension. The disciples waited in

prayer for the promised Holy Spirit. 'They all joined together constantly in prayer, along with the women and Mary the mother of Jesus, and with his brothers' (1:14). It is a fascinating question to consider *what* they prayed for and *how*.

The early church undoubtedly used the psalter as the prayer book of the church (Eph 5:19; Col 3:16). But the content of these corporate prayers (Acts 1:14,24; 2:42,47) is not revealed until we are given a compressed summary of the prayers offered when Peter and John were released from imprisonment by the Sanhedrin and returned to the waiting disciples. 'They raised their voices together in prayer to God' (4:24). This prayer purportedly uttered together and out loud is a remarkable combination of Scripture, thanksgiving and petition. I do not think it necessary to assume that this spontaneous prayer, obviously not in the psalter and undoubtedly not composed in some written manual, was uttered simultaneously by the whole group in perfect unison with no premeditation. More likely we have a summary of prayers offered out loud by various ones who, being led by the Spirit in their prayers, contributed to a symphony of prayer on a single theme.

The prayer starts as a typical Jewish prayer and then, quoting the second Psalm, marvels at the paradoxical meaning now apparent to them, that whatever the enemies of Jesus do against Jesus and his followers can only *further* God's pre-ordained purpose in Jesus. Herod, Pilate, the Gentiles and the Jews, all unwittingly served God! So, following Jesus' pattern of moving from certainty to petition, these believers now bring their requests. They *do not ask for protection*, or grace to obey the command 'not to speak or teach at all in the name of Jesus' (4:18). Rather they pray, 'Now, Lord, consider their threats and enable your servants to speak your word with great boldness. Stretch out your hand to heal and perform miraculous signs and wonders through the name of your holy servant Jesus' (4:29–30). These early disciples asked that they might identify boldly with the continuing service of God's Suffering Servant. We know they were heard because of the physical shaking of the room, the manifest filling of the Spirit and their empowerment to speak the word boldly, the very thing they requested. They asked what God wanted and were given what they most deeply wanted. Such is the mystery of wills in prayer. Undoubtedly, the timid church today is not praying this way.

This case-study in early church corporate prayer is a powerful illustration of the promise Jesus gave: 'Again, I tell you that if two of you on earth agree about anything you ask for, it will be done for you by my Father in heaven. For where two or three come together in my name, there am I with them' (Matt 18:19-20). Corporate prayer is not merely prayers said together in unison but prayers made together in which God himself, through the Spirit, orchestrates and harmonises the various contributions made by individual members of the body of Christ. Corporate prayer takes us into the social life of God himself. Corporate prayer is not unified speech but persons who are discovering unity while they pray. In the light of this much that passes for corporate prayer is promiscuous, not in the sexual sense but in its relational depth: it is idle verbal chatter in the context of superficial if not anonymous relationships.

Christian unity, as we have seen in the high priestly prayer, is not something believers must achieve among themselves in order to get God's work done. It is the work God is doing among believers. This principle is illustrated not only in the *practice* of the early disciples but in the *content* of the prayers of the Apostle Paul.

Paul's prayers in Ephesians (1:3-23; 3:14-21) are passionate prayers for unity. He longs that the Ephesian Christians will know who they are in Christ *together*. Laced throughout the letter is Paul's sense of vocation, to be a steward of the mysterious and transcendent unity of Jew and Gentile in Christ (3:6), making a new humanity (2:15). In chapter four he starts with the 'given' unity the Ephesians have in God the Father, Son and Holy Spirit

(4:3–6) and then prays that godly leadership will equip the church to attain 'unity in the faith and in the knowledge of the Son of God' (4:13). Spiritual gifts (4:11–12) are given precisely so that the church will attain a deeper unity.

Paul's prayer for and exhortation to the Ephesians is not directed to a bouquet of individual believers, each needing edification and equipping, but rather to the body. So he prays that 'Christ may dwell in your hearts through faith' and 'that you, being rooted and established in love, may have power, *together with all the saints*, to grasp how wide and long and high and deep is the love of Christ' (3:17–18 italics mine). We read this prayer as a prayer addressed to God on behalf of our individual hearts but Paul prayed that for the community. For Paul, individual Christians, in the isolated Western sense, do not exist. If we are in Christ at all, we are in Christ together, even if we come one by one. The believer cannot be filled with the fulness of God (3:19), be filled with the Spirit (5:18), or have the mind of Christ (1 Cor 2:16) alone, but only together with other believers.

So, once again, unity is not a means of mobilising, to get God's mission going on earth. Unity *is* his mission. As we have already seen, spontaneous personal prayer to the Father, through the Son and by the Holy Spirit, is corporate because we are being included in the life of the Trinity. What makes prayer truly corporate is the divine Conductor orchestrating the praying community to find a common mind and life through the unifying process of their prayer. There is a divine synergy in this, not only because the whole of the believing community is more than the sum of the individual parts, but because when we pray together we are drawn into the prayers of our heavenly high priest (Heb 4:14) and the Spirit's interpretive intercession (Rom 8:26–27). So we are most Christ-like and most united when we are together in our prayers. There is much wisdom in the old maxim that the church moves forward only on its knees.

Until now we have been examining the prayers of Jesus, the early disciples and the apostles to discover a prayer spirituality. We tried to get inside the Lord's prayer life to discover the source of his spontaneity. We found that source in the Father who as a loving and righteous judge (Luke 11:11–13; 18:9–14) inspires the disciples to approach him with expectancy and childlike candour. In the same way we examined the corporate prayers of the early church. We found that these too are inspired by the character and communal love of the triune God. But now we must explore one final dimension of truly Christian prayer: it takes us to the last book of the New Testament.

Praying Imaginatively

The Apocalypse of John (the Revelation) ushers us into a world of dragons, beasts, angels, cosmic catastrophes and martyrs chanting hymns. We are swept from one riveting vision to the next as we are transported from heaven to earth and back again, in an upstairs–downstairs drama. Bowls of judgment are poured out on the earth while cringing multitudes call on the hills to cover them from the wrath of the Lamb. There is a final battle, a wonderful wedding supper, and an exquisite garden city. Understanding all this is complicated by the fact that apocalypse is a lost literary genre to the modern Western Christian.

Apocalyptic prayer

Apocalypse was to the first century what science fiction is to the twentieth. Imagine trying to explain science fiction to a first-century tentmaker in Ephesus, or apocalypse to a cab-driver in Boston, Toronto or London. Comparisons may, however, be made. The Revelation of John can be compared with a dissolve-fade slide show (the Lion dissolves into a Lamb standing as though slain), a drama (organised in dramatic form with overlapping sequences of seven seals, trumpets and bowls, with the major pastoral messages offered at the moments of maximum dramatic intensity), or a symphony (it has more songs than all the rest of the New Testament). But none of these comparisons does justice to the unique form of literature that flourished between 200 BC and AD 100.

John uses apocalypse to help people to pray. He wants people to learn to pray and worship on the job, in the marketplace, at the trade-union meeting, in a neighbour's house. So John presents a thoroughly 'lay' spirituality, intended for ordinary Christians compelled to worship Caesar in Pergamum, and Christian bronze-workers in Thyatira struggling with the orgies and idol feasts of the pagan guilds to which they were forced to belong (Rev 2:20–26). Lay spirituality must deal not only with the ecclesiastical life (Rev 2–3) but with power, politics, economics, marketing, and social responsibilities in secular or religious society. This John does. The stillness he seeks is not quietude but the triumphant voice of God himself as in Psalm 46:10 – in the context of our conflict-ridden life in this world. God commands all the powers of evil: 'Be still, and know that I am God.' In this case stillness is discovered right in the centre of life rather than at its circumference.

John demonstrates this by pulling back the curtain of 'normal' perception to let us see a transcendent reality that is actually present in our everyday existence, to see *through* the eye, as Blake proposed, not merely with it. The Lamb has triumphed even though the Harlot appears to reign supreme. Heaven, for John, is not up there, or later, but bursting into the here and now. He shows us how the world looks to a person in the Spirit. Its 'otherworldly' atmosphere is precisely what makes it so relevant when the church is facing persecution from a hostile culture or is being seduced by a friendly culture. It tells us that behind either hostility or seduction is a sinister personage called the beast that is really Satan's puppet. Behind that, is the plan and purpose of God who is already overruling (13:7; 17:17) and will eventually be seen to rule everything (19:1). The Revelation is much more than a book of predictions. It provides our praying spirits with an imaginative vision of the realities that will evoke prayer and consistent living, realities associated with the second coming of Jesus.

The praying imagination

Revelation is to the second coming of Jesus what the Ignatian exercises and inner healing prayer are to the first coming of Jesus: they involve an imaginative presentation of the affective, emotional, and spiritual meaning of the appearance of Jesus in a way designed to evoke a deep and personal encounter with him. This cannot be done without imagination. Indeed Cheryl Forbes says 'We cannot have faith (belief in what is unseen) unless we have imagination; imagination is the vehicle through which faith is expressed.'[10] Our prayers are often fitful and half-hearted because we cannot 'see' the One to whom we pray, and we cannot envision what we are praying about.

A story is told about a kindergarten teacher who asked a boy what he was drawing. Without pausing to look up he said, 'A picture of God.' The teacher smiled and responded, 'But nobody knows what God looks like.' The boy carefully put down his crayon, looked her squarely in the eye, and declared, 'After I am finished here they will.' There is more than a half-truth in the child's boldness. But it is not only fear of idolatry that makes this story hard to accept as anything more than a 'figment' of a child's imagination.

Since the Renaissance, the Industrial Revolution and the advent of high tech society, our lives have been de-imaged and stripped of imagination. This is tragic, not only because of the aesthetic loss this entails for our personhood, but because of the loss, more critically, to our faith. Imagination relates to our essential dignity as made in the 'image' of God (Gen 1:27). We are a visual and social metaphor of God himself. Human beings are God's imagination incarnated, icons of God, just as Christ was his Word incarnated. God expressed his glory in creation not primarily through propositions but persons with imaginations. Mystery can be understood only through

imagination. So Jesus, who is God's perfect image, used
metaphors and images to express the deepest truths
about God, himself and the Kingdom. And John in Revelation uses imagination to invite prayerful participation
in Christian hope and radical discipleship. S. S. Fiorenza
suggests, 'The strength of Revelation's language and
images lies not in the theological argumentation or historical information but in their evocative power inviting
imaginative participation.'[11]

With marvellous reserve John describes the throne of
God, and the effects of God's presence without actually
describing God, the indescribable, thereby enlarging our
faith without seducing us into idolatry (4:1–5). 'Come,
Lord Jesus' (22:20) is the epicentre of prayer in this book,
yet the prayer is evoked not by persuasion or doctrinal
instruction but by an imaginative presentation of all the
realities associated with the second coming of Jesus. The
repeated exhortation, 'He who has an ear, hear', is a call to
converse with God imaginatively. John evokes prayer not by
telling us to pray, but by appealing to our imaginations to
grasp the transforming beauty of the Lord's final victory. He
invites us to join the angels, the living creatures, the elders
and the believing multitude to shout, 'Hallelujah! For our
Lord God Almighty reigns' (19:6). Equally remarkable is
the fact that Revelation encourages us to attend to God in
prayer by envisioning a God who attends to us; God keeps
a half-hour silence in heaven to receive the prayers of the
saints (8:1–4). If that does not bring us to our knees then
nothing in heaven or on earth can!

Praying spontaneously. Praying corporately. Praying
imaginatively. It is not tacking 'in the name of Jesus' on
the end that makes a prayer Christian. Rather, Christian
prayer is evoked by the God and Father of Jesus Christ,
to come to him through Jesus, as we are equipped to do
so by the unseen prayer-companion in our heart – the
Spirit. True prayer, as James Houston says so clearly in
The Transforming Friendship is simply friendship with
God, communion-prayer for God's sake.

A true friend can never have a hidden motive for being a friend. He can have no hidden agenda. A friend is simply a friend, for the sake of the friendship. In a much greater way, love for God is love for God's own sake. Bernard of Clairvaux wrote that our natural inclination is to love for our own sake. When we first learn to love God, we still love him for our own sake. As we grow in friendship with God, we come to love him not just for ourselves alone, but also for God's sake. At last, we may reach the point where we love even ourselves for the sake of God.[12]

CHAPTER FIVE

PARTNERS IN THE FELLOWSHIP

If ever a word has been devalued, this is it. 'The fellowship hour' after church turns out to be ten minutes worth of watery coffee which most of the congregation have skilfully evaded. 'Where do you fellowship?' means 'Where do you go for an occasional hour to hear the choir sing and the minister preach?' It all tends to be very superficial. We in the West know very little of sharing our lives in deep and costly fellowship. Our consumerism infects our religion. We even pick and choose our place of worship: there is often no lasting commitment to it. We know little of having our hearts deeply knit to others, not only because of our hedonism but also because of our independence. This determination to paddle our own canoe lies behind our entrepreneurial attitude to business and our take-it-or-leave-it attitude to the church. If we have a serious disagreement with the leadership, in England we opt out: in North America we go and found our own church. Consequently we know little of sharing the joys and sorrows, the strains and triumphs of our fellow Christians. We tend to live in our little box of a house, keeping ourselves pretty much to ourselves, watching our James Dobson tapes about the development of the nuclear family, and giving little consideration to the quality of life that can be found in the family of God.

It was not always thus in the Christian church, nor is it still in many parts of the Two-Thirds World, particularly in the great continent of Africa where they would never dream of putting their old folks in an Old People's Home, or their orphaned or illegitimate children in a Children's Home.

Imagine the scene at the very start of the Christian movement. Here are twelve men in an upstairs room, celebrating the strangest of passover meals: the lamb is not on the dish but at the head of the table! The meal, though mysterious, sad and very special, marks the climax of three years' shared life on the road, through the countryside, in the boat. Years when they had laughed and cried, prayed and toiled together. That was Christian fellowship – so deep, so committed, that when one of them left it they for ever remembered with ignominy the name of Judas.

Or come with me to one of the homes in Jerusalem in AD 33. It was a hotbed of love and sacrifice, of sharing and thoughtfulness. The nearest I have seen to the teaching and fellowship, the breaking of bread and prayers that marked these first Christians was a cell of the Christian counter-culture in Toronto in the sixties, where nobody had any personal possessions, and love simply overflowed. Two people broke that Jerusalem fellowship in a surreptitious way. It would not have been noticed in today's church. Nobody would even have gone round to visit the two people in question. But such a contrast did they present to the quality of fellowship in that earliest church that the whole world knows the shame of Ananias and Sapphira.

Or let us join a group sitting relaxed under a tree in the midday sun of Miletus, on the coast of Turkey. A weatherbeaten, hook-nosed, dark-eyed Jew with a wonderful smile and large, workworn hands, is deep in conversation with a number of men who look at him with a mixture of awe and deepest admiration. 'I have been with you three years,' he says. 'These hands have ministered to my needs and to those who were with me.' And he commissions them to care for the flock of God over which the Holy Spirit had made them overseers. That is Christian fellowship.

Or let us share in the hospitality of a large country

house at Colossae, in the glen of the Lycus valley. An aristocratic lady and her sunburned, distinguished-looking husband are entertaining a crowd of believers, many of them off their estate, in their roomy farmhouse. There has been wine by the fountain in the courtyard, dinner in one of the rooms overlooking it, and then they turn to welcome the guest of honour for the evening, Tychicus, who comes with news and letters from their dear, imprisoned friend, Paul. He brings with him one of the slaves which all great estates had in those days, Onesimus. He had robbed his master, run away, and landed up in prison with St Paul, who led him to Christ and then sent him back to his old master, in the company of Tychicus and a covering letter, the Epistle to Philemon. This was a tremendous risk to take. Torture and death awaited a runaway slave, if caught. But Onesimus is welcomed back with a hug by Philemon, his master. He had left in darkness and theft. He returns as a beloved brother in Christ. Only the Jesus fellowship made something like that possible. There was nothing to rival it anywhere in antiquity.

Of course, there were various different expressions of fellowship in the ancient world. Athens in the fifth century BC had almost invented it, with its *polis* and its democracy. But disenchantment set in, as it did with Jewish institutions. The ordinary people were excluded from meaningful relationships and from any exercise of real power. Increasingly, therefore, if you were a Jew in the ancient world, you resorted to one of the *haburoth*, brotherhoods where you could enjoy some togetherness. If you were a Gentile, you would turn to one of the trade guilds, or partnerships to prepare your funeral expenses: both were commonplace. Or you might turn to one of the mystery religions in which you tried to make some sense of your existence through participation in secret rituals of death and rebirth.

In one sense, therefore, Christian communities would cause no surprise. They were part of a growing movement towards voluntary associations in the ancient world. Often these unofficial associations were called *koinoniai*, fellowships, and the Romans were tolerant of them. But actually there was a qualitative difference in the fellowship of the Christians. Here were associations in which aristocrats and slaves, Roman citizens and provincials, Jews and Gentiles, rich and poor, men and women mixed without distinction and on equal terms. Here were societies which possessed a quality of care and love which amazed and attracted those who saw it. That is why, among other reasons, we find not only the New Testament writers but Ignatius, Clement and Tertullian in the second and third centuries laying such store by unity. It was a harmony which demonstrated something of the unity-in-diversity of the God they worshipped. It was only a church which was manifestly united, where each member was free to share as the Holy Spirit moved him or her, that could convince the visiting observer that God was among them. There is, in fact, no doubt that many were convinced in this way. Tertullian, for example, notes the affection and purity which marked these Christian fellowship groups, fittingly called 'brethren' because of their common relationship to the heavenly Father.[1] Worship, fellowship and feasting are all carried out under the Father's eye. The lowly, the needy, the sick are shown particular consideration. 'One in mind and soul, we do not hesitate to share our earthly goods with one another. All things are common among us except our wives' – the very area, Tertullian unkindly pointed out, where pagans were most willing to share. There was a great deal of love flowing in these Christian meetings, and it was sustained by 'the sacred words with which we nourish faith, animate hope, make confidence assured, confirm good habits, and administer rebukes and censures'.[2]

What was the secret of this remarkable fellowship? There are a number of New Testament words which give us some insight into it, particularly *agape* and *philadelphia* (love and care for the brotherhood): but perhaps the most significant word is *koinonia*, fellowship.[3]

Koinonia, fellowship, basically means 'joint participation in', and is not inherently a religious word. Like most important New Testament words it is scandalously and intentionally secular. So you get it used of being partners in business (Luke 5:10), or sharing in an enterprise (Phil 4:15), and Paul uses it of his fellow workers (2 Cor 8:23). But, with explosive force, the first and main meaning of fellowship erupts from the pages of the New Testament.

Fellowship Means Sharing in God

This is expressed in a number of ways in verses like Romans 15:27, 1 Corinthians 1:9; 2 Corinthians 13:13, Philippians 2:1 and 1 John 1:3. The most breathtaking example in the New Testament is 2 Peter 1:4 where the recipients are saluted as being *koinonoi*, participants, in the very nature of God himself!

This fellowship with Jesus and his heavenly Father, in which the earliest Christians exulted, can be looked at in two ways.

The way the words are used could mean that we share our lives with him. He is our friend, our brother with whom we can share our feelings and requests at any time of day or night. We can share our ordinary, humdrum lives with God himself!

But there is a deeper sense in which this *koinonia* can be construed. We share in his life. We share in his suffering (Rom 8:17), in his death and resurrection (Rom 6:8; Phil 3:10). We are raised with him (Eph 2:5–6). We will reign with him (2 Tim 2:12). We will share his future glory (2 Thess 2:14). Not only, then, does he share in *our* problems and difficulties: we have a share even now in *his* own risen life, with touches of its power and traces of its glory. So 'When Christ who is our life shall appear, you too will appear with him in glory' (Col 3:4). What a prospect!

Needless to say, fellowship with God is impaired by human wickedness and failure. It is spoiled (1 John 1:6) but not abrogated. When we are conscious of wrongdoing in our lives, we need to confess it and ask for pardon (1 John 1:9; 2:1).

We will find God *faithful* in forgiving – after all, we are in the family. We will also find him *just* in forgiving – after all Christ took the accusing load of evil on our behalf on the cross. 'We have an advocate with the Father, Jesus Christ the righteous.' And the word used of Jesus in this verse, 1 John 2:1, is, significantly, *parakletos*, the word used of the Holy Spirit in the farewell discourses in St John's Gospel. The Holy Spirit is the Father's paraclete with us, to plead the Father's cause in our hearts. And Jesus is our paraclete with the Father, to plead our cause in the courts of heaven! For he is the propitiation, *hilasmos*, that has dealt with our sins once and for all. By his presence he presents his completed task of sinbearing to the Father. What a God, who thus in perfect justice and incredible love allows us selfish mortals to have the inestimable privilege of fellowship with him!

But our fellowship is never from the alone to the Alone. It is jointly held with others. The Christian faith is so different from all self-improvement cults and the faiths that seek fulfilment or enlightenment 'for myself alone'. It is inescapably corporate. You cannot have fellowship with the triune God who *is* fellowship without that fellowship spilling over to others in the same family. Naturally, therefore:

Fellowship Means Sharing with Believers

Paul referred to this as 'the right hand of fellowship' (Gal 2:9). He was referring to the reality behind the handshake. From the Day of Pentecost onwards the believers found themselves plunged into the apostles' fellowship (Acts 2:42). We do not choose our fellowship in the Christian family. The choice has been made for us. After all, we cannot choose our brothers and sisters! Significantly, *adelphoi* is a favourite term for Christians in the New Testament – brothers. The Spirit teaches us to cry 'Abba, Father', but never in isolation. The One to whom we cry is *Our Father*! So fellowship in the New Testament means partnership both with God and with fellow Christians. And that double fellowship is perfectly expressed in the Eucharist. 1 Corinthians 10:16–17 sees the bread and wine as expressive of our relationship with Jesus and at the same time with our fellow Christians. Both the church and the sacred bread are described as 'the body' in which we all share. Christianity is inescapably corporate.

That word 'body' is very important in the self-understanding of the early Christians. We are one body in Christ (as Paul insists in Romans 12, Ephesians 4 and 1 Corinthians 12), and we are individually members of it. There is no room for superiority in that body, for we did not choose or merit our incorporation. Nor is there room for inferiority complexes, for God takes special care of the apparently less attractive parts. Least of all is there any excuse for absenteeism, for we are members one of another, and if one member suffers, all the members suffer hurt.

So sharing in God inexorably means sharing with others in his family. That is why the church is so important, frail and sinful though it is. It is the body of Christ, of which we are limbs. It is the flock of Christ in which we are sheep. It is the Bride of Christ which we help to constitute and adorn. That is how the New Testament church sees itself.

The church has three main aspects in the New Testament. It can mean, and often does, 'the church in the home' (Philem v2). It can mean 'the church in a town', comprising several such home associations (1 Thess 1:1). It can also mean 'the church worldwide' (Acts 9:31). The singular 'church' and plural 'churches' are used indifferently. The important qualifier is 'tou theou – of God.' It is God's church.

The origin of the word *ekklesia*, or church, lies in the Greek city state where it was an assembly. But it is often used in the Greek translation of the Old Testament to render the Hebrew *qahal*, meaning God's congregation. Christians at worship are not just a fortuitous assembly but part of God's heritage down the ages, stretching back to Abraham. So unity within that heritage is very important. The people of God already, they must still strive to become that people more and more. One in the Spirit already (Eph 4:3), they must strive towards it. It is the theme constantly repeated in the Bible: we are accepted by God because of his generosity alone. Then we must, by his power, become what he already sees us to be.

This has a powerful word to say to our casual denominationalism. There is no trace of denominations in the New Testament. They are part of the sin of the church. The temptation to sheer off into a Jewish Church, a Samaritan Church, a Gentile Church was seductive, to be sure. But they refused to fall for it. The early Christians went to enormous efforts to maintain their unity. And therein lay part of their strength. Even today we see something of the sort. When churches of widely different denominations sink their differences and pull together for a mission or some other joint enterprise in a city, there is great surprise and great impact on the whole community, and opportunities for the gospel are offered to them in their togetherness which none of them would have been accorded in their isolation. Fellowship with God must be matched by fellowship with other Christians.

Koinonia is used in a further sense in the New Testament.

Fellowship Means Sharing Each Other's Experiences

Joys and sorrows

It means sharing in each other's joys and sorrows. 1 Corinthians 12:26 shows our intimate interdependence in the Christian body. So just as a family would rejoice when one member succeeds or grieve when one member fails, so it should be in the church.

Financial needs

It means sharing in each other's financial needs. It was like that in the very earliest days when the Jerusalem

Christians shared their all (Acts 4:34–35). It was like
that in Antioch when the Christians heard of impending
need for their brothers and sisters in Jerusalem (Acts
11:27–30). It was like that when Gentile churches wanted
to make a collection for the Jewish Christians from whom
the gospel had reached them (Rom 15:26). The word used
is *koinonia*, fellowship. The meaning extended far beyond
sympathy: it meant sacrificial giving. Philippians 4:15 is
a good example of the same thing: a project of giving and
receiving is called *koinonia*, and the same holds good of
Galatians 6:6 and Romans 12:13. Christians did not see
this as some unwelcome tax: they longed to give and
to have a share in this sort of fellowship, although it
seemed beyond their means (2 Cor 8:4). Paul explains it
further in 2 Corinthians 9:13 (chapters 8 and 9 are full
of teaching on the privilege of giving). Christians give
to impoverished brethren out of obedience to the gospel:
the recipients long for them and pray for them because of
God's abundant generosity received through them. Thus
joy and partnership abound, and it all springs from God's
inexpressible generosity to them all (2 Cor 9:15).

If we were really to take this level of fellowship to heart,
it would be very noticeable. I heard of two examples from
Pakistan which illustrate it powerfully. After church, the
pastor gathered the wage-earners in the little church
together and told them of a brother who had been sick for
months and could not pay his rent. The men immediately
agreed to pay it for him, poor though they were. Would
that have happened in your church?

The other example shows how fellowship through
giving does not have to flow from the richer to the poorer.
It can go the other way. A poor Pakistani widow heard of a
missionary family who were, for some weeks, unable to go
outside because of anti-Western riots. 'Maybe they need
some provisions,' she thought. And so she bought vegetables from the local market and travelled a few miles by
bus to bring this gift to the missionary home. It was valued
far more highly than the cost of the vegetables! If this sort
of thing became the norm in our churches, society round

about us would sit up and take notice. Not only would
needs be met, but the bonds of gratitude and fellowship
between church members would be greatly strengthened,
and those who are not yet Christians would be profoundly
attracted.

Suffering

Fellowship also means sharing in suffering – and the
consolation God gives. Suffering is an inescapable part
of being human, and Christians are invited to be willing
for a costly sharing which will at times involve suffering.
2 Corinthians 1:7 is a case in point. Paul has suffered
greatly. He expects them to suffer too. But just as he
has known the comfort of Jesus, aided by their prayers
(vv5,11), he anticipates the same consolation for them.
St Peter, too, gives us the same juxtaposition of suffering
now and glory later, at the very outset of his letter (1:5).
It is a challenge to endurance. 'We shall sometimes be
publicly exposed to abuse and affliction, and sometimes
be *koinonoi* with those so treated' (Heb 10:33). But the
writer urges them not to throw away their confidence,
which awaits a great reward. After all, they follow a
crucified yet risen Lord. Their destiny, in both respects,
is to share in his.

Commitment

Fellowship means sharing in an exclusive commitment.
This sits ill with the happy-go-lucky Western world, so
prone to wanting to have our cake and eat it. But
there is a black and white aspect in Christianity which
simply cannot be reduced to various shades of grey. The
much misquoted 2 Corinthians 6:14 is stringent in this
requirement. 'Do not be mismated with unbelievers . . .
what fellowship has light with darkness? . . . What has
a believer in common with an unbeliever?' Tough talk
indeed, and it is clear that Paul is intransigent on the
need to safeguard Christian purity and distinctiveness
of life. So firm was he, that he laid himself open to
misinterpretation, as if he had been urging his followers

to come out of the world altogether, and he had to correct
this impression (1 Cor 5:9–11). 'But rather I wrote to
you not to associate with any one who bears the name
of brother if he is guilty of immorality or greed, or is an
idolater, reviler, drunkard or robber – not even to eat
with such a one.'

Paul was anxious to maintain the freshness and purity
of Christian living in all sorts of ways. Christians must
not share in any enterprise that is sinful (Eph 5:11; 1 Tim
5:22; 2 Jn. v11; Rev 18:4), but in particular he dreads that
those who take the sacred bread and wine of the Eucharist
should enter into *koinonia*, partnership, with demonic
forces (1 Cor 10:18, 20). The idols to whom sacrifice was
offered in antiquity may have been imaginary; but dark
forces, which were far from imaginary, were given the
opportunity, through idolatry, of invading the Christian's
heart, and inducing civil war there. How powerfully
this concern of the apostle's applies to the occult and
secret societies like the Freemasons. It applies, also,
Paul knows, to sexual immorality, such as prostitution,
when I 'wrench away' the 'limb of Christ' and make it
the member of a prostitute (1 Cor 6:15ff). Commitment
to Christ is exclusive of other total commitments: the
Lord is jealous over his bride, the church, and every
member of it.

Care

Fellowship means deep loving care for our brothers and
sisters in the church. *Philadelphia*, love of the brethren,
is a great New Testament word. In the ladder of virtues
in 2 Peter 1:7 it is second only to *agape* itself, the
undifferentiating, God-given love for all and sundry. The
difference between the two is simply this: *philadelphia*
is the heaven-sent family love for other members of the
family, while *agape* is the outworking of God's own love
for the unlovely. Love like this is beautiful when it marks
the life of any church. It is chilling when it is absent.
This attractive mutual love, springing from the heart, is
the fruit of reconciliation with the heavenly Lover (Rom

12:10; 1 Pet 1:22). New Testament writers take it almost for granted: it is, after all, taught and inspired by God himself (1 Thess 4:9). They are just concerned that it should be constantly lived out in consistent Christian attitudes: 'Let brotherly love continue' (Heb 13:1).

Fellowship Means Sharing God's Work

Koinonia is heavily tinged in the New Testament with the meaning of joint partnership in the work of the Lord (e.g. 2 Cor 8:23; Phil 1:5; Heb 10:33). Paul's closest friends were those who shared the work with him, men like Titus 'my partner and fellow worker in your service' (2 Cor 8:23). There is a profound spiritual truth that deep fellowship is almost a by-product of service. It is forged and bonded not by studying it and discussing it, but by joining together in service for God. I have spent some of my life in the smoke-filled rooms of the ecumenical movement, discussing Christian unity: an entirely admirable objective. But it is not achieved by talk, as is obvious from the state in which the World Council of Churches finds itself. I have spent some of my life in evangelistic enterprises and Christian social concerns with brother and sister Christians from widely different denominations, outlooks and backgrounds. And it is here that I have found really deep fellowship. It came through service.

Many churches are flaccid because their members want the joy of fellowship without the sweat of service. It is not to be had. For fellowship means sharing in the work of God and, in particular, evangelism. Paul speaks very clearly about this in 1 Corinthians 9:22–23 where he discloses the flexibility and consistency, the courage and imagination, the motivation and persistence with which he spreads the good news of Jesus to Jew and Gentile alike. 'I have become all things to all men, that I might by all means save some. I do it all for the sake of the gospel, that I may share in its blessings.' Note that *koinonia*, 'sharing' word again. You only really begin to taste the blessings of the gospel when you set out to give it away.

Churches need to learn that. Theological seminaries need to learn that. Individual Christians need to learn that. And so do you and I.

I have the impression that Philemon knew the truth of that. Paul writes, in an obscure allusion in Philemon 6, 'I pray that the sharing of your faith may promote the knowledge of all the good that is ours in Christ.' But it emerges with notable clarity in Philippians 1:7: 'I have you in my heart because you are partners in the same grace as I – both in my bonds and in the defence and confirmation of the gospel.' The Christians at Philippi shared with Paul in his bonds by means of a gift of money and provisions which they sent him in prison. They shared in his defence and prosecution of the gospel by doing the same themselves. The gospel needs a cool head to explain it, defend it, to show its inner consistency and its relevance to every side of life. It is sad to see how low Christian apologetics have sunk during the past half century, and encouraging to see just the beginning of a fresh interest in this most important part of evangelism. But if the gospel needs a cool head, it also needs a warm heart to seek out people who need this wonderful news, and to love them into the kingdom of God, come rain come shine. When Christians do that together, they engage in the work of rescue which is the supreme concern of the Holy Trinity, for the Father sent the Son to be the Saviour of the world, and the Spirit baptised him for that task. And as they enter into this crucial aspect of the life of the Godhead, serving poor needy sinners, so they come to understand a vital dimension of fellowship. It is co-operating with God in his gracious work of rescue for a fallen world. If you and I long for a deeper fellowship, maybe we should involve ourselves more deliberately in ministry and mission.

Fellowship in the church of Jesus Christ is a many-splendoured thing. It means sharing in the life of God himself. It means sharing with other believers. It means experiencing a wide range of the experiences of other Christians. It means sharing in God's work.

Perhaps the best way of experiencing these four main aspects of Christian fellowship is in the house group. There the horizontal and the vertical axes of fellowship intersect. We have fellowship with the Lord and with each other. And it comes about in three main ways.

First, there is the Godward side of it. We worship him in the house group as we praise and pray. We learn together from the Scriptures and from the way these Scriptures impact one another's lives as we reflect on them. This leads naturally into the second aspect of it, fellowship with one another.

For the house group is the natural place to share each other's joys and sorrows, and to enter into each other's experiences. In this way we not only get far closer to one another than we could in a month of Sundays simply by attending church, but we have the thrill of seeing and hearing of God at work in other lives. This level of sharing is impossible among folk who do not know each other well. People will only share intimate details of their lives with those they know to care, those they can trust. And how can this level of trust and caring be fostered? In a small, regular house group. Every church should encourage them. They are almost essential to its vitality and growth.

And of course such a group is a ready-forged unit to engage in ministry and mission in the neighbourhood. It begins, naturally, with ministry to one another and moves out from there. A missionary writes of a small house group in the Muslim land where he works. One of the group, an old man, was due for major heart surgery. He and his wife were understandably nervous. So the group prayed with them and for them. After the operation they took turns in visiting the old man and providing meals for him. So although this old couple had no family to support them, they were lovingly supported by their Christian family, the members of their house group.

But a house group which does not look beyond itself soon becomes stale and unhealthy. Ministry and mission need to take place beyond the confines of the group. A warm, cohesive group like this can easily split for a while in order to invite some friends in, and do an inductive series of Bible studies on, say, passages in St John's Gospel. Or it can be more ambitious, and hold a few evangelistic supper parties with an appropriate speaker and plenty of opportunity for discussion. For fellowship is not only with God and with other Christians. Its quality is enhanced, its purpose is fulfilled only when, like the God we serve, it reaches out beyond its comfort zone to those who are strangers to the divine love. No wonder the house group is an invaluable part and embodiment of true fellowship in every congregation. We each need to take seriously the need to belong to a house group. And we need to take no less seriously the outward thrust of such a group if we are to enjoy its greatest dimension of fellowship.

CHAPTER SIX

AWARE OF THE STRUGGLE

Only he who understands that sin is inexplicable knows
what it is.
Emil Brunner

The Stevens and the Zimmermans were driving through downtown Nairobi, Kenya on July 8, 1990. A people's movement was taking place at that time. Thousands of people were bringing pressure on the government to allow more than one political party. But the real reason for the riots that had begun the day before, was the fact that one-third of the people of the city, where the average age is seventeen, were unemployed. We were about to lead an urban church seminar in Nairobi, and had hoped to bring a measure of redemption to the city. We did not expect the riot to last into the second day. But as we turned into a roundabout, and then into a one-way street, we were attacked by about fifty people with rocks and clubs who attempted to turn the car over and set it on fire. Through an amazing deliverance, I was able to do a U-turn in a single-lane street and get the car going in the opposite direction as the rioters caught up with the vehicle. One large stone was hurled through the window and grazed my neck, smashing the windscreen. Had it been a centimetre to the left I would have been knocked unconscious and our escape would have been impossible.

The real reason for the rage was not the issue of black and white, but of rich and poor. We were driving a car, and were therefore obviously rich. Many of the rioters were members of the church and, as part of their 'fulfilling righteousness', were expressing their outrage about an unjust system against the symbols of that injustice, two rich couples who had come to help bring redemption to the city. As it happened, our home church was praying for us at the very time of this encounter. Two years earlier one of the members of the church had a vision of one of the couples escaping from an African city, and prayed against this for two years. What was going on there? An encounter with fallen human nature? Unjust and unredeemed social, economic and political structures? Direct harassment by Satan? Did angels – unseen by us – surround our car? Did God answer our sister's intercessory prayer for us offered over a period of two years?

A few misguided teachers claim that becoming a Christian solves all your problems and makes you effortlessly happy and trouble-free until you enter the final bliss of heaven. But they are lying. Following Jesus is a victorious battle, not a victorious life. And beware of anyone who tells you there is a simple explanation for the struggle. They are probably wrong. Indeed there are so many confusing messages around that the gift of discernment may be one of the most important gifts needed in the church today.

Some people maintain that you can gain sinless perfection and a totally victorious life. Spurgeon once heard a person at a conference claim that he had entered into sinless perfection and an untrammelled experience of peace. Spurgeon said nothing at the time. But the next day at breakfast a pitcher of milk was poured over the speaker to test his doctrine, which was shown, quite definitely, to be false! The reality is that the most godly saints still struggle. In fact we fight a multi-front battle: the world, the flesh and the devil, as the Prayer Book defines it. And for this multi-front battle the New Testament offers a multi-front victory. First, in the world.

The World: the Trouble Outside

A Canadian commercial artist works for a prominent advertising firm that keeps careful control over the kind of clients it accepts. While the senior partners in the firm are not Christians they are moral men and women and do not wish to become involved in advertising products that are harmful to human life, or to use advertising methods that are, in their view, overtly manipulative, or appeal to drives and appetites that would swamp any rational decision-making. A Christian working for this firm has particularly enjoyed doing the advertising for a fast-food chain over the years and won several awards for his imaginative representation of the food chain's new products. But the company branched out into some new investments that are known to be linked with highly questionable products. It is rumoured in the office that there is mafia money behind the food chain now, in spite of the high level of public acceptance of its products. In order to keep this influential client the Christian commercial artist will have to advertise products he believes are destructive to the moral fabric of society. But, as his boss says, 'In our society you are no longer dealing with a single customer but with multinational networks in all shades and colours. The only way to stay in the business world is to work in the system and don't ask too many questions about where the money is coming from.' What is going on here? One thing for sure, life in secular society is a spiritual battle.

The trouble with the world

Whether in a large corporation or a small business, work takes believers into a society where it is difficult to live by Kingdom principles. They do not feel in control of the circumstances of their work, surrounded as they are by structures, powers, authorities, influences and systems that either compel them to lower their standards or seduce them to compromise. The personal use and abuse of freedom by their superiors or workmates does not seem to account for the complexity of living for God in the secular world. The problem is deeper than personal sin, or even 'the flesh'. Indeed Paul says 'our struggle is *not* against flesh and blood' (Eph 6:12 italics mine). There is something more to the opposition we face in the world than the mere sum of all the sinful attitudes and actions of people. It involves a system. Jesus taught that the world cannot receive the Spirit (John 14:17), hates Jesus, and hates believers (15:18). Believers have been chosen 'out of' the world (15:19) and are not 'of' the world (17:14) even though they must live 'in' the world (17:15). 'In this world,' Jesus says, 'you will have trouble' (16:33).

The trouble is multifaceted and comes to us through unjust or unloving structures, systems of business and finance, principles of conformity, social patterns, customs and traditions that marginalise the life of faith or positively oppose it, and the ever-present influence of the media. At some personal risk, my friend who teaches marketing in a university wrote a scholarly article to show that the advertising world appeals to the seven deadly sins: wrath, lust, avarice, gluttony, sloth, envy and pride. Studies have shown that the average North American is exposed to fourteen hundred advertisements each day: fourteen hundred messages, by and large, from 'the other side'. The complexity of life in our neo-pagan society, is so confusing that some misguided people feel that the only safe haven is to work for the church or a Christian organisation. What they find – to their extreme disappointment – is more of the same, though often more cleverly disguised because the institutions claim to be redeemed and Spirit-led. There is no simple explanation and no easy escape. But the Bible provides an indispensable framework for understanding our trouble and dealing with it.

God so loved the world
Scripture uses 'world' to describe the created order about which God could say, 'It is very good' (Gen 1:31). But

there was more than mere matter involved in making the world. God's creative activity involved placing humankind in a structured universe which included time (seven days), space (a sanctuary garden), relationships (covenant marriage and family), structures (the tree of knowledge), and other creatures (animals and the serpent). Imagine a world without marriage, family, government, and without national borders (Acts 17:26)! All these are designed by God for our protection and to give meaning to life.

What are called in Scripture, 'principalities', 'powers', 'virtues', 'dominions', 'thrones', and 'names' (Rom 8:38; 1 Cor 15:24; Eph 1:21; 3:10; 6:12; Col 1:16; 2:10,15), are words used to describe the structured and ordered way that God has created the world. These terms imply government, human authorities, national structures, family and tribal structures, priorities within relationships of peers, and angelic realms. Far from being the result of 'the fall' and a necessary restriction of man's fleshly nature to protect humankind from himself, these powers are part of God's *good* creation. They are not innately evil. They are made by Christ and for Christ! Paul claims that through Christ 'all things were created: things in heaven and on earth, visible and invisible, whether thrones or powers or rulers or authorities; all things were created by him and for him' (Col 1:16). Hendrik Berkhof describes this brilliantly as the invisible background of creation: 'The dykes with which God encircles His good creation, to keep it in His fellowship and protect it from chaos.'[1]

These good gifts of God (Col 1:16) were intended to form a framework in which we serve God. But they have now, through the sin of humankind and the civil war that took place in the universe (Jude v6), become broken, hostile, resistant to God's rule, and intransigent. Some of these powers have taken on a life of their own, making idolatrous claims on human beings: government, religion, culture, 'isms' and the demonic, being symbolised by the 'names' and 'titles' (Eph 1:21) that dominate the news. Scripture speaks of the predicament of the 'principalities

and powers' in various ways. Sometimes we are told to
regard these pretentious, tyrannical powers as 'weak
and miserable principles' that make god-like claims even
though they are 'no gods' (Gal 4:8–9). In Ephesians, Paul
says that our struggle is not against human problems –
flesh and blood – but against 'the spiritual forces of evil
in the heavenly realms', suggesting that the devil himself
has co-opted these powers, or 'colonised' them for his own
ends (Eph 6:10–13). It is impossible for human beings
to function in this world without encountering these
habitual, fallen patterns, which will be experienced in
competition, compelling forces of conformity, and, in its
worst form, in direct satanic attack through witchcraft
and satanism.

Some Christian authors treat the New Testament witness to the powers *only* as structures of our worldly life,
having no relationship with the devil or fallen angels.
Other authors concentrate exclusively on warfare with
the demonic. But the Christian in the world must deal
with *both*. And Scripture witnesses to the complexity of
systemic evil: structures, spiritual hosts, and the last
enemy, death (1 Cor 15:24–27) – all arenas of spiritual
warfare. But the Christian is not powerless in this
spiritual warfare because Christ has already won the
victory over the powers.

The powerless powers

Oscar Cullman compares the powers to chained beasts,
kicking themselves to death. Between the resurrection
of Jesus and the second coming they are tied to a
rope, still free to evince their demonic character but
nevertheless bound. This is certainly the perspective of
the last book of the Bible (Rev chs 18–19). Christ's relation
to the powers is crucial for lay spirituality. Christ was
voluntarily 'victimised' by the powers when he submitted to a human crucifixion. The seeming victory of the
powers was symbolised by the three-language title over
his cross: Latin for government, Greek for culture and
Hebrew for religion. But ironically, Christ's death put

the principalities and powers in their place as instruments, subject to God's sovereignty. His cross was a victory not only over the sin of humankind but also the powers. The cross was a political act and a cosmic victory. Christ 'disarmed' the powers, 'made a public spectacle of them', thereby showing how illusionary their pretensions were, and 'triumphed over them' (Col 2:15). Speaking of this, Berkhof says 'Whenever [the cross] is preached, the unmasking and disarming of the Powers takes place.'[2] Without the eye of faith, these powers still seem almost omnipotent. But to the eye of faith they are vanquished even though they continue to press their claims and therefore complicate even the Christian's life in this world.

The first and most effective strategy against the false claims of the powers is preaching the gospel. Our duty is not to bring the powers to their knees: this is Christ's task. Our duty is to arm ourselves with Christ (Eph 6:10–18) and to preach his cross. However much we attempt to 'Christianise' the powers, we must not bypass preaching the gospel and calling people to embrace the reign of Christ through repentance and faith. Some of these powers deserve the loyal submission of Christians (Rom 13:1). Some of them should be Christianised by the involvement of Christians and the church in creational tasks: subjugating the resources of the world in education, politics and culture to serve man, as defined by God's intention. Some powers will be shown to be unmasked by the martyrdom of faithful believers (Rev 12:11). But Christians and the church must be under no illusion. As Markus Barth says,

The power of filling, subjugating, and dominating 'all things', including these powers is reserved to God and Christ alone. But the function of demonstrating God's dominion and love is entrusted to the church. She is appointed and equipped to be a public exponent of grace and unity . . . the beginning of a new heaven and a new earth.[3]

The power of public discipleship

Christ's complete victory over the principalities and powers, over Satan, sin and death, assure us that there is nowhere in the universe so demonised that a Christian might not be called to serve there. We fight a war that is already won. Therefore as far as is now possible Christians should Christianise the powers, to make peace with the powers through involvement in education, government and social action, all the while knowing that the task of subjugating the powers is reserved for Christ alone (Eph 1:10; Phil 2:10–11). We work on the problems of pollution, food distribution, injustice, genetic engineering, and the proliferation of violence and weaponry, knowing that this work is ministry and holy. In the short-run this work may seem unsuccessful, but in the long-run it will be gloriously successful because we are co-operating with what Christ wants to do in renewing all creation. In this they must live with heavenly-mindedness knowing that Christ said 'all power is given to me in heaven and on earth' (Matt 28:18). While the beast is master here for a moment (Rev 13:1–18), all dimensions of social unity will be ultimately restored according to God's design. And in the New Jerusalem the 'principalities and powers' will provide structure for our common life and work (Rev 21:24).

So we have seen that our struggle in the world is not merely the sum of the effect of all the sinful human beings in the world. We deal with systemic evil and systemic evil calls for spiritual warfare, a ministry for which we are gloriously provisioned. But we still must come to terms with ourselves, with our own tendencies toward evil, with our 'flesh'. Words attributed to G. K. Chesterton are *also* incisively accurate: 'What is wrong with the world? I am wrong with the world!'

Flesh: the Battle Within

A pastor who loves preaching finds that when he stands up to preach his eyes connect with a particularly attractive woman in the congregation. He feels she reciprocates with an equal intensity. Something mysterious is happening between them. While he preaches eloquently and convincingly, there is something electric going on between him and this woman. Both are married to other spouses, and he knows that he should not even be entertaining fantasies about another woman but she frequently appears in his dreams and they have an affair of the eyes each Sunday. His secretary has just told him that she is coming this afternoon for marriage counselling. What is going on here?

It is a fact that Christians struggle until the day they die. And part of that struggle *is* with flesh and blood, with human nature as it has become through sin. The word 'flesh' (*sarx*) is a complex word in Paul's writing and we must attempt a short explanation.

The flesh against the Spirit
In passing we might note that Paul sometimes uses *sarx* merely to denote what is human about us. Once we regarded Christ 'from a human point of view' (2 Cor 5:16). 'By human standards' not many of the Corinthians were wise and educated (1 Cor 1:26). Paul claims he does not make plans 'in a worldly manner' (2 Cor 1:17) meaning, according to the flesh. Sometimes 'flesh' simply refers to one's bodily life (Rom 2:28) which is normally good, or at least neutral. Paul firmly rejected the Greek view of the body as a hindrance; he adhered to the biblical view that believers can glorify God *with* and *in* their bodies. Our ultimate future is not to be holy souls floating around eternity but to be resurrected persons experiencing complete, personal, bodily and human life in the presence of God and his people in a new heaven *and a new earth* (Rev chs 21–22). So 'flesh' is not always pitted against life in Christ, or the Spirit.

On this point it is remarkable that the works of the flesh Paul lists in Galatians 5:19–21 are largely non-physical: impurity, idolatry, witchcraft, hatred, discord, jealousy, fits of rage, selfish ambition, dissensions, factions and envy. These are generally psychological,

spiritual, and relational. The war going on inside is
not mainly between our physical body and our human
spirits, but between something else which 'desires what
is contrary to the Spirit' (5:17). It is true that four of the
listed works of the flesh – sexual immorality, debauchery,
drunkenness and orgies – involve the physical body. But
the root of these destructive activities is to be found in
our minds and in what Scripture calls the heart. Sexual
problems are not primarily physical problems. Our root
problem is not our sensuality but something deeper and
more comprehensive.

While many modern translations use the words 'human
nature' to translate *sarx* they must not be understood to
communicate that we have *two parts* to our personhood,
one good and one bad, one higher and one lower, one
given to God and the other given to sin. No, it is our
whole person – body, soul and spirit – that struggles
to live under the reign of Christ and in the Spirit.
Biblically we do not 'have' a body, 'have' a soul, and
'have' a spirit, as though we were three compartments
on a train. We *are* bodies, souls and spirits – integrated
wholes. Touch someone's body in a sexual affair and you
have touched that person. So the sexual sins listed in
the 'works of the flesh' are personal sins, and arise not
from an irrepressible instinct in our bodies, but something
wrong in our persons. 'Idolatry' and 'sorcery' involve
the secret tampering with the powers of evil through
drugs or witchcraft. 'Enmity', 'strife', 'fits of anger',
'selfishness', 'dissensions', 'party spirit', and 'envy' are
relational sins – persons out of sync with others, seeking
their own advantage or cherishing pain when someone
else is honoured. Even 'drunkenness' and 'carousing'
are, in the end, not physical problems, because they
both involve giving one's consciousness to a chemical,
a profoundly personal matter. So the works of the flesh
are not to be located in our physical drives and appetites
but in something related to the fundamental orientation
of our lives.

This brings us to the special way Paul sometimes uses

'flesh' in his letters, for example, in Romans 7:18 ('I know that nothing good lives in me, that is, in my sinful nature [*sarx*]') and Galatians 5:16–17 ('For the sinful nature [*sarx*] desires what is contrary to the Spirit'). 'Flesh' stands for human nature as it has become through sin. It is life lived as though Christ had not come, died and been raised. It is life outside and against the Spirit. 'Flesh' describes – but does not ultimately account for – the oft-repeated situation where a person knows what to do but feels helpless to do it (Rom 7:18). There is a great range of interpretations of Paul's striking and troubling confession in Romans 7:15 – 'For what I want to do I do not do, but what I hate I do'. They include on one extreme the view that Paul was speaking of his pre-Christian state, and on the other extreme, that he is confessing his present experience of struggle as a Christian (and is therefore an exponent of our own struggle). The debate on this text will probably never be concluded. But James Denney offers a helpful pastoral comment in these words: 'It is safe for a Christian like Paul – it is not safe for everybody – to explain his failings by the watchword, 'Not I, but indwelling sin . . .' A true saint may say it in a moment of passion, but a sinner had better not make it a principle.'4 It is my view that this is precisely the emphasis Paul brings in Galatians 5:16–26.

The Spirit against the flesh
Seldom noted in Paul's correspondence – sometimes because of the translation – is the fact that Paul's most common use of 'Spirit' and 'Spiritual' involves the use of a capital 'S'. The war within is not between a lower nature (flesh) and a higher nature (spirit), but between the flesh and Spirit, between human nature as a whole, organised against God's purposes and thus turned inward, and God's presence and power. Paul's point in saying that flesh and Spirit 'are in conflict with each other, so that you do not do what you want' (Gal 5:17) is not to underline that a war rages within, a war over which the believer is helpless, unable to live for God

wholeheartedly. The passage is spoken to people who are already 'in the Spirit'. They have received Christ. They have found justification not by works of the law but by faith in Jesus. They are reminded by Paul that they began their Christian life not by human effort but by believing what they heard about Jesus and receiving the Spirit (3:2–3). Having begun with the Spirit they *still* cannot attain the goal of the Christian life by performance, religious or otherwise. The gospel not only takes us to heaven; it also equips us to live triumphantly now! It is faith and Spirit all the way.

So Christians are under obligation to live according to the Spirit and not to gratify the desires of the flesh (5:16). 'Flesh' in this context is not merely human nature, but human life lived outside of the reality of Christ's having come. Living 'according to the flesh' and living 'according to the Spirit' are not two factions warring inside the beleaguered and troubled Christian. They are two ways of living that are completely inconsistent and incompatible. Paul does not deny that people who have begun to follow Jesus may live 'according to the flesh'. What he denies is that they *need* to.

Gordon Fee notes that the burden of the passage is not that the believer is helpless before the volcanic forces of flesh within. Fee argues forcefully that we cannot interpret Galatians chapter five in the light of Romans chapter seven. We must find out what Paul was saying to the Galatians. And what Paul insists to these misguided believers is that the Spirit has brought them to life. Therefore walking in the Spirit *precludes* making provision for walking in the flesh and gratifying the desires of their former way of life. 'Spirit people cannot do whatever they like. Freedom is not freedom for the flesh; it is freedom for the Spirit, so that they serve one another in love.'[5]

The possibility of a Christian giving in to sin from time to time remains. The flesh has been crucified with the cross of Christ but a Christian might still live according to the flesh. A Christian might live as though he or she had not been redeemed, adopted, forgiven and indwelt by God's own Spirit. *But it is inconsistent so to do.* The fact that we continue to struggle makes it imperative not only to understand the nature of the conflict but also to learn how to deal with it. So we must now ask how to walk in the Spirit and not gratify the desires of the flesh.

Walking in the Spirit

What Paul teaches in Galatians is how to live victoriously in the thick of battle, not how to live the victorious life. He starts with the fruit of the Spirit and gives an *ad hoc* list of benefits from being in Christ, some aspects of the fruit being experiential (such as joy), some attitudinal (such as patience), and some behavioural (such as self-control). What is remarkable about this list is that Paul does not regulate the Christian life by a series of rules and behavioural requirements. For the Christian there can be no law against Spirit-fruit (Gal 5:23). There is also no law to regulate food, clothing, religious practices, entertainment and recreation. Human commandments have no value at all. What Paul proposes, rather, is letting the Spirit bear his own fruit in our lives. The contrast of 'works' of the flesh, and 'fruit' of the Spirit (actually a seven-fold fruit) is often noted. Works must be accomplished; fruit comes with very little effort from ourselves when there is the irruption of life within. Ironically the first and foremost strategy for refusing to live by the flesh is indirect: to turn from concentrating on the flesh to concentrating on the Spirit.

In a shocking, anonymous article entitled 'The War Within: An Anatomy of Lust' an American spiritual director revealed his long-standing struggle with pornography and voyeurism. He admitted that lust is fully pleasurable and has its own compelling rewards. He despaired that time after time when he repented in prayer and cried out to God to take away his desire, nothing changed. Then he chanced on a line from Mauriac – that there is only one reason to seek purity. Mauriac said that purity is the condition for a higher love – for a possession superior to all possessions: God himself. Whereas all the negative arguments against lust had failed, and guilt had provided no power to change, 'Here,' this Christian leader discovered, 'was a description of what I was missing by continuing to harbor lust: I was limiting my own intimacy with God.'6

Fruit-bearing is also the context for Paul's second strategy, a strategy which is also positively motivated. Crucifying the flesh is not first and foremost a negative work. It is like repentance. C. S. Lewis once remarked that repentance 'is not something God demands of you before He will take you back and which He could let you off if He chose; it is simply a description of what going back is like'. Paul's repeated exhortations in Galatians should be understood this way. He says, 'Those who belong to Christ Jesus have crucified the sinful nature with its passions and desires' (5:24). 'After beginning with the Spirit, are you now trying to attain your goal by human effort?' (3:3). 'May I never boast except in the cross of our Lord Jesus Christ, through which the world has been crucified to me, and I to the world' (6:14). These statements are not appeals to self-crucifixion, mortification of one's bodily life, or self-hatred as though these negative 'good' works could accomplish anything more than positive 'good' works. Paul appeals for a full and continuous agreement with God's judgment on our autonomous, self-justifying life. It is worthy of death; it puts God to death, murdering him in our hearts. John Stott reminds us that a crucifixion is pitiless (and we should not treat the flesh as respectable), painful (even though the pleasures of the flesh are fleeting) and decisive (as suggested by the aorist tense in the Greek – fully accomplished). Here, as everywhere in the Christian life, we move from the indicative (what exists) to the imperative (what ought to be done). Jesus *has* died for us and the flesh *has* been substantially overcome; therefore we should maintain a crucified perspective on the flesh. But mortification is less than half of living a victorious battle.

Once again Paul preaches good news. We do not have

to live defeated lives. 'So I say, live by the Spirit, and you will not gratify the desires of the sinful nature' (5:16). 'But if you are led by the Spirit, you are not under law' (5:18). 'Since we live by the Spirit, let us keep in step with the Spirit' (5:25). Here again we move from the indicative to the imperative. We *are* children of God and by the Spirit call God 'Father' (Rom 8:14–15). We *are* led by the Spirit (an image used to describe a farmer leading cattle, or soldiers escorting a prisoner to court). We have a continuous, gentle pressure towards goodness, because the Spirit leads we *do* the walking. Two words for walking are used – the ordinary word for 'walk', and *stoikeo* which means to draw people up in a line, or to line oneself up with the Spirit's initiatives. Both suggest an action on our part but it is an action that is responsive to the constant and creative initiative of the Spirit in our lives. In contrast to 'sowing to the flesh' which results in destruction, 'sowing to the Spirit' results in reaping eternal life (Gal 6:7–8).

Negatively, walking according to the Spirit means *not* setting the mind on the things of the flesh (Rom 8:5) or doing the deeds of the flesh (Gal 5:19–21). We put these desires and deeds to death by the Spirit (Rom 8:13, Gal 5:16–18, 24–26). Involved in this is repudiating our boasting in human achievement, human wisdom or human law-keeping as ways of achieving righteousness. Positively, walking according to the Spirit implies that the Christian 'keeps in line' (Gal 5:25) with what the Spirit is already doing. This involves setting one's mind on the things of the Spirit (Rom 8:5), allowing the Spirit to produce his character fruit in us (Gal 5:22–23), and receiving the Spirit's power for works of holiness (Rom 12:9–21; cf. Isa 58). Until Christ comes again and introduces a new heaven and a new earth, we will never cease to experience tension and struggle. But we need not live defeated lives. As surely as Christ has come, as surely as Christ has died and has risen, we are now living in the age of the Spirit. And we *can* live by the Spirit. Indeed we *will*. New Testament 'spirituality' is Spirit-uality. So Paul says, if translated literally, 'live by the Spirit, *and you will not gratify the desires of the flesh*' (5:16 italics mine). But there is more to living victoriously than overcoming the flesh.

The Devil: the Invisible War

A Christian oral surgeon went through the trauma of having three patients die in one year through a series of strange accidents. In each case the anaesthetist, not the surgeon, was directly responsible for the patient's life. But the presiding surgeon was held responsible. In one case the patient died of an undiagnosed heart problem while having a routine oral procedure under general anaesthetic. In a second, faulty equipment was to blame. Each autopsy showed that the oral surgeon had performed his procedure with professional competence. But a specialist's business depends entirely on the good-will of referring physicians and this broke down when the media got hold of the story. It was covered in tabloid newspapers and on local radio stations, so his 'record' as a surgeon became a matter of public conversation. While the accrediting body for oral surgeons investigated and found that he was not at fault, and while his friends were convinced that it was an almost incredible sequence of accidents, none of his former medical friends felt free to refer their patients to him. As things went from bad to worse, he finally had to leave the country and start again somewhere else. The experience forced him and his family to go deeper with God as they struggled against public opinion and tried to ignore the media people hiding at the end of their driveway. But this doctor whose career was being destroyed could not help but wonder if this was not a direct attack by Satan. What was going on here?

Know the enemy
We come now to a further dimension of the struggle, one we struggle even to understand! *Western society has largely rejected the spiritual interpretation of life.*

Even the church turns to social analysis to find out what is going on and leaves out the spiritual realities behind and within the visible and present. Years ago James Stewart traced the intellectual history of this demise of our biblical framework in these brilliant words:

> St Paul's 'principalities and powers' – the 'spirit forces of evil' whose malignant grip upon the souls of men called forth 'a second Adam to the fight and to the rescue' – are now known, we are told, to have been mere apocalyptic imagination. To this result Newton, Darwin and Freud certainly contributed. For Newton's work left no room for an irrational principle in nature; and the devil is essentially irrational, teleologically indefinable – as St John marks by his significant use of *anomia* (1 John 3:4) and St Paul by the phrase 'the mystery of iniquity' (2 Thess 2:7) . . . Darwin's picture of the biological struggle for existence was hailed as radically superseding the Biblical picture of the cosmic struggle between the demons and the kingdom of the Lord. Finally, Freud banished the powers of darkness from their last stronghold, the soul, by successfully dissolving them into psychological complexes, neuroses, and the like: so that the good fight of faith becomes simply a matter of inner individual adjustment.[7]

The ultimate enemy is a malevolent spiritual being who is totally opposed to God and God's purposes. He is called by various names: the prince of this world (John 14:30), the devil (Matt 4:1), the great red dragon (Rev 12:3,9), the ancient serpent (12:9), Satan (12:9), and the accuser (12:10). His strategy is *derision* through making clergy and the Christian church look stupid, *destruction* by harassing believers and robbing them of joy (Rev 12:10), *diversion* into sensualism, secularism, relativism and bitterness (2 Cor 11:3), *division* by splitting God's family, often starting with gossip (James 3:14), and *deception* through getting people to depend on human leaders

(Gal 4:17) or through seducing believers into accepting a compromised lifestyle (1 Pet 5:8). As the next chapter will deal with the specific ministry of exorcism I will restrict myself here to other aspects of spiritual warfare.

Don the spiritual armour through prayer.

Paul uses an elaborate metaphor for arming ourselves, in Ephesians 6:10-18, by using the pieces of armour worn by a Roman soldier. Perhaps he was chained to one as he wrote. The belt of truth means living with integrity. The breastplate of righteousness involves having right relations with God, and living righteously. The 'shoes' of the gospel implies that we are ready and 'on the way' to share the good news – there is more than *defence* here! The shield of faith deflects the enemy's attacks, and the helmet of salvation brings assurance to our minds that we belong to a God who will never divorce us. The sword of the Spirit is the word of God, read, obeyed and spoken. All these are ways of 'putting on Christ': Christ's righteousness, Christ's message, Christ's faith, Christ's finished work on the cross, and Christ's word. All of these are put on by prayer: prayer on all occasions and all kinds of prayer (6:18).

Living a life of prayer and constantly putting on Jesus protects us from threats we cannot see. Sometimes we do not even know how we have been protected until long after. Earlier I mentioned our deliverance in Nairobi. We did not see angels around the car, but I believe they were there. God has an invisible host of angels at his disposal. A year ago a student at Regent College received a letter from a friend in England. She had been walking across a campus by herself when a seedy and threatening-looking man appeared in front walking alone. She put on the armour, crying to the Lord, 'Please help me'. When she got safely home and turned on the television, the local police were asking for help in identifying the very man she had seen on the campus, a man who had already molested several people. She immediately presented herself and identified the person.

'Why then,' she asked, 'did you not touch me?'

'I would not have dared,' he said. 'There were two strong men with you, one on the right and one on the left.'

Spiritual warfare involves direct confrontation with the demonic – a subject to which we will shortly turn. But more commonly it involves putting on Jesus day by day and living the gospel. A crucial dimension of this is forgiving those who have hurt us, and even forgiving ourselves.

Practice forgiveness and intercession

Forgiveness plunders hell and sends Satan's hordes screaming for cover. It brings peace to the soul, and makes peace between people. It secures freedom from the past, opens up a new future and permits people to live heartily in the present. It is the most significant healing of the soul, the most profound victory in the cosmic battle. When we forgive we do several things: *remember* that we ourselves have been forgiven by God and therefore empower ourselves to forgive others; *forget* the original hurtful meaning of offences against us and regard them now, like the wounds in the body of Jesus after the resurrection, as the means of faith for others; *cancel* the debt others owe us and refuse to offer an easy repayment schedule or a trade-off; *prize* the value of the relationship even more than the behaviour that hurt; and *create* a new future (John 8:11) unencumbered by the sin. Lewis Smedes says that 'our only escape from history's cruel unfairness, our only passage to the future's creative possibilities, is the miracle of forgiveness'.[8]

Paul ends his magnificent metaphor of donning the armour with this simple request: 'Pray also for me' (Eph 6:19). Karl Barth once said that 'to clasp the hands in prayer is the beginning of an uprising against the disorder of the world'.[9] It is also the beginning of an uprising against the disorder we see in others and in ourselves. Intercessory prayer, of which Ephesians 1:15–23 and 3:14–21 are stunning examples, is hard work. It is hard to hold people in our hearts and then to take them to God in our praying hearts. But understood from the perspective of the New Jerusalem some very important things happen when we pray for others. First, we receive God's thoughts about the person or the situation we are holding before God. Secondly, we piggyback on the Spirit's intercession since our prayers, even the most eloquent ones, are mere groans and babblings in comparison to the eloquence of the Spirit (Rom 8:26). Thirdly, in some mysterious way that offends the secular mindset, we get in touch with persons on a deeper level than we might otherwise. Bonhoeffer explains that direct relationships between people are impossible. But Jesus as our mediator puts his hand on each and brings both together. So the most direct way to our brother is indirect — through Christ. Finally, something happens when we pray for people. Pascal said that 'prayer is God's way of providing man with the dignity of causality'.[10] P. T. Forsyth agrees that the earth is shaken daily by the prayers of the saints.

> The real power of prayer in history is not a fusillade of praying units of whom Christ is the chief, but it is the corporate action of a Saviour-Intercessor and His community, a volume and energy of prayer organized in a Holy Spirit and in the Church the Spirit creates.[11]

Engaging in spiritual warfare may well start with praying for ourselves. Our colleague and friend, Dr James Houston offers a prayer for the struggle:

> So we cry out to the Father: lead me through all the evil tendencies of my heart. Help me to overcome the temptations of my temperament. Change inside me the evil tendencies of my own personality as it relates to other people. Protect me from the temptations of my own age group in the phases of life: passionate when young, cynical when middle-aged, self-pitying when old and lonely. Save me from the temptations

of our culture, the modern world in which we live.
For in all these realms, and above all to my sinful
heart, I am seducible.[12]

The world, the flesh and the devil – each is fought differently. We deal with the world through nonconformity
with the world and conformity with the will of God (Rom
12:2). We deal with the flesh by mortification (identifying
with Christ's crucifixion) and aspiration (breathing in the
Spirit). We deal with the devil by resisting and fleeing
(James 4:7; Rev 12:11). It is a battle fought on three
fronts: the world, the flesh and the devil. And our Lord
meets us on each of these fronts. He *transfigures* us from
within (Rom 12:2) so we can transform the world rather
than be conformed as we penetrate the world in our work
and mission. He *bears Spirit fruit* through us (Gal 5:22,25)
as we determine to walk in the Spirit and regard the flesh
as crucified. And he *overcomes the evil one*, the devil
(Rev 12:10) as we put on Christ's armour through all
kinds of prayer (Eph 6:13–18). During one of our many
trips to Kenya I was travelling with a pastor in a remote
rural area. I am always anxious to learn from African
Christians because, by and large, they really believe in
God, really believe in angels and the devil, and really
believe that Christ can empower us to live triumphantly.
They have a biblical world-view.

'Do you cast out demons as part of your ministry,' I
asked naively.

'No, never!' was his surprising answer. And then he
added, 'Only Jesus does!'

CHAPTER SEVEN

HEALING AND DELIVERANCE

Healing

Examples of healing are everywhere apparent in society. Healing through conventional medicine is the most common, and where would we be without it? But sometimes healing occurs through alternative medicine, such as acupuncture, and sometimes without medical means at all. In this context I want to look at divine healing, for there is no question that Jesus and his disciples saw this as an important part of their spiritual lives, and an evidence of the break-in of the Kingdom of God. The healings, so notable in the ministry of Jesus, are continued in the Acts of the Apostles (e.g. 3:1ff.; 9:18; 14:8ff.; 20:9–10; 28:8 etc). They are alluded to in the Epistles (e.g. 2 Cor 12:12; 1 Cor 12:9, 30; James 5:16). And despite the claims of dispensationalists that healing, along with other remarkable gifts of the Holy Spirit, ceased at the end of the apostolic age, this is demonstrably false if we are to credit the testimony of the Fathers who were well aware of divine healings from time to time in their midst, and expected them. Here are some examples: they have been conveniently collected by John Wimber as Appendix A of his book *Power Evangelism*.[1]

Justin has much to say on the subject both in his *First* and *Second Apology*. He speaks of 'many of our Christian men exorcising demoniacs in the name of Jesus Christ, who was crucified under Pontius Pilate. They have healed, and do heal . . .' (*2 Apol.* 6). Irenaeus, one of the greatest second-century leaders, remarks 'Some certainly and truly drive out devils, so that those who have thus been cleansed from evil spirits frequently join themselves to the church. Others heal the sick by laying their hands upon them, and they are made whole' (*Adv. Haer.* 2.32). Tertullian is no less explicit on the subject, giving examples of deliverance from evil spirits and naming some distinguished personages (such as Severus, the father of Antoninus Pius) who were healed of various diseases as Christians prayed for them (*Apol.* 23). Bishop Ambrose of Milan bears testimony to the Father bestowing 'the grace of healing . . . and the gift of tongues'. But it is his celebrated and learned follower, Augustine, who is most confident in writing about divine intervention to heal and to set people free from dark forces. 'It is sometimes objected,' says Augustine in *The City of God* (22.28), 'that the miracles, which Christians claimed to have occurred, no longer happen . . . The truth is that even today miracles are being wrought in the name of Christ, sometimes through his sacraments and sometimes through the intercession of the relics of his saints.' And lest anyone should regard that as pious generalisation, Augustine gives a whole catena of examples from his own experience: the healing of a blind man, a rectal fistula, paralysis and a hernia, gout; along with the liberation from demons for a young girl in Hippo, for some of Augustine's neighbours, and for a demonised boy whose eye was ripped out under demonic frenzy and was left 'hanging by a tiny vein, as by a root.' The eye was restored. He concludes 'It is a simple fact that there is no lack of miracles even in our day. And the God who works the miracles we read of in the Scriptures uses any means and manner he chooses.' And to that claim the church throughout the ages has to say Amen, even though in the more rationalistic periods of its history these manifestations of divine power have been much rarer than in periods of vital faith.

Of course, we all know many examples of devoted believers who are not healed, despite prayer, the laying on of hands and an attitude of deep faith. We are face to face with a deep mystery, and no slick generalisations about healing will avail. It is both cruel and naive to attribute this failure to experience physical healing to prayerlessness or lack of faith. Suffering and death remain the ultimate mysteries which we must all face and to which there is no final solution within the bounds of this mortal life. However, the biblical account does have a good deal to say on this subject of healing, and it was clearly something which the early Christians expected to see in their midst.

God's will for mankind

The Genesis account makes it plain that God made humankind perfect, the man and the woman together. He put them in a garden. There is no hint that suffering and death were part of his purpose for them. On the contrary, it is made very clear that suffering, disease, sin and death are all part of that disastrous fall of man from pristine innocence and obedience. And that same chapter, Genesis 3, where we dimly discern some of the ravages wrought by human rebellion, shows us God himself stepping in as Saviour. He covers their nakedness with skins – the earliest hint of sacrifice in the Bible and the earliest suggestion of the cost of redemption. And, consonant with that early picture, throughout the Old Testament we see God's concern for the whole man: there is nothing ethereal and 'spiritual' about 'salvation' or 'wholeness'. It is embarrassingly physical. It means rescue from death (e.g. Ps 6:4,5), crippling fear (Ps 107:13), sickness (Isa 38:20), and trouble of many kinds (e.g. Jer 30:7). It means rescue from enemies (e.g. 1 Sam 14:23), often brought about by a 'Saviour' whom God specially raises up, such as Samson and Gideon: sometimes by divine intervention alone. But always we see God at work seeking to remove anything that inhibits and threatens the wellbeing of his covenant people. That is the basic meaning of the root '*yasha*', to save, or heal. It aims for the restoration of the whole person.

And Jesus underlined that understanding.

The healings of Jesus

There is a studied ambiguity in the use of the word 'save' in the Gospels. It means both to heal and to rescue in a deeper sense. This is very apparent from the story of the paralytic in Mark 2:1–12 and in verses like Mark 5:34;10:52. Faith is a gateway to physical healing: it also brings spiritual restoration with God, the deeper meaning of 'salvation'. The biblical writers know nothing of our post-Enlightenment dichotomy between the sacred and the secular, the physical and the spiritual. The word 'save' is most frequently applied by the Gospel writers to the healing miracles of Jesus. Thus 'as many as touched were saved' (Mark 6:56 Gk). Blind Bartimaeus was 'saved' by believing in Jesus (Mark 10:52). So was the Samaritan leper (Luke 17:19), the man with a withered hand (Mark 3:3–4) and a host of others. Normally, but by no means always, Jesus is said to have healed *in response to faith*. 'Your faith has saved you' is a constant refrain (e.g. Mark 9:23; 11:24; Luke 8:50). Equally, those healings were deliberately *messianic*. They were bound up with the person of Jesus the Messiah, and the irruption of the Kingdom of God under his leadership and in his person. It is by the words of Jesus, by the person of Jesus, by the total mission of Jesus, that men and women were saved or healed (John 5:34; 10:9; 12:47). This is nowhere more powerfully brought before us than in the story of Jesus and Zacchaeus. In Luke 19:5–6 we are told that Jesus came to Zacchaeus' house: in verse 9 that salvation had come to his house. The two are identical.

Healing continued ...

Jesus intended his healing ministry to be continued by his followers. This is very evident from the mission charge to his disciples where 'he gave them power and authority over all demons and to cure diseases, and he sent them out to preach the kingdom of God and to heal' (Luke 9:1–2). Again in the charge to the Seventy, Jesus says 'Heal the sick ... and say to them "The kingdom of God has come near to you"' (Luke 10:9).

The early Christians clearly regarded this as part of their mandate. The Kingdom of God, they were persuaded, was not a matter of mere talk, but of power (1 Cor 4:20). It is prominent in the Acts, as early as chapter 3 and as late as chapter 28. The Epistle of James expects God to raise a brother up in response to prayer (5:14ff). And so it has continued, in the second and third centuries, as we have seen above, and up to the present day.

Come with me in imagination to a quadrangle of an ancient Oxford college. In a room off that quad lies a young man on his bed. He has been there for weeks with serious trouble in his back. He read James 5:14ff, and in obedience he called together the Christian leaders in his College and me, his parish priest. We prayed for him earnestly, laid hands upon him, and then invited him to get up and walk. He did – right round the quadrangle several times, with evident joy. We hastened away to get him his first decent meal for weeks!

Or come to a hospital ward, where I had been summoned to visit an old woman in our congregation who was dying. She momentarily regained consciousness as I prayed over her, but the medical staff were clear that she would be dead in an hour or two. That evening I returned to find her not only on the way to recovery, but a changed personality: gone was the sharpness and complaining attitude for which she had been known, and a new gentleness and growing Christlikeness began to bloom in her as she lived on for a few more years.

I think of a situation in Malawi. It was a clergy conference and at the end a clergyman asked me to pray for his leg. It was clearly non-functional, and my faith was far from confident! I invited two others to come and pray with me, and we poured out our hearts to God in prayer as we laid loving hands on this man's leg. He then bounded to his feet and started to dance round the church, while we tried to urge caution – to no avail!

Or imagine the scene in an Intensive Care unit of a hospital. A 21-year-old girl has been knocked down by a bus and has serious internal head injuries. The prognosis is death or, as an outside chance, survival as a cabbage. My colleague and I ask for admission to go and pray over her. It is granted. As we arrive she seems to recognise us for a moment from the depths of the coma in which she has been for four days, since the accident. As we begin to pray in tongues the nurses move away, mystified, and the restlessness of the patient abruptly abates. After a while we have a conviction that God will heal her completely. We leave. That was about 5.00 p.m. That girl was sitting up and having breakfast next morning (having eaten nothing, of course, since the accident). She was up at lunch. She was back in the ward in a day, and home a few days later. And now she is a missionary overseas! Her healing was the talk of the hospital, from consultants to porters. It was a marvellous exhibition of divine power, confounding human prognostications.

However, we know it is not always like that.

Failures in healing

Stories such as I have just mentioned, all from my personal experience, are a glorious indication of the Lord's power to heal. But that is only half the story. And so it has been from the first days after the ascension of Jesus. For the healings brought about by the disciples were not of the same quality as those of their Master, although they were continuing his gracious work. For one thing, Jesus had no failure rate, and no reversions afterwards. All Christian healers experience both. For another, his healings seem to have been complete and instantaneous, apart from two recorded incidents where there was a short delay and renewed ministry before the cure was complete. Healings by the church are not like that, unfortunately. Often there is delay. Often there is failure.

Why is it that we so often experience failure when we pray for healing? The problem is not new. Even the Apostle Paul had to say 'Trophimus I left ill at Miletus' (2 Tim 4:20). He has to record unanswered prayer in his own situation, as he begged the Lord to remove some affliction which he calls a 'thorn in his flesh' (2 Cor. 12:8ff). All in vain. His prayer was not answered in the affirmative – though the Lord provided his strength, the strength which is brought to fruition in human weakness, to enable him to face the situation. And that is often the case today.

Francis MacNutt in *Healing*[2] and John Wimber in *Power Healing*[3] face this issue head-on, and with great honesty. Both of them have been much used in a ministry of healing. Their writing on the subject comes from deep reflection and much experience, and is full of wisdom. Failure to secure healing is not because God is indifferent to the ailments of our bodies. And it is not always because of unconfessed sin or inadequate faith. No. To make that claim is to add insult to injury and heap gratuitous agony on the person who is already suffering greatly (though sometimes it may be the case, and if so needs to be exposed). But four major reasons stand out in my mind as obstacles to the healing grace of God.

First, it will often be the case that we do not have because we do not ask (James 4:2). Many churches and pastors seem not to believe that God heals today, and it nowhere figures in their teaching and church life.

Second, we have a great outside adversary, so the Scriptures teach. Satan is involved in sickness. Think of the hunchbacked woman in the Gospels (Luke 13:16): Satan had bowed down that back of hers for years. Think of Paul's thorn in the flesh – it was a messenger of Satan to buffet him. I remember an illness of mine which vanished when friends came in, sensed the presence of evil, and challenged Satan to release his grip and go. We often fail to allow for this possible demonic dimension to suffering.

Third, we must always remember that Jesus was divine, and we are not. There is indeed a continuity between his ministry of healing and ours. It is afforded by the Holy Spirit. But there is also a discontinuity: it is afforded by the ascension.

Fourth, there are three *tenses* to salvation, as it is set

out in the Scriptures. There is a sense in which salvation has already been achieved and appropriated. There is a sense in which we experience it constantly. And there is a sense in which it is still to come – and these are the references which predominate in the biblical teaching on the subject. Salvation and healing are always imperfect in this life. Think of it this way. It is not the will of God that we should suffer disease and suffering, just as it is not his will that we should sin. However, in this mortal life he tolerates both, though he desires neither. If we are to get a balanced view of the situation, we must return to the scriptural insight that our present condition is neither what it was originally when God made the world, nor what it will be finally, when we go to share his home in heaven. To put it in a Pauline way, we remain 'in this age' and subject to its attacks and weaknesses, even while we enjoy some of the invasive and healthgiving powers of 'the age to come'. One day we will be immersed fully in the 'age to come'. For now, we taste occasional fruits from it to assure us it is real and to incite our appetite for it.

The Christian attitude
Christians who, like the first disciples, believe in divine healing, might usefully keep the following reflections in mind as they approach particular cases of illness and disease.

First, God is the supreme source of healing, and he plans wholeness (*soteria*) for his children. We shall experience many a taste of that wholeness as we go through life, but it will only be complete after our final deliverance from disease and death. Then, and not till then, will wholeness be complete.

Second, it is important to remember that God is the healer. Sometimes he heals through the natural recuperative powers of the body, sometimes through medicine, sometimes without. Exodus 15:26 reminds us, 'I am the Lord, your healer'. It is not better if healing comes through prayer than through medicine; neither is it worse. God is sovereign to use whatever way he chooses

— or to withhold healing if he sees it to be in our best ultimate interests. The important thing, when we get sick, is to learn to turn to the Lord before we turn to anyone else, and surrender the whole problem into his hands. This will then free us up to see either medication or Christian ministry as his possible avenue of healing.

Third, following on from this, we need to search our hearts before God when sickness strikes. There may be something he longs to teach us through the experience. Confession of sin, and openness to whatever he may send is called for, even if it be the final healing of all mortal ills in death. Only thus can God bless us as he longs to. Only thus can we be confident that our prayers for healing are according to his will, rather than ours. We must never forget that God is sovereign. Our prayers are not to twist his arm, but to co-operate in his purposes. And we can come to him in confidence, assured that not even death can rob us of complete wholeness at the last. We need to come in faith to the God who is well able to heal. We need to seek and accept his purpose and his timing. We need to have our sins forgiven and put away. We need to be open to gifts of healing, from whatever source they come.

Finally, it is worth reflecting that healing is of different kinds. We are so infatuated with our pleasures and our bodies that we seek physical healing above all else. But it is not the ultimate good. Heaven, not health, is our goal. And a lot of sickness is not physical in origin or nature. Much is related to conflict between body and mind, the conscious and the unconscious, home and work, the individual and society; conflict within the family, conflict between our ambitions and our achievements. When the tension in any of these areas becomes intolerable, we get sick, and need healing. The Lord expects his body, the church, to be one of the agencies in human healing. Healing of frustration and disintegration by coming to Christ. Healing of anxiety by trusting Christ. Healing of painful memories by the touch of Christ. Healing of animosities by the reconciliation Christ brings. Healing of fear by the presence of Christ. These are palpable areas of human need to which Christ is profoundly relevant here and now in this life. The ultimate healing lies beyond the grave.

Deliverance

We come to a dark and controversial area of spirituality which was very familiar to the early Christians, as it is to believers in many parts of the Two Thirds World, but of which I, along with millions of Western Christians, was utterly ignorant, until I was brought face to face with it — in one of the most sophisticated cities of the world. Many Christians deride the whole idea of the demonic. Others see demons under every bush. What does Scripture say?

1. *There is a supreme anti-God force* known in the Bible as Satan, the devil, the prince of this world, the prince of the power of the air, Beelzebul, the liar, the slanderer, the murderer — and other names. He is taken with great seriousness by the biblical writers. It seems to me that there are at least seven considerations which point strongly to the existence of this anti-God force: considerations of philosophy, theology, the environment, the occult, personal experience of temptation, the uniform testimony of Scripture and the clear teaching of Jesus. I have filled out these headings in chapter 1 of *I Believe in Satan's Downfall*,[4] and I shall not rehearse them further now. I find it significant that Jesus himself has more to say about the devil than any other teacher in the whole of Scripture (e.g. Matt 4:1–11; Matt 6:13; 12:22–45; Mark 3:22-26; Mark 4:15; John 12:31; 14:30 etc). It is only possible to evade the force of his testimony by having recourse to the theories of accommodation or kenosis, neither of which can withstand rigorous examination. If Jesus was clear and unambiguous about the awesome reality of Satan, that should be good enough for the Christian disciple.

Scripture is restrained in its treatment of the devil. But it does indicate that Satan is a fallen angel whose arrogant pride led to his being cast out of heaven (Ezek chs 26–28; Isa 14; Luke 10:18; Rev 12). The Book of Job makes it very plain that Satan is not equal and opposite to God: he remains God's devil, with comparative freedom, but at the end of a long chain. His aim is to spoil God's world: in society by war, in the home by broken relationships, in the body by disease and in the soul by sin. Powerful though he is, his destiny is destruction (Rev 20:10). In the meantime he wages unceasing war against all that is good – and supremely against God.

2. *Satan has demonic allies*. And these allies afflict human beings. Once again the Scriptures are clear that God is the source not only of human but of angelic life. There are angelic beings in God's world, and they figure greatly in the Bible. Some of them joined Satan's insurrection against God, shared in his fall, and became his allies, and agents against God (Rev 12:7–9; 2 Pet 2:4; Jude v6). These spiritual forces of darkness assail human beings. There appears to be a wide variation in the extent of the grip they gain, though the common distinction between 'oppression' and 'possession' has no basis whatsoever in Scripture where the word most commonly used is *daimonizesthai*, to be demonised, i.e. affected by a demon. It would appear that these demonic beings may have knowledge (Mark 1:24; Acts 19:15), emotions (Mark 1:24; James 2:19), speech, willpower (Matt 12:44) – yet they are constantly referred to in the neuter gender in Greek. If all this seems bizarre to us, it could be because we have been imprisoned within a rationalistic post-Enlightenment world-view which discounts the supernatural – at the same time as millions of our citizens are involved in the fascinating, dangerous and real world of the occult! It is at least worth examining the biblical alternative.

3. *Jesus came to set people free*. He came to destroy the works of the devil (1 John 3:8). He came to free the captives (Luke 4:18).

There are many general statements in the Gospels about Jesus liberating demonised people (e.g. Mark

1:32–34; 1:39; Luke 4:41; 6:18). Demonic activity may underlie some diseases: blindness, dumbness (Matt 12:22), epilepsy (Matt 17:14–17), mental illness (Luke 8:27) and physical illness alike (Luke 13:11ff) *may* be thus caused, but the Bible never suggests that this is normally the case. It never suggests that *all* illness is caused by demonic activity. In fact it makes a careful distinction between healing diseases and casting out demons (Luke 13:32). In Luke 4:40ff we have a general picture of Jesus' liberating work, and find that whereas he often laid hands on the sick and healed them, he did not lay hands on the demonised (that would be to express solidarity with the demons), but rebuked them and cast them out. Demons are expelled. Diseases are healed. The distinction is clear. Jesus came to destroy both aspects of the work of the devil, and we find him doing it throughout the Gospels.

In addition to these general references, there are seven accounts of Jesus liberating individuals from demonic grip (Matt 9:32; Mark 1:21–28; 3:22–27; 5:1–20; 7:24–30; 9:14–29; Luke 13:10–17). Three of these, the Gerasene demoniac, the epileptic boy, and the Beelzebul controversy, appear in all three Synoptic Gospels.

Certain significant principles emerge.

First, Jesus did not go around seeking confrontation with the demonic: people brought the patients to him.

Second, Jesus seems normally to have cast the demons out with a word of command (Mark 9:25) and not to have entered into parley with them; indeed, he often forbade them to speak (Mark 1:34). The only exception to this refusal to discuss with them is the case of the Gerasene demoniac.

Third, there was considerable variety in Jesus' very direct approach to demons. Sometimes he 'muzzled' them (Luke 4:35), sometimes he 'bound' them (Matt 12:29) and sometimes he had to repeat his command (see Mark 5:8; and the Greek of Luke 11:14).

Sometimes he seems to have made a point of forbidding the evil spirit ever to return (Mark 9:25). He was well aware of the danger of reinfestation (Matt 12:43–44). And in his forthright approach to the problem, he always addressed the demon, not the person.

Only once do we find him exorcising at a distance (Matt 15:28). It happened to be a situation of exceptional faith and persistent, single-minded request.

Of course, the cross was the supreme exorcism. It was here that Satan and his demonic allies suffered rout. Matthew 8:16–17 is a significant hint of this; but the clearest expression of it comes in Colossians 2:15. 'He disarmed the principalities and powers and made a public example of them, triumphing over them in it [the cross].'

4. *Jesus empowered and commissioned his followers to continue his work of liberation.* We find this is true of the Twelve in Luke 9:1, and of the seventy in Luke 10:17. It continued in the apostolic church (Mark 16:17; Acts 16:16–18; 19:11–17), and it was a major strand in the advance of their successors. One of the early second-century writers, Justin Martyr, for example, can make a claim like this:

> Many of our Christian men have exorcised in the name of Jesus Christ, who was crucified under Pontius Pilate, numberless demoniacs throughout the world, and in your city. When all other exorcists and specialists in incantations and drugs have failed, they have healed them and still do heal, rendering the demons impotent and driving them out.[5]

It has always been part of the practice of the church to seek deliverance from demonic infestation both of places and people. It is a very delicate area of ministry, because it is so easy to go wrong. To diagnose demonic interference when there is none can raise in the person concerned all manner of fears. It should be the last resort, not the first, in Christian ministry. Nevertheless this work of liberation is a proper part of the all-round ministry of the church, and therefore I propose to address some of the practical issues which will confront us as they did the first Christians.

Practical issues

1. *Is there an increase in demonic activity these days?* There certainly is. It was a deliberate feature both in Hitler's Germany and Stalin's Russia. There is a massive preoccupation with the occult in our generation, leading often to ritual Satanic worship. There are reasons for this growth: the emptiness of materialism, the religious instinct of man, and the deadness of the church to the issues of the Spirit. There is also a hunger for thrills and significance in a society where the individual seems to matter less and less, along with a desire for power over other people and group coherence in a crumbling society.

2. *What is the purpose of occult involvement?* It is threefold, to correspond with the three main divisions of occult activity. Magic, be it white or black, seeks to control the spirit world. It is all about power. Fortune telling, whether by palmistry, tarot, clairvoyance, or horoscopes, seeks to penetrate the future. It is all about knowledge. Spiritism, through ouija, trances, séances and mediums, seeks to break through to the world beyond. It is all about contact with the dead.

3. *Is there anything wrong with it?* There is. It is expressly forbidden in the Bible. Deuteronomy 18:9ff forbids the children of Israel to be cajoled by their pagan neighbours into any of these three divisions of the occult. It was a capital offence (Exod 22:18). In the New Testament the prohibition is no less stringent (e.g. 1 Cor 10:20–21) and the Satanic origin of the occult is clearly exposed (Rev 16:12ff). Why this hard line? Because you are submitting yourself, in the occult, to a power which is not from God and may well be in active revolt against him. What is more, it betrays a lust for knowledge we are not supposed to have, along with an illicit power over people. It seeks to break the barrier of death which is God-given. It is dangerous and can become destructive, as it was to

King Saul and Manasseh. Worst of all, involvement in the occult is hateful to God because it is direct disobedience: 'Rebellion is like the sin of witchcraft' (1 Sam 15:23).

4. *Is occult involvement the only way in which demonic infestation comes?* No, but it is the main way. It also seems that deliberate, persistent sin may sometimes allow powers beyond ourselves to force an entrance. Sexual sins and involvement in nature-worship or the worship of false gods may render people vulnerable. Sometimes the possession of a charm or decoration offered to heathen gods can have this effect, as can a curse and even trouble in the family tree.

5. *Can Christians be thus infected?* Indeed they can. The conviction that this is unthinkable springs from the unbiblical distinction of 'oppression' and 'possession', coupled with the conviction that if Christ's Spirit possesses you, an evil spirit obviously cannot. If you look at it in 'possession' terms, that argument holds good. But that is not what *daimonizomai* means in the New Testament, as we have seen. There is no reason why believers should not be influenced by dark forces: they are in fact a prime target, as the prince of the apostles found just after a moment of high spiritual insight! (Matt 16:23). Sometimes there has been prior demonic influence in a life which becomes Christian: and unless it is dealt with at the time of initiation it may well lie low and cause trouble for years to come, like neglected clumps of weeds in an otherwise lovely garden.

6. *How should Christians approach this matter?* In general we need to appreciate that the critical victory over all the forces of evil has been won – by Jesus on the cross. That is the key to the understanding of all history: the Lamb once slain is in the midst of the throne of God (Rev 5:1–12). In Satan we confront a defeated foe (Rev 12:7–11).

The specifics are laid out in the famous passage on spiritual battle in Ephesians 6. We are to stand firm (v14) in an attitude of determined rejection of any strand of evil in our own lives. We must approach this ministry with no compromise, no defeatism and no fear. We then need to take and don the whole armour of God (v13), claiming the Lord's protection. We need to pray and to get others to support us in prayer (v18). And we need to watch, to have our wits very much about us as we minister (v18).

7. *How are we to discern forces of active evil*? Discernment is a gift (1 Cor 12:10) and it is a great help if someone in the little group ministering possesses this gift. Some indicators are: abnormal aggression and strength, preternatural knowledge, violent reaction against the name of Jesus, or when confronted by a cross, the Communion, the Bible, or entry into a church. Any involvement with the occult, Christian Science, TM, and all animistic religions, may alert us to the possibility of demonic presence, as may a series of suicides among close relations, or spiritism in a previous generation (often a grandmother). Unnatural bondage to sexual perversion, or other compulsive habits, unsought blasphemy, and uncontrollable mockery of God are also characteristics that should arouse our suspicion, as may strange behaviour – the fluttering of eyelids, changes in voice and laughter, compulsive inability to pray, and the grip of a nameless fear.

These characteristics are not exhaustive, nor do they necessarily denote demonic grip. Some are found in conjunction with mental illness; some with people who have never learnt what it is to 'crucify the flesh'. It is extremely unwise to jump to hasty conclusions in ministry of this sort. But evil spirits like to remain hidden. They are normally driven to manifest themselves most in lively charismatic worship, at the Holy Communion, or in the presence of several deeply committed Christians. Often the persons concerned will display that love– hate response to Jesus which the Gerasene demoniac showed. They are very much torn in two, and we need to help them find freedom. If we do make a mistaken diagnosis it need not be disastrous, particularly if we have established easy relationships. Explain that you are not clear whether or not dark forces are present, but will challenge them in case they are. The result will be obvious. One further word: if someone claims to be demonised – take leave to doubt it.

8. *How can we prepare for a time of deliverance ministry?* Quite simply. We need to go with at least one other person who is experienced in this work. It is important to operate only with the goodwill of those who are over you in the Lord: the forces of evil seem to be very aware of levels of authority and will not leave if we have not submitted ourselves to those in authority over us. Prayer is of course vital. And it is good to have a group of people praying in the background while ministry is actually being carried on. It is helpful to take with you oil for anointing when the job is done, elements for an informal Communion if appropriate, and a cross – all emblems of the victory of Jesus in whose name you go. Incidentally, it is important not to be rushed, and never to use a larger ministry when a smaller one will do.

9. *The ministry of deliverance.* There is no set way: it is interesting to notice the variety in Jesus' approach to different demonised people. But we should begin by setting fears at rest and getting the person relaxed and keen to co-operate. That will save much time and trouble. Be matter-of-fact about the job of liberation to be done: I find it helpful to allude to it as a very normal part of pastoral ministry.

Explanations over, it is time to move into a time of honest confession, with detailed renunciation of every form of activity through which the grip of the demonic might have entered. This should be followed by the absolution, and encouraging verses from Scripture. I have found that fear and resentment are two of the most common blockages on the road to freedom. I often ask 'Is there someone you cannot forgive?' That has to be dealt with before proceeding.

Together we claim the armour of Christ, and then quietly but firmly command the evil thing to go, in the name of the Trinity and with explicit mention of the blood of Christ shed upon the cross. 'Resist the devil,' we are told 'and he will flee from you' (James 4:7). Command it to leave and never to return. It may go immediately. It may temporise, with strange voices emerging from the person, offering defiance, swearing it will never leave, insulting you, or whining not to be cast out. The insistent command to leave must then be repeated. Verses of Scripture may come to the mind of one of those ministering: that can help. So of course does praise (often in song), repeated recourse to prayer, the use of the gift of tongues, or perhaps of holy water (which I have found to be very effective) or some representation of the cross. We need to be prepared for anything, and to watch very closely to see what appears to be happening. Violence, deceit, a cynical smile, mockery, vomiting, animal behaviour — any of these things may happen.

I find it most helpful to ask the person concerned how they are feeling as we proceed. They always know when there is more work to be done, and they know when they are free. If you can get the persons concerned to call upon the Lord themselves for deliverance, that is best of all. They then see themselves as partners in the ministry, not just objects of it. I have not found it necessary to name the evil influences, though it is often obvious what they are and they sometimes name themselves. When they do, it is an advantage: there is power in knowing the name. It may take some time before freedom comes. It is important not to hurry, but to wait on God for his illumination while the ministry is going on. God may guide by a conviction, or a picture coming into the mind of someone ministering. His Spirit will lead you, as you trust him. If there is no progress in an hour or so, claim Christ's power to bind whatever evil force is there, and set another time for renewed ministry, after the person has had a time to reflect on the possible cause of the blockage, and you have had time for prayer and perhaps advice from those more experienced. Avoid a long, protracted session which is exhausting for all and deeply disappointing if it does not end in success.

The persons concerned always know when the thing

has gone, and there are usually tears of joy and relief.
Afterwards they need love, food and rest. It may well feel
as exhausting as an operation, and rest is essential. Make
sure that tender loving care is continued.

A final word to those engaging in this ministry. Do
not get hooked on it. It is so dramatic that it can easily
become unhealthily addictive. I find it wise not to do it
at all except among people to whom I am ministering in
other ways.

Conclusion
If all this sounds like Alice in Wonderland to the reader, I
can sympathise. It sounded like that to me. Unfortunately
I have discovered that it is painfully real. The church has
known this down the ages. It is only in this century that
Christians in the West have ceased to expect deliverance
for the demonised. The consequences of this failure of
ours are great. People thus affected go to doctors, who
cannot help them, or into mental hospitals which are not
appropriate for their condition. Only Christ can set them
free, by his lifegiving Spirit. And the church is charged
by her Lord not to fail people by neglecting this ministry
of liberation.

Renewal, spiritual warfare, expectancy, and the power
of God. These are our weapons. And remember Luke
10:19–20, 'I give you authority . . . over all the power
of the enemy . . . Nevertheless do not rejoice in this, that
the spirits are subject to you; but rejoice that your names
are written in heaven.'

CHAPTER EIGHT

ZEALOUS FOR GOOD WORKS

*It is only by living completely in this world that one learns
to have faith . . . By this-worldliness I mean living
unreservedly in life's duties, problems, successes and
failures, experiences and perplexities. In so doing we throw
ourselves completely into the arms of God.*
Dietrich Bonhoeffer

New Testament spirituality is essentially subversive.
It sneaks into the centre of our lives rather than
remaining at the periphery – in 'quiet times', church services and retreats. If spirituality does not make an actual
difference in the concrete details of our lives, it is fraudu-
lent. The Letter of James brings this crucial dimension
to our study. But before examining this fascinating letter
we will briefly explore some of the theological reasons for
insisting on down-to-earth holiness. Essentially there are
four reasons.

First, God himself is a Trinity, three persons in one
social, complex unity. This is the ultimate mystery and
we humbly confess that we cannot 'explain' God. But
what is revealed to us is that God exists in relationship, a
covenant love relationship of Father, Son and Holy Spirit
that existed even before there was a world (John 17:24).
Contrary to the popular idea that God created humankind
because he was lonely, the Bible reveals the exact opposite: God created us because he was *not* lonely. He is love,
and we are the fruit of his love. To say 'God is love' (1 John
4:16) is not merely to describe an attribute of God, but to
confess that God *is* a lover and that love exists constantly
between the Father, Son and Holy Spirit. Therefore, true

spirituality in those who would be God-like must involve authentic, covenant love relationships in which the rich are not preferred for their wealth and power and the poor are not despised because of their apparent uselessness. James makes some searching statements on this subject. Biblical spirituality is intrinsically relational. It is not what a person does with his or her solitariness.

Second, the Incarnation (God becoming a man) is the paradigm for the spiritual life. The Word became flesh and genuinely came among us in every conceivable way: physically, emotionally, spiritually, cosmically, culturally and aesthetically. God slipped into the human family in a little Jewish baby and grew up to make wooden yokes, to speak with a Galilean accent, to tell jokes with a wry Jewish humour, and to die on a Roman gallows. Jesus had a real and recognisable human body after his resurrection. How much more human can God get? In one sense Christ is not interested in 'spirituality' as an exalted state of mind in which one becomes released from the struggles and pressures of life in the real world. That is an essentially Buddhist idea. True spirituality has to do with work, money, sex, relationships, values, family, politics and neighbouring. And the ultimate goal of the Christian life is not 'heaven' but a 'new heaven and a new earth'.

Typically, evangelical spirituality has focused on three marks: Sunday service attendance, the Wednesday night prayer meeting and personal daily devotions. Today these are almost dead issues and largely not practised. Catholic spirituality has traditionally been monastic (the contemplative life is lived away from the normal pressures of life), mystical (in the narrow sense of exalting transcendent experiences of God that lead to what is called a 'spiritual marriage' with God), and clerical (those who handle the things of God in sacrament and word are invited to live a superior life not possible for those who live and work in normal society). The Protestant version of this is not very different! So spirituality has become mystified, clericalised and privatised. In contrast, biblical spirituality is down-to-earth, practical and embodied. As we will see, James is eloquent on this subject.

Third, the New Testament view of the human person is consistent with that presented in the Old Testament. In contrast to the Greek dualistic view of personhood (body and soul as two separate compartments in the person) the inspired authors took an essentially Hebraic view that the human person is a unity. Body, soul and spirit are not compartments but dimensions of one human being. We *are* bodies, souls and spirits. Touch a body and one has touched a person. So Paul says the shocking thing that a person who 'married' his body to a prostitute is joining Christ (in his person) to a prostitute (1 Cor 6:15). Sexual sins affect the personality, not just the body (6:18). And James says that faith without works is dead (James 2:26). There is no sense in having Jesus in our hearts if he does not affect our bodily life! So James will tell us that spirituality has little to do with seeing visions or having rapturous experiences. Rather it has to do with how we spend our money, how we speak and listen, and how we treat the poor. Holiness has to do with eating and sleeping, working and playing, laughing and crying. True spirituality is an embodied spirituality. The ultimate destiny of the Christian person is not to be a disembodied spirit floating around in eternity but, through the resurrection of the body on the last day, to have a complete bodily existence in the presence of God, his people and his recreated world forever.

There is a fourth reason for the insistence of authors like James for a down-to-earth holiness. The New Testament views the consummation of the former (old) covenant in Jesus as an invitation to live the paradox of the Christian life: strength in Christ through emotional and physical weakness. God's strength is made perfect through bodily weakness; God's glory is revealed through the reality of our earthen vessels (2 Cor 4:7; 12:9). The success, wealth and health gospel has a deep hold on a large part of the world. But it is essentially heretical. God does not deliver us *from* problems so much as he delivers us *in* them. That is the first of ten themes we will explore in the Letter of James.

The spirituality of problems (James 1:1-18; 5:7-12)

'Consider it pure joy, my brothers, whenever you face trials of many kinds' (James 1:2). At first this might appear somewhat bizarre, unrealistic and perhaps even sadistic. But James is not counselling *enjoying* our problems, but counting them pure joy, a much deeper thing. What he is claiming is that a Christian life-view, countercultural as it is, determines *to count* trials as a joy in anticipation of the good things God will do in the hardest moments of our lives. Some trials come from our family background and personality. My own trials illustrate both the diversity and the 'joy' which ultimately can be experienced through our struggles. I grew up in a non-affirming family environment (a factor that has already turned into a blessing as I look to God for my affirmation). I had difficulty in public speaking, a handicap which led, during my secondary school years, to a determination to learn how to speak. I won several public speaking contests!

Some trials arise from decisions we have made believing we were doing God's will. A few years ago I decided to take up carpentry/joinery for a living in order to support the ministry of church-planting in which we were engaged. It turned out to be a very difficult experience, but it gave me a deep appreciation of the fact that most people invest an enormous amount of energy providing for themselves and their families. In job after job I have been faced with increasing administrative responsibilities, which I have usually accepted reluctantly, and sometimes I have resigned from these positions in order to be released from administration. But these 'trials' have led me to consider that administrative roles – such as I now enjoy – to serve others without public recognition are gifts from God. Some trials arise from our own personality – such as my shyness – or short-circuited character development – such as my oversensitivity to criticism. Unprovoked trials because we follow Jesus, and

seemingly random problems – such as almost being killed
in a riot in Nairobi – add to the list of 'trials of every kind'.
What is extraordinary about the message of James is that
trials are considered sacramental.

As distinct from temptations (1:13–15), trials test our
faith to reveal what is real, as fire tests the metal
and removes the dross. We cannot have a trouble-free
life. Trials are the necessary environment for developing perseverance (1:3–4) and patience (5:7,10). God is
the ultimate equipper. He uses the day-to-day experiences – especially the hardest experiences – to develop
endurance, what Eugene Peterson calls 'a long obedience in the same direction'.[1] Trials are the God-given
context for developing singlemindedness. In contrast,
the doubleminded person is unstable in all his ways
(1:8). 'Unstable' is not used here in the psychological
sense (emotionally unstable) but in the life-orientation
sense – dashing here and there, being swept along by
circumstances, succumbing to trials rather than profiting
by them. God's goal is that we will not be governed by
circumstances but by the promise and the word of God.
God desires that we will be undaunted by competing
pressures and not confused by competing 'calls'.

To become a mature person we must get beyond allowing our contentment to be dependent on our circumstances (1:9–11). God uses our problems to accomplish
this character development and to build perseverance. It
is impossible to learn perseverance in a classroom, on a
retreat, in a momentary transcendent experience of God's
presence or even by prayer. We learn perseverance by
meeting trials with faith and counting them 'pure joy'.

Patience (5:7,10) is similar to perseverance but there
is a slight difference. With perseverance we are able to
persist; with patience we are willing to wait. Set as we
are in an 'instant gratification' culture, we need patience
to wait for the full realisation of our faith, our service to
God and our life work. But there is no way to become
equipped for patience other than by experiencing trials
with the perspective of faith. Job is James' example of

perseverance (5:11). Job pestered God with his questions which might appear to be a lack of patience. But Job never gave up believing that God would justify him. In the end, Job's handling of his painful trial revealed that wisdom (1:5) is not keeping silent in trials – while seething on the inside – but looking to God *in* them. Job's friends talked *about* God; Job talked *to* God.

So the mature person is able to profit through trials and can deliberately count it pure joy when new trials surface. Such a person does not gravitate to self-pity when things do not go well, but rather prays to see God's purpose in it. The mature person stays at the task until it is finished. The long view on life anticipates that we will receive the 'crown of life': knowing God better and experiencing the life of his Kingdom (1:12; 2:5). We can receive the crown by embracing the trials with faith and seeking God's wisdom in them (1:5–6), or we can miss the crown by resenting the trials, feeling sorry for ourselves and becoming a victim instead of victor. What has holiness to do with problems? Everything. In the same way holiness has everything to do with listening.

The spirituality of listening (James 1:19–21)

Every disciple of Jesus has the same basic anatomy: two ears and one mouth. This is a powerful argument for doing twice as much listening as we do speaking! James' emphasis is not on 'twice as much' but on being twice as ready. 'My dear brothers, take note of this: Everyone should be quick to listen, slow to speak and slow to become angry' (James 1:19). Being a good listener is more crucial for Christian ministry than speaking. Even evangelism should be done with the ears as well as the mouth.

One finds good listeners in unusual places. Sometimes people who are quiet are poor listeners while others who talk a lot may be good listeners. It has to do with enjoying people and wanting to discover the mystery of each person, not with the volume of speech. Good speakers have listened deeply to the struggles and joys of others and can discern an entry point for spiritual movement.

They have listened to their own hearts and discerned the movement of God in their own life experiences. Then, with the truth of God wrung out of their own experiences, they can sustain others by their words. Pastoral care involves offering our own life experience to others and so, as Paul Simon sings, laying ourselves down as a 'bridge over troubled water'. Like the Servant in Isaiah's songs we can say, 'The Sovereign Lord has given me an instructed tongue, to know the word that sustains the weary. He wakens me morning by morning, wakens my ear to listen like one being taught. *The Sovereign Lord has opened my ears* . . .' (Isa 50:4–5, emphasis mine).

Furthermore, good speakers not only listen to people; they have learned to listen deeply to Scripture. A medieval Augustinian canon, Walter of Hilton, described the inattentive Bible reader as gnawing on the outer crust of Scripture and missing its heavenly meaning which is disclosed by the Spirit of God even to the illiterate if they seek God as lovers and listeners. It is not surprising that in our entertainment-oriented culture there is a famine not so much of speaking the words of Scripture but of *hearing* God's word. It is a day about which both Jeremiah (Jer 23:16–36) and Amos prophesied (Amos 8:10–12).

James not only explores the timeless principle of earning the right to speak by listening, but also the relationship of being 'quick to listen' and 'slow to become angry' (James 1:19). If we are slow to speak – refusing to finish people's sentences for them and not assuming we know what is going on inside – we are less likely to get angry. We have tried to understand the person and have not merely reacted. 'For man's anger does not bring about the righteous life that God desires' (1:20). So the patient tongue – 'slow to speak' – comes from open ears and a listening heart – 'quick to listen' leads to greater peace – 'slow to become angry'.

But there is more in this passage than good techniques in communication or a psychological description of the relationship of empathetic listening and anger. This is a matter that concerns our spirituality. By listening to others we position ourselves to attend to God. The converse is also true: by listening to God we learn how to attend to others. So listening is an act of worship. By listening we recognise our creatureliness and accept that we are neither autonomous nor self-sufficient. We need the viewpoint and presence of others. By listening we renounce control of others, including our pretence of controlling God. By listening we prize others and therefore communicate the most important thing of all: their worth. Perhaps God himself shows his love for us best not by speaking to us, but by listening to us as we pour out our hearts to him.

Not having earlids to match our eyelids turns out to be a good thing for spiritual formation. Having a continuous stream of sounds enter our consciousness is an everyday opportunity to cultivate an embodied spirituality. So is the everyday opportunity of speaking.

The spirituality of speaking (James 3:1–12)

James' argument for a holy tongue can be summarised in four points. First, the tongue is revelatory (James 3:2). It reveals, as Jesus said, what is in the heart (Matt 12:34). 'If anyone is never at fault in what he says, he is a perfect man, able to keep his whole body in check' (James 3:2). Once while walking down the hall with my colleague, Phil, I blurted out, 'Do you know why I plan so far in advance, Phil?' 'No,' he said. 'Because I do not want anyone to make plans on my behalf!' It was an unpremeditated self-disclosure. To the Hebraic mind the person stands behind the word and is revealed by the word. Therefore the person literally comes out of the mouth, as it did that day in the College halls.

Second, the tongue is hard to control. 'No man can tame the tongue' (3:8). The reason is simply that *persons* are hard to control. Third, the same tongue can both praise God and curse men (3:9–12). This indicates that the 'source' of the speech is not as pure and undefiled as might be thought. Finally, most people should not aspire to teaching 'because you know that we who teach will be judged more strictly' (3:1). It is not just the teaching that will be judged but the person of the teacher.

We should make sure that the source of our words – the inner person – is being sanctified. In biblical anthropology the person comes out of the mouth. Every word begs the question, what kind of person is this who is speaking? Bitter people produce bitter words. Gracious persons bring grace in their speech. So in preaching, the preparation of the preacher is more important than the preparation of the sermon.

The three vices of the tongue in Ephesians 5:4 are expressions of three vices in the Christian person. *Aischrotes* is obscenity or ugly speech that comes from a shameless person. *Morologia* is foolish, silly talk or, as Bengel said, fishing for a laugh. There is no salt in this person's speech (Col 4:6) because there is not salt in the person (Mark 9:50). *Eutrapelia* is coarse joking, or facetiousness. Instead, says Paul, let there be thanksgiving (Eph 5:4). James agrees, 'Can a fig tree bear olives?' (James 3:12). It is a two-way street: what we say reveals ourselves; what we say also affects ourselves. So deciding to practice thanksgiving and a life of blessing God and humankind, will simultaneously be a ministry to *ourselves* and to others.

James has deep reasons to regard even ordinary conversation as a spiritual discipline. Our speech reveals the integration or disintegration of our inner lives. It also is directly related to the depths of our relationship with God. 'If anyone considers himself religious and yet does not keep a tight rein on his tongue, he deceives himself and his religion is worthless' (James 1:26). Our words are powerful. 'One word of the truth,' Solzhenitzyn said, 'outweighs the whole world.' The proverb says, 'The tongue has the power of life and death' (Prov 18:21). With the tongue, James notes, we can actually make a difference to God when we bless him (James 3:9) and we can affect people negatively by our speech about them and to them, especially when we curse them. A controlled tongue is an accurate gauge of the self-controlled person under God.

As we grow in maturity we become increasingly free from the fear of being controlled by others or from wanting to control others by our words. All of this is consistent with another theme in James' letter.

The spirituality of doing (James 1:22–27; 2:14–26)
James repudiates any polarisation of doing and being. He argues that we *do* what we most truly *are*, and we *are* what we most truly *do*. Consistent with this, James also repudiates any polarisation of *believing* and *acting*. It is often noted that this letter has a distinctively Jewish character and was probably written very early in the history of the church by James the Just, brother of Jesus, who was converted after a personal encounter with the risen Christ (1 Cor 15:7) and became a leader of the Jerusalem church (Acts 15:13). But neither James nor the Old Testament teaches salvation by works or by Christian activity. The message of this letter is not anti-Pauline, in spite of Luther's unfortunate remark that it is a 'right strawy epistle'. What James repudiates is the intellectualisation of the faith and 'only believism' – faith interiorised but not exteriorised. In full agreement with Paul, James assumes that salvation comes by faith like Abraham's hearty trust in God (James 2:23–24). Also, as with Abraham's faith, the disciple's faith must be realised in the action and deeds of life. 'You see that a person is justified by what he does and not by faith alone' (James 2:24). Unexpressed faith is not faith in Jesus. Therefore, the prostitute Rahab (2:25) may have more faith than well-published theologians, because orthodox doctrine without orthopraxis is not Christian orthodoxy. We know God's word to the extent to which we have lived and acted upon it – no more and no less! And the single, most conspicuous indication of our real faith and knowledge of the law of love (2:8) is our treatment of the poor (1:27; 2:5; 2:15–17).

James is not promoting works *per se*, but works that arise from faith and, in turn, inspire faith. Luther's 'Treatise on Good Works' makes the same point. Both James and Luther plead for a spirituality of Christian action. In James' letter, three fundamental points emerge. First, we may come to God as genuinely through action as by thinking and reflection. Faith and works are not only related but interdependent. Each should lead to the other and both to God. Evangelism for us, as it was for Jesus, must involve both 'do this' (Matt 19:21), and 'believe this'. Second, our actions are not only evocative but revelatory. Excessive, lustful Christian service may express a failure in faith, in the same way as does dry intellectualism or contemplation without compassionate action. But third, the solution for the hyperactivism of most Western Christians is not contemplation, but faith. For James and for Jesus, whose teachings James expounded, it must never be either–or, but both faith *and* works. It is now appropriate to explore one concrete dimension of faith-in-action.

The spirituality of neighbouring (James 2:1–13)

James dwells on the problem of favouritism because it is a very revealing sin. It shows that we have not grasped the law of love enough to live by it. In the Christian community this failure to show neighbour-love is revealed in preferential treatment of the rich and the powerful. 'If you show special attention to the man wearing fine clothes and say, "Here's a good seat for you," but say to the poor man, "You stand there" or "Sit on the floor by my feet," have you not discriminated among yourselves and become judges with evil thoughts?' (James 2:3–4). Such discrimination is made on the basis of external appearance – clothes and jewellery – and results in positions being given to those who are recognised for their power and influence (2:3). But this unchristian favouritism in the first century and today, ignores the timeless truth that James dares to explore: usually wealth comes by the exploitation of others (2:6).

There are real reasons for favouring the rich and powerful, even in the Christian community. Sometimes we fear what will happen if powerful people are not given what they want. So we comply. At the same time we fail to recognise our own blindness to the spiritual gift that the poor and powerless are to the community. 'Has not God chosen those who are poor in the eyes of the world to be rich in faith and to inherit the kingdom he promised those who love him?' (2:5). We misunderstand the nature of true religion, which is 'to look after orphans and widows in their distress and to keep oneself from being polluted by the world' (1:27). If in contrast we showed neighbour-love to the poor we would treat them truly as equals (2 Cor 8:13). Failure to do that is to break the law of love.

If there are deep reasons for breaking the law of love, there are deeper reasons for keeping it. James speaks of the law of love as a 'law that gives freedom' (2:12). Our response to both the rich and the poor, the powerful and the powerless, reveals whether we have found security and freedom in Christ. If we have not found this we will cower before the powerful. And, faced with the poor we will either take advantage of our neighbour, or because our poor neighbours' existence poses such deep questions about our own wealth, we will ignore them because they reveal our own vulnerability. Neither Jesus nor James will let us off the hook. God himself not only loves the poor but *became* poor (2 Cor 8:9; Phil 2:1–11). So our attitude to the poor and powerless reveals our true attitude toward Jesus, as Jesus himself hinted in the parable of the Rich Man and Lazarus (Luke 16:19–31). If that is not an incentive for spiritual formation what can be? God meets us in Jesus when we reach out in mercy and compassion to our hurting and helpless neighbour.

Francis of Assisi would normally swerve his horse around the lepers that met him begging on the road. But one day there was something in his heart stronger than fear: the love of Jesus. So he jumped off his horse and, taking a coin, pressed it into the hand of the man. Then he kissed the leper's hand. It was an act of great courage since it was believed in that day that by touching the man he would instantly contract the dreaded disease. It was also an act of reverence since the kiss on the hand was normally reserved for the priest. But supremely it was a moment of revelation, for Francis saw in the surprised face of the leper, the face of Jesus, our ultimate neighbour who is loved through the neighbours we meet in this life (Matt 25:31–46). To unpack this we must get inside our motivation, which James is most anxious to do.

The spirituality of desires (James 3:13–18; 4:1–3)
James gives a spiritual test for Christian maturity and leadership. 'Peacemakers who sow in peace raise a harvest of righteousness' (3:18). What qualifies a person to be considered 'wise' is relational grace: relationships that are 'considerate, submissive, full of mercy' (3:17) rather than a head full of knowledge; an orientation to community-building (4:11–12) rather than self-promotion; and contentment rather than envy (3:14; 4:2). All of these James speaks of as wisdom – indeed, two kinds of wisdom, one from below that is 'earthy' and 'unspiritual', and another from above that is 'pure' (3:17). What the Spirit does in Paul's letters, wisdom (from above) does in James'. It helps one stand, delivers one from the flesh and brings what Paul calls the fruit of the Spirit. Wisdom is the way a believer lives when rightly related to God and his final purpose for the world.

That wisdom is a gift from God but one for which the believer must pray. Indeed it should be the major focus of our requests. Without this orientation we are liable to ask amiss. 'You do not have, because you do not ask God. When you ask, you do not receive, because you ask with wrong motives, that you may spend what you get on your pleasures' (4:2–3). Failing to seek this wisdom from above, we end up yielding to the desires that battle within us rather than yielding ourselves to God.

Simply put, the state of our desires reveals how deeply we love God and how much we have allowed ourselves to be transformed by his wisdom and Spirit. Do we love God enough to be content? Discontentment and covetousness are indications of a failure to love. The covetousness that so concerns James can take many insidious and subtle forms: desiring someone else's experience of God, someone else's spiritual gifts, someone else's experience of marriage, or someone else's health. Paul's example and direct teaching in Philippians 4:4–19 suggests that we should wage war on discontentment by practising thanksgiving and taking direct, creative action where we can. There is no room for 'poor me' thoughts in either Paul or James. 'Thanksgiving,' said Calvin, 'is the chief exercise of godliness.' And James would add that it *results* in 'a good life', in 'deeds done in the humility that comes from wisdom' (3:13). But the next theme touches on how these godly desires are expressed.

The spirituality of personal expressiveness
(James 4:4–10)
There is a complicated verse in James that is one of the thorniest interpretative problems in the whole letter. After accusing some of his readers of being adulterers because of their love of the world, James says, 'Or do you think Scripture says without reason that the spirit he caused to live in us envies intensely?' (4:5). In his superb commentary, Peter Davids argues convincingly for the alternative reading in the footnotes of the NIV: 'God jealously longs for the spirit that he made to live in us.' This means that God's yearning for us is even greater than our spiritual adultery (4:6). If we turn to him God will be even more responsive than we will be willing to draw near (4:7). Therefore, in the light of God's passion for us James calls for a total response in repentance. It includes the will ('submit' and 'resist' – 4:7), the spirit ('come near' – 4:8), the mind ('purify your hearts, you double-minded') and the emotions ('grieve, mourn and wail' – 4:9). When did we last hear shouts of hilarious joy or wailing over sin expressed in our services of public worship? Have we settled for a spirituality that is balanced and tidy but almost dead? Are we afraid of losing control?

The problem of passionless spirituality is deeper than the paralysis of our emotions or the fears we have of being rejected by others because of our unconventional behaviour. It is caused by spiritual double-mindedness. We want God but we also want to keep control of our relationship with God, something which even Peter was not allowed to do in the presence of Jesus (John 13:8–9). But for those who are willing to let go, James offers a great promise: 'Humble yourselves before the Lord, and he will lift you up' (James 4:10). Humility is Godwardness not self-depreciation. So often the attempt to put ourselves down enough – a negative form of 'good' works – appears to be humility, but in reality this disguised self-centredness is the cloak of pride turned inside out. It is false humility. When our passion – inspired by God's jealous love for us – turns us wholeheartedly Godward, a great exchange takes place. Our identity once founded on our performance, either good or bad, is now founded in God. 'He will lift you up' (4:10) means that we no longer need to prove or disprove ourselves, for we are proven in God. That surely is the ultimate source of liberation for the human personality. It frees us, additionally, to plan our life with God.

The spirituality of planning (James 4:13–17)

I am a planner. There are both good and bad reasons for my interest in plotting my future as far as possible, sometimes two or three years in advance. So I am challenged by James' probing words: 'Why, you do not even know what will happen tomorrow' (4:14). The issue at stake, however, is not forethought – which is a good thing – but, as Jesus taught (Matt 6:25–33), the question is whether we are planning with or without God.

When we plan without God our goal is usually personal advancement and our assumption is that *we* are in charge of our destiny. That is why James asks, 'What is your life?' (4:14). When *our* plans are not fulfilled we struggle to be flexible; our pride is wounded and we sink into disappointment.

In contrast, planning *with* God is based on solid spiritual realities. First, our future is in God's hands. Therefore, James advises, we should say, 'If it is the Lord's will, we will live and do this or that' (4:15). Second, we are aware of our human frailty and limitations. James compares our life to a vanishing mist (4:14). Third, our deepest desire is to glorify God, not to boast and brag about our own accomplishments (4:16). Finally, we are willing to abandon our own plans to see God's purpose realised at every point. But implicit in these four summary statements is the truth that the believer is not passive before the sovereignty of God, refusing to do anything until God acts. The disciple of Jesus is freer to be decisive and purposeful than the person who is not a disciple. Faith in Jesus delivers us from the twin decision-making terrors of worry and arrogance. It does not deliver us from planning. But we plan with a difference because even our mistakes can be redeemed.

This last point is beautifully illustrated by the manner in which handmade Persian carpets are made. A band of weavers down each side of the loom insert the various colours of wool as they are directed by the weaver who sees the 'good side'. Only the master weaver, standing on the other side of the carpet at the head, can see the overall design. When someone inadvertently makes a mistake, the master weaver does not withdraw the coloured wool but rather incorporates the mistake into his now slightly revised overall design. God apparently does not have a wonderful plan for our lives that must be discerned detail by detail. He has something far better: a wonderful purpose. Within that purpose there is freedom to change the plan.

So planning is a spiritual discipline. One reason is that our style of planning will be determined by our convictions about the future. The theologian Jürgen Moltmann states that eschatology – the study of last things – is the most pastoral of the theological disciplines. Most people in Western culture foresee no worthwhile end to which the travail of history might lead. They must either fabricate a future or live as though there were no future. But the disciple has a destiny. He or she knows that God will bring the whole human story to a worthy consummation. This gives meaning to the warp and woof of everyday decision making. Biblical spirituality, as we will discover later, cultivates the simultaneous readiness for Jesus to come back at any moment and the willingness to wait for centuries if need be. The parable of the Wise Virgins (Matt 25:1–13) is instructive on this point. Both the wise and the foolish virgins *wanted* the Bridegroom to come to the wedding. Both *slept* with impunity when there was a delay. Both had *lamps* and oil for the night watch. But only the wise virgins had enough oil for a long wait. That is planning in faith. Failure to plan – because one believes the future is unthinkable, or because one anticipates an immediate evacuation – is no more spiritual than the compulsion to map out the future as an act of arrogant authority.

Further, our style of planning indicates whether our security is found in controlling our circumstances and people around us or in God. If our security is in God then we can be free to change our plans, even the plans we make in faith, perhaps especially those. Only idols are entirely predictable (Ps 115:3–8). Our willingness to abandon our plans and to embrace God's sovereign intervention is a practical daily act of faith, hope and love. Most of the ministry of Jesus took place in the interruptions of what he set out to do. The same may be true for us. Planning in faith reveals what we treasure most, and that is the next theme we discern in the letter of James.

The spirituality of accumulating (James 5:1–6)

Wealth is an especially deep test of our faith. For every ten people that can thrive spiritually in the face of adversity, only one can stand in the face of prosperity. In this passage James moves from addressing the merchant class within his community – addressed indirectly in 2:1–7 and 4:13–17 – to castigating the landholding class which is either at the edge of the community of faith or even outside it. He calls upon them to bewail the coming punishment (5:1). 'Your wealth has rotted, and moths have eaten your clothes. Your gold and silver are corroded. Their corrosion will testify against you and eat your flesh like fire' (5:2–3). The context of this withering judgment is the imminent return of the Lord. James views the church standing at the overlap of this age and the age to come. Just as trials can be embraced with joy (1:2) because the reward is soon coming, so the Judge-friend 'standing at the door' (5:9) will soon bring comfort to the poor Christians and judgment to the rich ones. 'You have hoarded wealth *in the last days*' (5:3 italics mine). The issue at stake is not being wealthy *per se* but being wealthy because of the exploitation of the poor (5:4), and failing to help the poor with the resources we have. 'These people,' notes Peter Davids in his commentary, 'had treasured up as if they would live and the world would go on forever; but the end times, in which they have a last chance to repent and put their goods to righteous uses, are already upon them.'[2]

James, in harmony with the rest of the New Testament, raises some disturbing questions about the spirituality of wealth. Is it possible to get rich apart from the exploitation of others (5:4)? Why does the accumulation of wealth tend to make people insensitive to the suffering of others (5:4)? The parable of Lazarus and the Rich Man we saw to be a case in point (Luke 16:19–31). Why do both Luke and James maintain one cannot have abundance in *both* this life and the next (James 5:2; Luke 6:20–26)? What does it mean 'to store up treasures in heaven' (Matt 6:20), to gain friends for heaven (Luke 16:9)? What does it mean to be 'rich towards God' (Luke 12:21)? These probing questions call us rich Western Christians to a life of continuous financial repentance and stewardship. On this latter point, in the spirit of James' words, though expounding the parable of Lazarus and the Rich Man, the golden-tongued preacher John Chrysostom maintains that 'the rich man is a kind of steward of the money which is owed for the distribution to the poor'.[3] That is not merely a matter of spiritual justice but an issue for spirituality. Without addressing these questions, the rich cannot work out the salvation God so graciously is working in them.

This text touches me. Though most would say I am 'middle class', I must regard myself, in the light of global poverty, among the rich. In my meditation journal I noted for myself on this passage some conclusions on the question of how to be rich and thrive spiritually. First, I must regard my riches as a low estate, the way it really is: 'The one who is rich should take pride in his *low* position' (James 1:9–10). Second, I must realise that even relative affluence is short-lived and will pass away. There is no ultimate security in wealth and this is not a real Kingdom treasure (1:11). Third, I must accept that riches are a trial of faith, a testing intended to purify my spirituality so that what is left, when the dross is removed, is pure gold (1:12). Finally, I must reject the Latin view of ownership and embrace the biblical-Hebraic view of stewardship. I own nothing; I have been entrusted with God's resources. Faith requires such countercultural living. Love inspires it. And hope brings a future with promise to both the rich and the poor, and even to the middle class!

The spirituality of healing (James 5:13–20)

The Lord is 'full of compassion and mercy' (5:11) not only to rich and poor, but also to the sick who turn to the Lord for healing. James offers some fascinating perspectives on this ministry. It is, for James, an *official* ministry. There is no mention of people with the charismatic gift of healing as there is in Paul's letters. Rather the sick 'should call the elders of the church to pray over him and anoint him with oil in the name of the Lord' (5:14). It is a *divine* ministry. '*The Lord* [not the healer] will raise him up' (5:15). It is a *penitential* ministry, usually involving confession of sin (5:15–16) since sickness is often – though not always – related to sinful behaviour. And finally it is a *corporate* ministry. James does not envision a solo healer touching the sick to make them well, but a community characterised by mutual confession (5:16, 19–20) and communal prayer which is the vehicle through which God brings healing. James brings a unique perspective on this ministry which is controversial today but would have been considered normal in the early church and is today in the Two Thirds World. We are given some pregnant hints on why the ministry of healing profoundly touches the spirituality of the sick and the healer.

James argues that some sickness is a result of personal sin or the sins of others against that person. Personal sin can include an unhealthy lifestyle which should be confessed and mended. When emotional or sexual violence has been experienced there are profound hurts. Those hurts lead to sinful behaviour, usually in a related area. In time the person adjusts and appears to become 'normal' except for compensatory emotions and desires, such as excessive anger, defensiveness, addiction, a poor self-image or jealousy. Superficial ministry deals with the compensatory emotions. More probing ministry deals with the sinful behaviour that preceded the 'apparent' health. But James advises going to the root – the original sin or hurt that knocked the person's health off balance. Consistent with other epistles (1 Cor 11:30–32), this letter counsels confession of sin *publicly* in the context of community meetings and not merely privately to an elder. Bonhoeffer elaborates on the strategic importance of this in his classic *Life Together*.[4] Public confession disarms the power of the past (by naming it and removing its secret power over the person). But it also establishes a community based on truth and compassion.

James' contribution to the vexed debates over healing includes the role healing ministry plays in the spiritual formation of the community. It goes almost without saying that receiving confessions and dealing with sin and sickness in others forces members of the community to deal with their own unresolved hurts and sins. When this is not done people tend to condemn or condone when they hear about a real sin. Further, if seeking help increases the faith of the sick, being sought for confession and prayer increases the faith of the community. James encourages this by noting that it is the ordinary person – not just the elders – who will be powerful in prayer like Elijah (5:17–18). Finally, by making healing a community matter, ordinary 'lay' Christians share in the salvation of others, working it out *with* them though not for them. So James ends his letter with this beautiful promise: 'My brothers, if one of you should wander from the truth and someone should bring him back, remember this: Whoever turns a sinner from the error of his way will save him from death and cover over a multitude of sins' (5:19–20).

James brings holiness down-to-earth: everyday holiness – how we speak and what we do with our money. James will not allow us to locate the spiritual life at the circumference of our lives in quiet times, church services and leisured retreats. It must be at the centre, or it is not Christian spirituality. But James also insists on another fundamental truth. We need each other to embrace a fully Christian spirituality. John Wesley, before he became a Christian, was advised in this way: 'Sir, you wish to serve God and go to heaven? Remember that you cannot serve him alone. You must therefore find companions or make them; the Bible knows nothing of solitary religion.'[5]

James would agree. True spirituality is not a leisure-time avocation reserved for moments of transcendence in our free time away from work. Nor is it a solitary pilgrimage. God meets us where we are in the nitty gritty of the daily round, transforming even troubles into a sacrament.

CHAPTER NINE

COMMITTED TO THE SACRAMENTS

The Christian faith is the most earthy of all religions: after all, it is rooted in the Incarnation. Among other things, that supreme miracle insists that the physical matters a great deal. It matters so much to God that he expresses himself through it. He did so uniquely when Jesus took human flesh. But the same principle of divine life through physical means remains central to Christianity. That is why the faith of the New Testament is unashamedly sacramental.

A lot of confusion gathers around the term 'sacrament'. Some Christians are shy of it: others can speak of little else. Basic Christian usage is to see a sacrament as a physical token which expresses a spiritual reality: as the old Anglican Catechism put it, 'an outward and visible sign of an inward and spiritual grace'. It rightly goes on to say that Christians use this word 'sacrament' of two ordinances 'ordained by Christ himself, as a means whereby we receive the same [i.e. his grace] and a pledge to assure us thereof'. The word derives from the Latin, where it was used of a soldier's oath of allegiance. All of this helps us to understand the normal Christian usage of the word.

Clearly the sacramental principle runs through the whole of life: a kiss, for example, or a handshake are 'outward and visible signs' which should, and normally do, convey the 'inward and spiritual grace' of love and friendship. But of course they may not do so – depending on the attitude of the donor and the recipient. It is like this with the two great sacraments Christ left us. Baptism and the Lord's Supper are outward and visible signs of the inward and spiritual grace of God which enables us to begin and to continue the Christian life. They are meant to be channels of his unseen but very real grace to us. And we can certainly rely on the attitude of the Donor. But that may prove ineffectual if on our side there is no response: if we grasp the hand, so to speak, but not the friendship proffered; if we accept the kiss but reject the love. The sacraments, then, like the Incarnation whose influence they continue, are not only pledges of God's lasting grace to us but should be, and normally are, channels of that love. Most Christians restrict the word to describe the two great outward actions with inner meaning which Jesus himself inaugurated, namely the Communion and baptism. Some denominations, rather unhelpfully, it seems to me, add five more which were not inaugurated by Christ and which are five among many other external acts with inward meanings. We will here therefore concentrate on baptism and the Lord's Supper.

Baptism

One baptism – or three?
There is one baptism (Eph 4:5), but you'd never guess as much from the way Christians talk about it. For the Catholic, it was his baptism as an infant which brought him into the church and made him a Christian. For the Baptist, her baptism was by immersion, administered after profession of faith. For the Pentecostal, baptism was in or by the Holy Spirit, normally accompanied by the gift of tongues: this eclipses all else.

All three are saying something important. All three are stressing one aspect of what Christian baptism is.

The Catholic sees baptism as the gateway into the people of God. Just as you entered the old-covenant people of Israel by circumcision, so you enter the new people of God by baptism (Acts 2:40–41; Gal 3:27–29). A noble view, strong on God's act of incorporation, but

weak on response. If we think of it as the only strand in
Christian initiation, it degenerates into magic.

The Baptist sees baptism as a seal on the profession
of faith, and that is clearly the emphasis in Acts 16:31.
The church is the company of believers. This view is
strong on response, but very individualistic. It makes
human commitment almost more significant than divine
initiative. Moreover it is very cerebral: it gives little room
for those too young or too handicapped to make a decisive
response.

The Pentecostal sees it very differently. The church is
not so much a historical continuum (which may well be
apostate), nor a company of believers (which may mean
little more than intellectual assent). No. Reception of
the lifegiving Spirit of God is the authentic mark of the
church. Baptism with the Holy Spirit is the only baptism
worth having (Rom 8:9). Important though this emphasis
undoubtedly is, it too is deficient. Cut off from historical
continuity it can be, and often is, very divisive. Cut off
from any serious emphasis on the content of the faith, it
can easily go off the rails in doctrine or morals. There is
such a thing as church history. There is such a thing as
Christian doctrine. The Spirit of God, the word of God
and the people of God need to walk hand in hand.

These different strands belong together. We find them
all in Acts, where baptism is sometimes seen as the
agency of salvation (Acts 2:38), sometimes as the seal on
faith (16:31–33) and sometimes as the sovereign anointing
of the Holy Spirit (10:44–48). All three strands are needed.
For baptism is a big thing. The Catholics are right to see
it as the objective mark of God's great rescue achieved
on Calvary, to which we can make no contribution or
addition. The Protestants are right to see in it our
personal response to the grace of God, in repentance
and faith. The Pentecostals are right to see baptism
as the way whereby we are ushered into the world of
the Spirit. Without that divine enduement, you can be
baptised until you are blue in the face, you can profess the
creeds with unfailing zeal, and still be a stranger to the

love of God. Baptism is as deep and broad as the salvation of which it is the sacrament.

What can we learn from the baptism of John?

It caused an immense stir, and for a number of reasons. It was a mark of repentance. No pedigree, no good deeds could bring you into the coming kingdom of God: the only path lay through the baptismal waters of repentance. And that was very humbling.

Moreover it pointed ahead to the forgiveness of sins and the gift of the Spirit that Jesus, the Messiah, would bring.

It was also a very public and a very humiliating act. Never before had Jews been baptised: baptism was the initiation ceremony for Gentiles joining the people of God.

And finally, it was decisive. Either you went through the waters of God's judgment on sin symbolically in the Jordan, or else you would have to face it in stark reality later on. In all these ways, John's baptism, a landmark in Judaism, was a trailer of the 'main film', Christian baptism.

What can we learn from the baptism of Jesus?

In his baptism Jesus identified with sinners, something which even John the Baptist found scandalous (Matt 3:14ff). It was, if you like, a dummy run for Calvary, when his cross was to be his baptism – in blood (Luke 12:50). We cannot enter with him into the unspeakable agonies of bearing the world's sin, but Christians can and should share in three other implications of his baptism.

It was an assurance of his sonship (Matt 3:17 and parallels). So it is with the Christian, adopted into the family of God (Rom 8:15–17).

It was an anointing by the Spirit (John 1:32, cf. Isa 11:2). So it is for the Christian, because 'Anyone who does not have the Spirit of Christ does not belong to him' (Rom 8:9).

It was a commissioning for costly service. The voice from heaven at Jesus' baptism, 'You are my Son; in you I am well pleased', was a combination of two significant Old Testament texts, the first from Psalm 2:7 and the second from Isaiah 42:1. Jesus, the Son of God, is also the Servant of God. Those Servant Songs in Isaiah, culminating in Isaiah 53, sketch out the path of ministry and suffering. And for the Christian, as for his Lord, ministry and suffering are inescapable: baptism points inexorably to that calling.

Christian baptism catches us up into the baptism of Jesus himself. This had three great dimensions to it. The baptism of repentance in the Jordan, the baptism of rescue on the cross, and the baptism of power in the Holy Spirit. And in my own baptism I see those same three realities. It calls me to repentance. It shows me where pardon is to be had. And it offers me the power of the Holy Spirit.

How are we to understand Christian baptism?

In the light of these precedents of John and Jesus, how are we to understand Christian baptism? It is no optional extra, by the way. Jesus solemnly enjoined it upon us at the climax of his life on earth (Matt 28:18–20).

1. *Christian baptism embodies God's challenge to repentance and faith.* It cannot be conducted without some expression of both. It says to us 'You are foul. You need washing. I can do that for you. But you must change your ways.' It takes us to the heart of the gospel.

2. *Christian baptism offers us the blessings of the new covenant.* God approaches us in utterly unmerited grace. We respond in repentance and faith. And baptism signs over to us the blessings of the new covenant: forgiveness, sonship, servanthood, the Holy Spirit, the new birth, justification, and the promise of life after death.

3. *Christian baptism plunges us into the death and resurrection of Jesus.* We are brought to the point of death to the old life, which had no room for God, and the dawning of new life as the Holy Spirit enters our hearts.

This dying and rising life is the essence of Christianity. It is what we are called to – and empowered for. It has a profound impact on the way we behave. So baptism is the gateway to a complete revolution in morals and lifestyle, even though we shall never achieve perfection in this life. It embodies our aim to live out the life of Christ in our own daily circumstances.

4. *Christian baptism initiates us into the worldwide church.* It is the adoption certificate into the family of God. It is the mark of belonging, the badge of membership. That may not always be obvious in traditionally Christian lands. But if your background is in Judaism or Islam your baptism is crossing the Rubicon. It is the essential dividing line.

5. *Christian baptism commissions us to work for the Kingdom of God.* It is God's commissioning service for his troops. For baptism is indeed a sign of the Kingdom of God. It shows that we have surrendered to him as our king, and it is the uniform we wear as we go about the king's business.

6. *Christian baptism* does *something*! This New Testament emphasis is often overlooked by Protestants: we prefer to think it *symbolises* something. But the New Testament uses some strongly instrumental language about baptism. It is through baptism that we enter the 'name' of the Trinity (Matt 28:19) and thus are saved (1 Pet 3:21) or regenerated (John 3:5) or united with Christ in his death and resurrection (Rom 6:3ff; Col 2:12), and incorporated into his body (1 Cor 12:13). To be sure, several of these references mention the Holy Spirit (the divine agency) or faith (the human agency), but there is an undeniably instrumental flavour about the language used by the biblical writers. This should not surprise us. Justification, regeneration, incorporation into Christ, baptism – these are all different images of the way God makes us his own.

Baptism, then, is an 'efficacious sign' of the new life. But of course it is not unconditionally efficacious, any more than a wedding ring is! It was not efficacious with

Simon Magus (Acts 8:13, 21ff) nor with some at Corinth (1 Cor 10:1–6). But it is intended to bring about what it symbolises. It is a palpable mark of belonging, like the wedding ring or the adoption certificate. Luther grasped this clearly. When he was tempted to doubt his own faith, he recalled the standing emblem of God's faithfulness marked upon him as an infant. He cried out in confidence *'Baptizatus sum'*, 'I have been baptised', realising that God's faithfulness was even more important than his faith.

How was baptism administered?

Did the early Christians sprinkle candidates for baptism, or immerse them? We are not as well informed as we would like to be, but it is not a matter of supreme importance. They insisted on baptising in water in the name of the Trinity, but the amount of water is nowhere specified. It is not a matter that should divide Christian brethren. Sometimes a river was to hand and they would doubtless immerse. Sometimes it would take place in a home, like that of the Philippian jailer, where immersion facilities would not exist. One of the early murals in the Catacombs shows John the Baptist and Jesus standing waist-deep in the Jordan, and John *pouring* water over the head of Jesus: both methods have prizes!

But does not the word *baptizo* mean immerse? Not necessarily: it can mean wash (Luke 11:38). Surely Augustine has it right when he claims 'A little drop of water may serve to seal the fulness of divine grace in baptising, as well as a small piece of bread and the least sip of wine in the Holy Supper'. The early Christians seem to have been very relaxed about the mode of baptism. The very early *Didache* says 'Baptise in the name of the Father and of the Son and of the Holy Spirit, in running water. But if thou hast not running water, baptise in other water. And if thou canst not in cold, then in warm. But if thou hast neither, pour water three times upon the head in the name of the Father and of the Son and of the Holy Spirit'.[1]

Who received baptism?

Adult believers, certainly, and they are primary in any theological reflection about baptism. But it seems that children, wives and slaves in the household were baptised also, when the head of the household professed faith. This, though not certain, is very probable and would not be in the least surprising to the first Christians. After all, children were sacramentally admitted to the Old Testament church (Gen 17). Whole families of proselytes, including children and slaves, were baptised into the Jewish faith. Households were baptised in the New Testament itself (Acts 16:31, 33). The attitude of acceptance which Jesus displayed to tiny children would have helped (Mark 10:13–16). The baptism of infants was the virtually unchallenged practice of the early and mediaeval church. Moreover, it emphasises the objectivity of the gospel: you have the mark of what Christ did for you at Calvary marked upon you, whether you choose to respond to it or not. And it emphasises the initiative of God, reaching out to us before ever we think of reaching out to him. That is why most Christians baptise the children in their families. But it is a practice open to gross abuse if it does not take place in the context of faith. It is only intended for the children of believers, not to be an indiscriminate charm. It should not be administered without careful teaching of the obligations it calls for and the blessings it offers. And it requires personal reaffirmation on behalf of the candidate when he or she is confirmed.

On the other hand, the Baptist case is strong. It stresses that baptism is the Christian badge of belonging, not a social ceremony for the very young. It gives a clear, dateable time of commitment. It produces far less in the way of fall-out than infant baptism does, and it is a powerful evangelistic occasion. My prayer is that Baptists and paedo-baptists may grow in mutual understanding of the strength of the other's position, and respect, rather than criticise one another.

Can you repeat baptism?

No. It is as unrepeatable as justification or adoption, of which it is the sacrament. The early Christians were clear about this. There is a strange lust for rebaptism today. People very often feel that their baptism as an infant was deficient. There was too little faith around, too little water, too little feeling, too little chance for public confession of faith. The desire to 'do it again, and do it properly' often springs from the modern cult of feelings. But strictly it cannot be done again, any more than birth can. It is ever to be remembered but never to be repeated. Baptism may be reaffirmed. It may even be re-enacted: 'If you are not already baptised, I baptise you . . .' But it cannot be repeated.

What is baptism with the Holy Spirit?

There are seven references to baptism with the Holy Spirit in the New Testament: (Matt 3:11; Mark 1:8; Luke 3:16; John 1:33; Acts 1:5; 11:15-16). All these six draw the distinction between John the Baptist's baptism which was looking forward to Jesus, and the baptism Jesus would himself give 'in' (or 'with' or 'by' – the Greek word can be translated in any of these ways), the Holy Spirit. All six point forward, then, to Christian initiation. It is precisely the same with the seventh, where Paul reminds the Corinthians, 'charismatics' and 'non-charismatics' alike, that they had all been baptised by one Spirit into the one body (1 Cor 12:13). So all the New Testament references to this contentious phrase are initiatory. None points to a second and 'more profound' experience. That is not for a moment to deny that such subsequent infillings may and do occur. Sometimes they are the most momentous spiritual experiences in our lives. But it does not help to call them baptism. It simply causes confusion. As we have seen, the Pentecostals are right about the importance of having the Spirit to come and flood your life: they are wrong to call that experience 'baptism in the Holy Spirit' in contrast to 'baptism in water'. That is not how the Bible ever speaks of it.

Although there are not a great many references to baptism in the New Testament, it was clearly critically important to them as the sacrament of initiation. It sealed for them the unrepeatable incorporation into Christ. It pointed them to the dying and rising life which Christians are called to live. It joined them to brothers and sisters throughout the world. And it released in them the power of the Holy Spirit, so long as they claimed in faith the gift God so generously offered them.

The Eucharist

Baptism is the sacrament of Christian initiation; the Eucharist is the sacrament of Christian growth and development. Both are vital. The early Christians were well aware of this, and they valued the Communion highly. Here again we are often impoverished by our own tradition. The very names used for it in Scripture hint at the breadth of meanings in this most wonderful sacrament. The 'Lord's Supper' takes us back to the Upper Room (1 Cor 11:20). The 'breaking of bread' (Acts 2:42) alludes to Jesus feeding the multitude. The 'Holy Communion' indicates a joint 'participation in the body and blood of Christ' (1 Cor 10:16). The 'Eucharist' speaks of blessing God for all that Jesus has done for us (1 Cor 11:24; *Didache* 9.1). And the 'Mass', though somewhat obscure in etymology, probably means dismissal of the congregation into the world for ministry and mission. Mass is not, however, a New Testament term, though the idea of sending out certainly is.

Imagine the setting

Most early Communions did not take place in a church at all, but a home. People begin to appear in the early evening with materials for a pot-luck supper. They are happy and relaxed: work is over. All are on a level here, men and women, Roman citizens and commoners, slaves and free. Candles are lit. Couches are set. Feet are washed. They have a meal, reclining round a courtyard,

or squashed into a room. They share news. Someone
produces a musical instrument and they begin to sing.
Indeed, they create new songs, snatches of which are to
be found in the New Testament, like 'Awake sleeper,
and arise from the dead: Christ shall give you life' or
'Holy, holy, holy, Lord God Almighty, who was and
is and is to come'. Meanwhile someone has brought
out the church box which contains their most precious
Christian belongings: some sayings of Jesus, perhaps
a letter from an apostle, or Communion vessels. The
praise is heartfelt. Tongues might well follow. There
could be prayer for a healing or a specific need of one
of the members. Certainly prayer, the reading of an
Old Testament scripture, the recitation of a story about
Jesus, and some words of encouragement from members
of the community, along with joyful singing, would all
feature. And as the evening comes to an end, they would
tell again the story of Jesus' passion, and break bread
and drink wine in remembrance of him. Every scrap is
finished. The prayer that Jesus taught them is recited.
They move round and embrace one another with a holy
kiss, and then go home. All very simple. No service books.
No priests. No altars. Every eye is on the unseen Lord, the
bread, the wine and each other. And then – out into the
night, spiritually refuelled for the journey of the coming
week.

What is this meal?

There have been many speculations. Some have seen
it as a *haburah*, a special religious meal held by a
group of friends. Others have sought to show that it
derived from a *kiddush*, a Friday evening family gathering to prepare for the sabbath. Others again have
looked to pagan sources for this meal. None of this
need detain us now. For the clue to understanding
this meal lies in the passover of the Old Testament,
and 1 Corinthians 5:7 makes this very plain. 'Christ
our passover has been sacrificed for us. Therefore let us
keep the feast.'

A passover with a difference

Joachim Jeremias persuasively demonstrated this passover background to the Communion in his book, *The Eucharistic Words of Jesus*[2]; and all subsequent scholarship on the subject has been beholden to him. He points out eleven elements in the account which substantiate this passover background. For example, the Last Supper took place in Jerusalem; it extended into the night; it was a small intimate gathering; they reclined instead of sitting; a dish preceded the breaking of bread; wine, an essential at passover, was drunk; the words of institution are an adaptation of passover *haggadah*; Judas went out, ostensibly to give to the poor – a passover custom; and so on. Jeremias piles up the evidence that the meal was an anticipated passover. He then deals with ten objections. There are two which he does not handle. One is the absence of any mention of a lamb. Was this due to the compression of the account as Christians recited what was special about that passover? Was it because they saw Jesus as the passover lamb? We may never know. The other of Jeremias' omissions was an explanation of how the annual passover celebration turned into the weekly (or even more frequent) Christian celebration. The frequency was probably due to the well-remembered fact that the Master had made a point of eating regularly with his disciples. They had a regular common meal (which turned in the early church into the *agape* meal). But all subsequent communal meals were impregnated with the meaning of this awesome night, repeated often, at his express command.

All the four accounts, despite their different nuances, are agreed that Jesus took bread, blessed and broke it, spoke interpretative words over it, and gave it to his disciples. There is no space to study in detail this meal which gave rise to the Holy Communion, but several factors are of great importance.

1. This was a complete meal, extended for a long time. Our accounts cover only the special Christian differentia

in this passover meal; the bread and wine were only selections from a much fuller mealtime together.

2. The annual Jewish passover was not a sacrifice, but it was the memorial of the first passover which certainly was a sacrifice when the lambs of Israel died, and their blood was painted on the door lintels to avert the angel of wrath. Equally, the Christian Eucharist is not a sacrifice, but is the memorial of that great sacrifice when the Lamb of God shed his blood to avert judgment on a sinful world.

3. The words 'body' and 'blood', clearly a pair, lead us back in Aramaic to the only pair that Jesus could have used: *bisra udema*. Both are sacrificial words. Each word denotes violent death. They point to his sacrificial death on the morrow.

4. By giving them the bread and the wine, he gives them a share in the benefits of his atoning sacrifice, just as the Israelites who ate the passover lamb shared not in making the sacrifice but in enjoying its benefits — in their case, rescue from bondage and death in Egypt. This is how sacrificial language came to be applied to the Communion. Properly, the Eucharist is not a sacrifice. It is the memorial of his atoning sacrifice, and a means of enjoying its benefits.

5. The change in the *halakah* (explanatory words about the passover) is truly amazing. Normally the president would (in obedience to Exod 12:25; 13:8) take bread and say 'This is the bread of affliction which your fathers ate in the wilderness'. Imagine the electric atmosphere when Jesus, presiding, says 'This is — my body, given for you'. In Aramaic this would have gone like this: 'This — my body . . .' leaving it open whether representation or identity was intended — an issue which has divided Catholics from Protestants for centuries. Do this in *remembrance* of me! The word *anamnesis*, remembrance, does not mean mere mental recollection, as we Westerners would interpret it. To the Semitic mind it meant representation. The Jews were accustomed to say, at passover, 'This the Eternal did for me when I went out of Egypt'.

They saw the past as in some way made contemporary. Similarly Jesus seems to have intended his disciples at the Eucharist to see his death as in some way made contemporary, however many years ago it happened. Here in this service I see afresh before my very eyes what the Eternal did for me to bring me out of a bondage and a doom far worse than that which befel the Jews in Egypt. The broken bread and the poured-out wine not only dramatically reminded the early Christians of what Jesus did for them on the cross: it showed them that this historical event has present power and relevance. They could enter into the experience to which it referred, sharing in the benefits of his death and resurrection for them.

The blood is as significant as the bread. The passover blood was originally applied to the houses of the Israelites, and brought salvation, rescue from the destroying angel who killed the firstborn of the Egyptians. That is why wine (to recall the blood) was an essential part of passover. The benediction before the 'cup of blessing' in the passover specifically praises God for that deliverance from Egypt and the covenant he made with his people. The *hallel* of praise which followed had Psalm 116 as its core, a psalm which spoke of gratefully receiving the cup of salvation. So there were profound associations combined here: the blood, the covenant, the exodus, the vicariousness, the cup and the appropriation.

6. The shocking language was intentional and was remembered. To eat human flesh and to drink blood was expressly forbidden in Judaism. We need to take seriously both the metaphorical and the realistic significance of this language. We feed on him in our hearts, really feed on him. But we do so by faith.

The meaning of the meal
Set as it is against the backcloth of the passover, both historically and theologically, the depths of the Eucharist begin to become apparent.

1. The passover had a *backward* orientation. The first

passover was a sacrifice. Indeed, it was the sacrifice which constituted Israel as a people. Succeeding passovers were not sacrifices, though they might loosely be called such, and they had no expiatory significance. But they brought that original sacrifice powerfully before the worshipper. It is like that with the Communion. Not a sacrifice in itself, it is the representation of his sacrifice, and we feast on the benefits he won for us through it.

2. The passover had a *present* orientation. The first passover had been a meal to strengthen the Israelites for their march from the land of bondage to the land of promise. This element was re-enacted annually. The theme of God's constant care and provision for them is prominent in the *haggadah* (the account of God's mighty rescue, recounted at the meal). The eating and drinking formed a sacred bond between the worshippers: one can see from Psalm 41:9 how heinous was the breaking of such table fellowship. It was the same with the Communion. It, too, has the effect of binding together all its participants into one (1 Cor 10:17). Its fellowship, too, cannot be violated without the most heinous sin and disastrous consequences (1 Cor 11:19, 20, 27–30). And it too strengthens pilgrims for the journey, for it feeds them on the body of Christ (1 Cor 10:16), and he is the nourishment and sustenance of all Christian lives (John 6:51).

3. The passover had a *future* orientation. It prefigured the ultimate feast of salvation as well as being the memorial of deliverance from Egypt. Passover would be the night when Messiah would come. 'On this night they were saved, and on this night they will be saved' mused the rabbis. This forward look is integral to the Christian passover, the Eucharist. In Luke's account (22:7–23) it is stressed almost to the exclusion of all else. It is also there in Matthew and Mark, and in the allusive language about the 'true' bread and vine in St John's Gospel. It is notable in 1 Corinthians 11:26, and the cry *Maranatha* ('Our Lord, come' 1 Cor 16:22) was used at the Eucharist, as we learn from the *Didache* (10.4). The passage is worth

quoting, since it shows something of the fervour of early Christians as they shared in the Communion.

> Remember, Lord, thy church to deliver it from all evil and to make it perfect in thy love; and gather it together in its holiness from the four winds to thy kingdom which thou hast prepared for it. For thine is the power and the glory for ever. Let grace come, and let this world pass away. Hosannah to the God of David. If any man be holy, let him come! If any man be not, let him repent. Maranatha, Amen.[3]

Just as the passover was the pledge of the coming of the Messiah, so the Eucharist is the pledge of his return, and of the Messianic banquet towards which every Communion points.

No wonder this is the central meal for Christians, the service important beyond all others. For it is the archetypal symbol of our redemption, past, present and future. We will grow deeper and deeper in its appreciation until we taste it new in the Kingdom of God. Our Master knew what he was doing when he left just two sacraments to his church – baptism and the Eucharist. Both are incandescent with all the colours of salvation's rainbow. The one points to its once-for-allness, and its need to govern the dying and rising life of Christians. The other calls and empowers for persistence on the journey, as pilgrims climb the upward path. It lifts our eyes to the Lord, our Bread and Vine, and it points us towards God's wedding banquet when Christ will marry his bride, the church, for ever, and there will be no more sorrow, no more crying, no more death. We shall see his face and share his likeness.

CHAPTER TEN

PILGRIMS IN FAITH

Were it needed, He would die again to possess you. As the Father loved the Son, and could not live without Him — so Jesus loves you.
Andrew Murray

Spirituality is a weasel word. Just when you think you have it in your hands, it slithers out. Because each person uses the word to describe different realities it is essential to define our terms. Spirituality sometimes means a person's search for God through disciplines, religious practices, meditation and retreats. All of this amounts to trying to get to God by human effort, an altogether hopeless approach. Biblical spirituality is substantially different. It is our response to the seeking Father. It is God finding us. It is Christ's persistent love. And spiritual practices are merely ways of removing obstacles in ourselves that keep us from being found. Simone Weil, a Jewess who became a follower of Jesus, described this as God crossing the infinity of time and space to visit our home and knock on our door as a beggar. And like a beggar he keeps knocking. We will never regret opening the door and giving what she correctly calls the nuptial 'yes'. But there is more, and that is the subject of this chapter. Spirituality is our experience of *God keeping us close to himself.*

We will focus on John chapter fifteen. But, as we will see, this chapter is consistent with the teaching of the entire New Testament. What keeps disciples following, what keeps believers believing, what keeps children of God *living* as children of God, and what keeps pilgrims 'on the Way' is not *their* faith, but God's loving tenacity in Jesus. To express this truth Jesus offered an allegory – the vine and the branches (John 15:1–12) – and a metaphor – the friend with his friends (15:13–17).

The Allegory of the Vine and Branches: the Double Abiding

As a master teacher Jesus uses an allegory to express a complex truth so that those hearing it will identify with the pictures and actions, and say, 'That means *me!*' He uses three everyday images from first-century Palestine: a gardener or vinedresser – representing God the Father (15:1); the vine or main trunk – Jesus the Son of God; and the branches or shoots sprouting from the vine – representing those joined in a living connection to the vine. Though this agricultural image would be supremely familiar to people in first-century Palestine, it is not difficult for us to grasp. The vine is a plant that needs continuous care, as its luxurious growth must be drastically cut back year after year in order to conserve its life and secure the maximum fruit. Dead, unproductive branches are cut off. That dead wood is completely useless for anything else. It could not even be used for making the fires in the temple sacrifice. Generally it was burned in a bonfire. But the scrubby branches burdened with tasty grapes are doing exactly what was intended: bearing fruit and not just 'looking great'.

The image has a history. The 'vine' was used in the Old Testament to describe Israel, almost always in a context of unfaithfulness (Ps 80:8–16; Isa 5:1–7; Jer 2:21; Ezek 15:1–8). So we must read John fifteen as an audacious assertion. Jesus is saying, 'Whereas Israel was supposed to be the channel for God's life in the world, I am. And those of you who stay with me are not the vine but branches, and I will dwell in you.' Most people miss the breathtaking and liberating truth implicit in this. The church is not the vine, fulfilling Israel's abortive mission for God. Jesus is the vine and we who are joined to Jesus in discipleship, worshipping God the Father in the powerful presence of the Spirit, are simply branches or shoots. What hope there is for the people of God in this provocative truth! The church, like Israel, can from time to time be a useless vine. The reason is simply that it is trying to be the vine instead of a branch or shoot. The church has no life in itself but only as it dwells in Christ who gives and sustains life. So the first step in becoming a true child of God and to have an authentic spirituality is *not* to join the branch but to join the vine.

This is not the only image Jesus uses to describe himself in the Gospel of John. He offers many metaphors to awaken faith in his transcendent identity. He speaks of himself as the bread of life (6:35) – a metaphor of ingestion; the light of the world (8:12) – a metaphor of penetration; the door (10:7,9) – a metaphor of permission and protection; the good shepherd (10:11,14) – a metaphor of relationship; the resurrection and the life (11:25) – an eschatological metaphor suggesting direction and destiny. Jesus speaks of himself as the way, the truth and the life (14:6) – metaphors of orientation. But no other metaphor in John expresses so well the full mutuality of double indwelling – I in Christ and Christ in me. 'Remain in me, and I will remain in you' (15:4). This double abiding leads to a continuous life transformation.

Earlier we said that we make a great mistake when we invite people – as their first step – to join the church. They should join God! But when they join God – through discipleship to Jesus – they discover a truly wonderful reality. Jesus joins them, abides in them and stays with them. He never lets go. He never stops abiding. He never cuts himself off. And this dogged determination on his part to penetrate us continuously with his lovely life inspires our abiding and remaining in him. One of the best words to describe this two-way abiding is the word communion. The word means to have a common life by mutually participating in one another's lives. As we will see, there are five dimensions to this communion.

Communion in life
The word 'remain' or 'abide' means to stay with, maintain one's attachment, continue, persist and find one's centre in someone else's life. This is heart-to-heart communion, life-to-life intercourse, something much deeper than having one's name on the membership roll of a church or being theologically orthodox. The branch abides in the vine; it is not glued on the bark of the vine. This is full communion: we find *our* life in Him; he delights to find life *in us*. Oswald Chambers expresses this beautifully.

> Determine to abide in Jesus wherever you are placed . . . It does not matter what my circumstances are . . . With our Lord the inner abiding was unsullied; He was at home with God wherever His body was placed. He never chose his own circumstances, but was meek toward His Father's dispensations for Him. Think of the amazing leisure of Our Lord's life! We keep God at excitement point, there is none of the serenity of the life hid with Christ in God about us.[1]

But there is an alternative.

Five things happen to a person who does not abide in Jesus (15:6). In the allegory, the non-abiding branches are thrown away, they wither, they are picked up, thrown into the fire, and burned. Jesus here deals with the simple fact that if a person is spiritually dead because they are out of connection with Jesus their ultimate fate will reveal this. This is consistent with the words of Jesus in the Synoptics: 'I never knew you' (Matt 7:23). There is surely no more horrifying prospect ahead of a human being – especially one who claims to be a Christian – than to have the Lord say on that day, 'We were never in communion and I do not know you'. Or, in terms of the allegory, 'You were a dead branch and never knew it'. But to be alive in Christ is to discover the supreme purpose of life. Jesus speaks of this in terms of fruitfulness.

Communion in fruit-bearing

'No branch can bear fruit by itself; it must remain in the vine. Neither can you bear fruit unless you remain in me. I am the vine; you are the branches. If a man remains in me and I in him, he will bear much fruit; apart from me you can do nothing' (15:4–5). Without the branch the vine can do nothing; without the vine the branch can do nothing. All the branch possesses belongs to the vine; all the vine possesses belongs to the branch. The branch exists for the purposes of the vine as a conduit of life for the world. In other words, the branch exists not to become a beautiful branch but to bear fruit. But that begs the question which is universally asked by people who read this passage: what is the fruit?

Of the various answers commonly given to this question some are even suggested by the text. Possibilities include the conversion of others, answered prayer (15:7), love (15:9), reproducing Christ's presence in the world, bringing life in Jesus' name, and demonstrating the presence of Jesus through the love of the Christian fellowship (13:35; 15:8). Jesus does not tell us what the fruit is, perhaps deliberately. If we focused on calculating the extent to which we have 'produced fruit' we would lose the point of it all – to live in Christ. Jesus does not ask us to inspect our own fruit or anyone else's but to see that we are abiding in him! Producing the fruit is his responsibility; bearing it is ours. But bearing cannot happen without pruning.

The word 'pruning' is not actually used. In its place is the word 'cleansing', a word used in John elsewhere (13:10) for the cleansing that the disciples had received through his words and would receive through his cross. There are two cleansings in this chapter. First, there is initial cleansing through conversion, or new birth (13:10). Of such people Jesus can truly say, 'You are already clean because of the word I have spoke to you' (15:3). Second, there is the continuing experience of cleansing through pruning or purging. So Jesus says, 'Every branch that does bear fruit he prunes so that it will be even more fruitful' (15:2). What are these pruning experiences? Are they ordinary hardships experienced by all Christians, or sufferings we experience because we are disciples? Are they special restricting and hard experiences which God ordains to help us concentrate our energies? Are they reductions in ministry opportunities in order to increase our personal dependence on Jesus? Are they 'natural' reductions of superfluous activities that come when people invest heavily in the work of the Lord? Are they day-by-day cut-backs, or traumatic and life-changing experiences?

Once again, Jesus does not tell us. It might be any or all of these. But two crucial truths that will be experienced by every fruit-bearing disciple are these. First, purging experiences are not chosen by the disciple but orchestrated by the Gardener, even if they may be inflicted by other disciples at the hand of God. And, second, pruning experiences are essential for fruitfulness. I was once working in a church that, for almost a whole year, did not ask me to teach or preach. It was what I wanted to contribute most of all. At the time I was angry and frustrated. But in time I realised the gracious Gardener was cutting me back in order to make me even more fruitful at a later time. It was a hard and yet a good lesson. Our part of the communion is to abide. We can trust the pruning knife to his wise and gentle hand.

Communion in prayer
'Ask whatever you wish, and it will be given you' (15:7). The assumption behind this amazing promise is obvious from the passage. If we are so abiding in Christ and therefore have his mind so that what we ask for is what he already wants to give, then our asking and receiving will be fully harmonised. Once again, Oswald Chambers writes with penetrating insight:

> The idea of prayer is not in order to get answers from God; prayer is perfect and complete oneness

with God. If we pray because we want answers, we will get huffed with God. The answers come every time, but not always in the way we expect, and our spiritual huff shows a refusal to identify ourselves with Our Lord in prayer.[2]

Elsewhere in the Gospel Jesus speaks of this as asking *in his name* (16:26–27). This is not using the name of Jesus tacked on the end of the prayer as a magic word, a divine 'open sesame', but rather we have become so intimate with the Lord, so much in harmony with his purposes that we find ourselves asking for what he already wants to give us.

Communion in love

This also is a mutual abiding: we abide in Christ's love for us; Christ abides in our love for one another. We will explore these one at a time. First, there is abiding in Christ's love. 'As the Father has loved me, so have I loved you. Now remain in my love' (15:9). The Christian experience of love is not merely restricted to what we observe of Christ's love for the world, for which he gave himself sacrificially. This love is the same love that the Father has for the Son. We receive the same love that has always existed within the Godhead and which gave Jesus his identity, vocation and worth while on earth. Andrew Murray speaks correctly when he says, 'The love of the Father to the Son is that divine passion with which He delights in the Son and speaks, "My beloved Son, in whom I am well pleased."'[3] We are a delight to God. He desires us. He seeks our fellowship. Were it needed, he would die again for us. We never know ourselves to be truly loved until we know ourselves to be loved by God.

But abiding in his love involves our loving one another, a mutual love in which he abides. 'My command is this: Love each other as I have loved you' (15:12). So abiding is not a mystical experience in the sense of ecstatic experience that is unconnected with ordinary life. Abiding means simple obedience to the commands of Jesus which in this verse are reduced to one: to love one another as Jesus has loved us. This is essentially the only place where the word 'new' is used by Jesus in the Gospel of John (13:34) and it refers to the new commandment to love. This commandment is new in motive because it is inspired by Christ's love for us, not our sense of obligation. It is also new in style because the love we are to show one another is to be characterised by the love within the Holy Trinity. Therefore it is not only redemptive – mending broken relationships and broken people – but it is unitive and creative like the life-giving, covenant love within God himself. It is not, as previously suggested, 'mashed potato love' where the identities of individual persons become merged in one great melting pot. Just the reverse: within the one God there are three persons. Within the community of the vine each branch, each person, has a gift, a ministry, an identity, and a presence – even more so because of the love.

Love is the final apologetic for the truth of the Christian cause. Reasons must be given for the hope within us. Demonstrations of compassion will give evidence of our concern for others, and God's concern for all. But if Christians do not love one another then the world has no reason to believe that the Father loves the Son. Two ancient writers commented on this fundamental message to the world. Tertullian says the heathen were saying, 'See how they love one another.'[4] But in the fourth century Chrysostom complains of the Christians in his day that they have too little love: 'Even now, there is nothing else that causes the heathen to stumble except that there is no love ... Their own doctrines they have long condemned, and in like manner they admire ours, but they are hindered by our mode of life.'[5]

Where the communion in love is experienced there is a gracious circle. The more we love our brothers and sisters, the more Christ is able to dwell in us with the love he enjoys with the Father; the more we abide in Christ, the more we are equipped to love one another as Christ loved us. All of this leads to joy.

Communion in joy

'I have told you this so that my joy may be in you and that your joy may be complete' (15:11). Once again there is a mutual abiding: we have joy as we live by the words of Jesus; it is, however, not our joy but *his*. We enter into the Lord's joy in being loved by the Father and in sharing that love with the world. Canon Stanley Evans once described a Christian as 'a controlled drunk, purposely intoxicated with the joy of the life which is perpetually created by God himself'.[6] Most pleasures are substitutes for this deep exhilaration of spirit. It is one infallible mark of the touch of God. So C. S. Lewis, before his conversion concluded that 'Christians are wrong, but all the rest are bores'. It was a backhanded but insightful compliment. Besides commending our Lord to the world by mutual love, we should commend our Lord to the world by being the most joyful people on earth. In this self-forgetful God-centredness, we will at last be fruitful, probably without our knowing it.

Now, having explored the allegory of the vine and branches Jesus adds a metaphor to deepen his invitation to belong to him.

The Metaphor of Friendship: Full Mutuality

'You are my friends if you do what I command. I no longer call you servants, because a servant does not know his master's business. Instead, I have called you friends, for everything that I learned from my Father I have made known to you' (15:14–15). Jesus is the friend of the disciples. That is almost too marvellous to understand. But the next statement is equally awesome: the disciples are friends of Jesus.

By using the word 'friend' Jesus underscores five more

dimensions of the mutual abiding of believers and the Lord. First, there is mutuality; it is a two-way street. Second, in our relationship with Jesus there is freedom from self-interest; friendship is not *for* anything, not even active service in the Kingdom. Once there is a commercial dimension in the relationship – when the relationship is primarily useful – it is probably not a friendship. Third, friendship involves mutual delight in each other's persons. Immediately, this makes some of us ask, 'What delight can Jesus have in me?' But he *is* our friend in just this way. Fourth, friendship involves a common interest and purpose, an intelligent and mindful participation in each other's lives. So Jesus reveals the Father's thoughts and will to the disciples, thus sharing his inmost experience with them; the disciples are his friends as they make decisions (in the light of what they know his mind to be) in order to please him and not merely to mechanically fulfil his will as slaves.

The use of the 'friend' concept greatly enriches the vine–branch allegory. The disciple is not merely a mindless channel for Christ's life, or a compliant slave. Christ calls forth our mind, our heart and our will, not into mere compliance but into joyful and responsible submission. Friends of Jesus do not wait passively for the Lord to decide everything for them. They can be the most decisive people on earth if they are really listening to Jesus and responding to the will of the Father revealed by Jesus. Tragically many Christians want to be servants of God when his wish is that they be friends!

Years ago I picked up an anonymous sheet describing Jesus as 'my best friend'. Among the statements are these:

- He initiated our friendship.
- He loves me unconditionally.
- He believes the best about me.
- He is always available when I need him.
- He desires the very best for me, knowing what that is, and leads me toward it, sometimes through difficult

paths, but always supporting me and staying close
to me.
- He never gives up on me.
- He brings out my spontaneity and enjoys me.
- He allows me to be free to come and go, never forces,
  never controls, never manipulates.
- He values me as a person and not merely for what I
  can do for him.
- He opens up opportunities for me to know his other
  friends.

Real friends will do his will, not because they *must*, but
because they *may*. Sometimes I overhear someone pray,
'Lord completely control me'. While I understand the
intent of that prayer, and delight that the Lord can piece
together a life that has gone out of control, I suspect that
it is a prayer that the Lord does not answer in the terms of
the request. What Jesus wants is friends with self-control,
not slaves under his control. So the old hymn now takes on
new meaning. 'What a Friend we have in Jesus.' May he
be able to say, 'What a friend I have in my disciple!'

Living the Metaphor

Taken together, the allegory of the vine and branches,
and the metaphor of the friend with the friend, offer five
exciting prospects for the pilgrim on the Way.

First, *the Christian life is essentially relational*. It is
impossible to be saved outside of relationship to Jesus.
Salvation is not a state, or something given to us, but
it *is* Jesus. It is finding our identity, our destiny, our
satisfaction and our meaning in life in relation to him.
Not even our work for him counts, since bearing fruit
is the responsibility of the vine not the branches. Our
responsibility is simply to abide or remain in him.

In John 13:1–17 Jesus, knowing who he was, where he
had come from, and where he was going, washed the feet
of the disciples. When Peter refused Jesus said: 'Unless
I wash you, you have no part with me' (13:8). It is not

possible for Peter to have the benefits of being with Jesus without being with him in an unconditional relationship. It is the indispensable condition of fellowship with Jesus that we must renounce control over our relationship with him. Merely to consent to be a branch. To be willing to be a friend. Relationship is not the *means* to a salvation end; it is the end.

Second, *the Christian life is purposeful*. The branch bears fruit for the vine. Other trees are planted for shade or for ornamentation; but this tree is planted only for the fruit. And the Lord will see that our life is not resultless. Andrew Murray expresses the purposefulness of the believer's life in this way: 'If Christ, the heavenly Vine, has taken the believer as a branch, then He has pledged Himself, in the very nature of things, to supply the sap and spirit and nourishment to make it bring forth fruit.'[7]

Third, *the Christian life is revelatory*. Jesus places our experience of being a branch in the context of the relationship of the Father and the Son: the Father is the gardener (15:1); the Son's love for the disciples is an expression of the Father's love for the Son (15:9); the Son remains in the Father's love (15:10) just as disciples are to remain in the Son's love. The love disciples are to have for each other – Trinity love, not just neighbour love – is an expression of the love between the persons of the Godhead. What we earlier called a 'gracious circle' is really a spiral of grace. We keep re-entering at a deeper level. As we love others in God's family, we open ourselves more to being penetrated by Christ's love. As we deepen our friendship with Jesus we spontaneously love brothers and sisters more deeply. Every moment of our life is an opportunity to know God better. God can be found not at the perimeter of the daily round but right in the centre.

The theological presupposition of this whole matter is the truth that God is love (1 John 4:16). For God to be love there must be someone to love. We have the privilege of being included in the mutual love, order and purpose that exists within the social life of the Holy Trinity. So

our spiritual life and ministry is derivative. Love starts
within the life of God himself. It precedes both creation
and the fall. Jesus prayed, 'Now, Father, glorify me in
your presence with the glory I had with you before the
world began' (17:5). 'Father, I want those you have given
me to be with me where I am, and to see my glory, the
glory you have given me because you loved me before the
creation of the world' (17:24). 'I have made you known
to them, and will continue to make you known in order
that the love you have for me may be in them and that
I myself may be in them' (17:26). 'We proclaim to you
what we have seen and heard, so that you also may
have fellowship with us. And our fellowship is with the
Father and with his Son, Jesus Christ' (1 John 1:3). In
the Synoptic Gospels, discipleship is presented as being
'with Jesus' and 'being sent out by him' (Mark 3:14).
But John allows us to view discipleship as a transcendent
experience. To be with Jesus means that we are drawn
into the mystery of God himself: Our life in Christ is
revelatory.

Fourth, *the Christian life is a responsive life*. God
the gardener and Christ the vine-friend constantly take
initiatives with the believer. Our abiding in Christ is
nurtured by his abiding in us. Our friendship with him
is inspired by his friendship with us. We are found people
and all our seeking is a sign of our already having been
found.

The Corporate and the Personal

What we have been exploring is consistent with the rest
of the New Testament. The allegory and the metaphor
in John's Gospel correspond to two great metaphors
in Paul's writing: the body of Christ, a metaphor of
corporate spirituality; and being 'in Christ', a special
metaphor to express the direct interpenetration of the
believer and the Lord. The vine–branch allegory gathers
up the truths expressed by both of Paul's metaphors.
The vine and the branches describes the full *corporate*

life of believers in relation to Jesus – developed in terms of 'the body' by Paul – and also the direct *personal* and *interdependent* relationship of the believer and Jesus – which Paul describes as being 'in Christ'. We will briefly consider each of these Pauline parallels.

The body of Christ expresses several relational realities that Christians should normally experience:

- The members of the body are interdependent with each other.
- Members and the Head are interdependent.
- There is a living, intimate connection of the Head with the body.
- Unity is experienced in the body only because of its relation to the Head.
- Unity is enriched by the diverse contribution and gifts of all the members.
- Unity in the body makes the whole more than the sum of the parts.
- Growth takes place systemically through integrating all the members with each other and the interests of the Head.
- Membership in the body is a living, heart connection rather than a formal organisational involvement.
- There is corporate solidarity: to deal with one member is to deal with all (since each is affected by the other) and to deal with the body is to deal with the Head. No one can be in Christ alone. He is not a disembodied head!

These few notes underscore that the vine and branch theme is entirely consistent with Paul's development of our *corporate* experience of living in communion with Jesus. And the 'in Christ' theme in Paul is consistent with the *personal* communion dimension of the allegory and the metaphor we have been considering.

Being 'in Christ' is a favourite Pauline expression for the Christian experience. He uses 'Christ in me' or 'I in Christ' 164 times. The heart of Pauline Christianity is a

Christophany. Christ discloses himself to us. 'Where two or three come together in my name, there am I with them' (Matt 18:20). James Stewart said, 'Every Christian is a mystic in the Pauline sense', in the sense of being capable of a daily, ever-renewed communion with Jesus rather than a transient rapture. Stewart comments,

> The notion which certain philosophies have almost taken for granted, that human personalities are mutually exclusive and impermeable, is disproved when the experience of love is taken into account ... It is the potential permeation of one personality by another which makes spiritual religion possible.[8]

In his classic treatment of the subject of Paul's mysticism, Adolf Deissmann distinguishes between 'union mysticism' and 'communion mysticism'. It is a useful and illuminating distinction. Union mysticism, says Deissmann, involves being absorbed into God or discovering divinity in ourselves – the current fashion with New Age religion. In the process we lose our identities. Communion mysticism, in contrast, involves a social intercourse in which we experience the gracious paradox of 'I, yet not I' (Gal 2:20) in the experience of the immanence of the transcendent Christ. So we discover our true identity in the context of the communion. Because Paul believed and experienced Jesus in communion mysticism he was more concerned with ethics than ecstasy.[9] This is entirely consistent with the vine and branches – through which abiding leads to loving relationship – and friendship – which leads to doing the will of the Father.

Deissmann made one other illuminating distinction, the difference between 'acting mysticism' and 'reacting mysticism'. Acting mysticism is the process through which the aspirant takes initiative to gain a transcendent experience through liturgy, disciplines, reason and other means.[10] Much that passes for spirituality is 'acting mysticism', the attempt to gain God-consciousness. Reacting mysticism is the process in which the person responds to the initiative of God himself. So Paul spoke of himself as a reacting mystic when he confessed that 'Christ Jesus took hold of me' (Phil 3:12). He confessed that 'by the grace of God I am what I am' (1 Cor 15:10). He spoke of how God 'was pleased to reveal his Son in me' (Gal 1:16). Christ was the initiator, the lover, the seeker, the evangelist. Deissmann suggests that, 'It was Damascus that transformed his acting mysticism into the reacting mysticism and the soul shaken and thrown open to the creative energy by that impact from that time onwards had its firm support in Christ.'[11] This is entirely consistent with the allegory and the metaphor we have been exploring in John. In John's Gospel, divine election is strongly expressed: 'You did not choose me, but I chose you and appointed you' (John 15:16). Indeed only in John's Gospel is it stated that the Father chose the disciples.

But here is a hard question. Can the disciples become un-chosen? Are there limits to the friendship of Jesus? Is it possible that a once-live branch could become a dead branch? There are dark hints of this in a later book in the New Testament: the Letter to the Hebrews (2:3; 3:6,14; 4:1–2,11,14; 6:1–9; 10:26–31). There in the context of the repeated exhortations to continue, to abide and to persist, the author says that 'It is impossible for those who have once been enlightened . . . who have shared in the Holy Spirit . . . if they fall away, to be brought back to repentance . . . (6:4–6). Apparently they cannot be brought to repentance because they have rejected the only means of receiving forgiveness, 'because to their loss they are crucifying the Son of God all over again and subjecting him to public disgrace' (6:6). Many feel this is consistent with the so-called 'unforgivable sin' mentioned by Jesus in the Synoptic Gospels (Matt 12:31; Mark 3:29). It is important to state that persons concerned about having committed the unforgivable sin *have not committed this sin* or they would be unconcerned that they had done so. If they had, their hard hearts would not care, nor ask for the hope of redemption. In contrast, those who have committed the unforgiveable sin cannot be brought back to repentance because they do not want grace. They have rejected fully, repeatedly and finally the one means of hope they have. Judas is a tragic and mysterious embodiment of this possibility. Had he come to the foot of the cross and begged for forgiveness, he would have been forgiven. But he never asked. He could not. I am reminded of the comment made about the two thieves who died beside Jesus. 'Never despair, one thief was saved. Never presume, the other thief was damned.'

My friend and co-author, Michael Green, surveys the New Testament literature on this subject in *The Meaning of Salvation*. After considering all the statements that assure believers of their eternal salvation, Green admits there is a contrary body of evidence even within the New Testament, most of which relate not to a single sin but presumption and apostasy. He concludes:

The answer is that we can *know* we are forgiven, saved, in Christ, justified. Assurance of salvation is the birthright of every Christian. It would only be presumptuous if it rested in any way on human achievement. But it cannot be presumption to take God's word of acquittal, of adoption, of salvation as the truth, to believe it and to live by it. But this adoption, this acquittal, this salvation of which we can be assured here and now is only proleptic of the age to come; it is only the first instalment of heaven. As soon as I regard salvation as a possession, as something that now belongs to me, I have gone far from the biblical picture of inaugurated eschatology, and fossilized God's future into a past experience. It is perfectly true, moreover, that Christ will never cast out the Christian, that he will be 'with us always, even to the end of the age'. No foe can pluck us out of his hand. No sin can drive him from our hearts. The believer's security in Christ is absolute, for in Christ alone is salvation ... Although no power of circumstance, or force of evil, can separate the Christian from Christ, there is one thing that can; his own free will.[12]

These passages, however, emphasise abiding and continuing, not the probability of becoming deserters. And I think it is the spirit of the New Testament that, while warning of a tragic possibility, we should emphasise the grace that keeps us. We are dealing with a mystery that eludes simple doctrinal statements. Instead of speaking of eternal security we may be better to use a phrase suggested by our study of John fifteen – *the eternal tenacity of God*. Jesus says in John 6:37–40 'no-one can snatch them out of my hand' (10:28). I am a follower of Jesus today not because I have been faithful in abiding or a faithful friend, but because of his gracious, persistent and friendly hold on me. His hold on me is stronger than my hold on him. Andrew Murray's words capture the spirit of this chapter beautifully.

Shall I not, instead of thinking of only how hard and how difficult it is to live like a branch of the True Vine, because I thought of it as something I had to accomplish – shall I not now begin to look upon it as the most blessed and joyful thing under heaven? Shall I not believe that, now I once am in him, he himself will keep me and enable me to abide? On my part, abiding is nothing but the acceptance of my position, the consent to be kept there, the surrender of faith to the Strong Vine still to hold the feeble branch. Yes, I will, I do abide in Thee, blessed Lord Jesus.[13]

CHAPTER ELEVEN
CHILDREN OF HOPE

The only ultimate disaster that can befall us, I have come to realize, is to feel ourselves to be at home here on earth.
Malcolm Muggeridge

The Christians who did the most for the present world were just those who thought most about the next . . . It is since Christians have largely ceased to think of the other world that they have become so ineffective in this. Aim at heaven and you will get earth thrown in; aim at earth and you will get neither.
C. S. Lewis

C had Walsh once said that orthodox theology has not abandoned eschatology (the study of the end times). Rather, theology has embalmed it! Too often it has been embalmed in elaborate charts on the Revelation or in books claiming to provide a schedule for the presumed timing of events leading up to the new heaven and the new earth. These books feed on a deep human anxiety that the world and our work within it, have no meaningful result and, to quote T. S. Eliot, the world will end not with a bang but a whimper. So popular writers like Hal Lindsey make a fortune on claiming that this is the terminal generation.

The Theology of Hope

It is not surprising that the popularity of theologies that promise an instant evacuation come at precisely the moment in history when there is so much despair about the future. There was once a time when secular 'prophets' preached a glorious future while Christian prophets preached hell-fire and brimstone (though I cannot honestly say I have heard such a sermon). But today, while secular 'prophets' preach doom, Christians have the privilege of announcing both the hope of glory and a glorious hope. It is this which is the focus of the chapter.

Defining eschatology and futurology

We must start by defining our terms. Eschatology can be defined as the study of the end (*eschaton*). It has been suggested that the Christian trying to understand the teaching of the New Testament about the end is like an early explorer of the Rocky Mountains or the Alps. Coming from the east and not having a detailed map, the explorer would see multiple ranges and peaks without knowing how deep are the valleys between. In the same way, the New Testament reveals six 'peaks' about the end without giving us a detailed map of their order, or the distance between them. These are: the second coming of Jesus, the resurrection of the body, judgment, eternal life, the full realisation of the Kingdom of God, and the new heaven and the new earth.

When we speak of these six eschatological dimensions we are not using the word 'hope' as we do in normal conversation, as, for example, when we say 'I hope to see you sometime in the future'. Unlike human wishful thinking, *this* hope is as certain as Christ's first coming, as certain as God himself. So the New Testament speaks of Christ as our hope (1 Tim 1:1); it affirms that 'Christ in you, [is] the hope of glory' (Col 1:27); it says that the calling of every Christian is to one hope (Eph 4:4); it insists that to live without God means 'to have no hope' (Eph 2:12; 1 Thess 4:13). This is eschatology. Futurology is related but very different.

Futurology is a term that describes how we are to live on planet earth until the end. Futurologies run the full range from future bright to future night, and everything in between. There are a few secular futurists that hold out the promise of a limitless, unpollutable world in which everyone will be middle class, well-fed, and well-entertained. Marxism held out the hope of a classless society in which justice and prosperity would be evenly and universally distributed. Future bright proponents believe that human beings can bring in Utopia. But most futurists today forecast the exact opposite: a future night. They envision a gloomy end through the final depletion of the world's resources, a deadly irradiation of the race through the gaping hole in the ozone layer, or the insane detonation of the world's nuclear stockpiles by people who have never signed nuclear disarmament treaties. Lesslie Newbigin, capturing the mood of the day said, 'We are without conviction about any worthwhile end to which the travail of history might lead.'[1] Reflecting on the evening newscast, someone said, 'Who can absorb any more bad news?' The question strikes a deep chord within us.

A 64-year-old man in Britain, being teased by his sons about his failing powers, told them to wait until they were his age and see how fit they'd be. There was silence, after which one son said, 'None of us is going to get to 64 and we all know that'. One obvious result of this short-circuited future is the proliferation of an instant gratification culture. People try to squeeze every pleasure they can out of the moment because there may not be another one. If there is no certain tomorrow, and if today is all one has, then it makes sense. Even Christians seem to be caught up in this, which is a certain indication that eschatology has been embalmed. As we will see, a person's futurology is dependent either on whether or not that person has an eschatological hope, or on the kind of eschatology he believes.

Relating eschatology and futurology

The relating of eschatology and futurology is critical. When Christians are profoundly influenced by short-term future thinking and, if they forget the glorious prospect of fulfilment in the new heaven and the new earth, they try to get 'the best of both worlds' by squeezing

everything they can out of this life while they wait –
albeit without any real hope – for the next. Sometimes
our spontaneous remarks betray the inner reality. A
church warden was once asked what he thought would
happen to him when he died. 'I will immediately depart
into everlasting felicity,' he replied, but he continued
along this line, 'but I wish you wouldn't ask me about
such unpleasant subjects!' The spirituality of hope had
not permeated his soul. Some Christian couples are not
sure they should conceive children and bring them into
this kind of world, or whether they should keep the
children they have conceived. Young Christians worry
about whether there will be jobs upon graduation, and
whether their marriages – if they marry at all – will last.
It is hardly surprising that such world-weariness drives
many young people to consider that the only thing worth
doing in the world in these last days is to go into full-time
ministry in the church.

In contrast, followers of Jesus in the early church could
not wait for the future to come. They felt the pressure
of the future as a positive pressure. They developed
a futurology that related to the certain hope of their
eschatology. They welcomed the future. They wanted not
only to live in the light of the end, but to hasten the coming
of the Lord Jesus. They believed that the second coming
was such a positive goal for themselves and for God's
creation, that their whole view of the future was shaped
by that eschatological perspective. Peter said, 'You ought
to live holy and godly lives as you look forward to the day
of God and speed its coming' (2 Pet 3:11–12). The Roman
Empire was, at the time, not too different from our own
society. It was in rampant decay. There was widespread
homosexuality; families were fragmented; marriage was
despised; each man had a mistress for pleasure and a wife
for domestic purposes. Slavery and poverty abounded. To
become a Christian meant joining a radical and despised
sect, to be persecuted at any moment, to experience losing
one's job or to suffer social rejection. Nevertheless these
Christians lived *in hope*.

The Apostle Paul modelled a person living for the end *in an unhurried way*. He spent fourteen years preparing to become a missionary and when he was finally commissioned to his 'world-wide' mission to the Gentiles, he spent forty or more hours each week making tents by hand as part of his service to God, while he knew all along that thousands were still unreached. Nevertheless he never indicated that he was wasting his time or wasting his life, even when he was shuffled from prison to prison. To live this way one must have a futurology formed around a biblical eschatology.

Some Christians have an eschatology with *no* futurology. They believe that Christ will come tonight, or tomorrow at the latest. So there is nothing to do in this world except put on the white clothes and prepare for the coming of the Lord. Other Christians have an eschatology with a *limited* futurology. Like Hal Lindsey they believe this is the terminal generation and we have, at best, a short time to wait. Needless to say this results in an otherworldly perspective in which work on the problems of ecology, or unjust food distribution in the world seem to be pointless exercises. Preparing for a life of service to God as an educator, a scientist, a craftsperson or a business person seems secondary to the imperative of preaching God's word, preferably in so-called full-time Christian work. Obviously we cannot all live this way, especially if the end does not come soon.

It is often argued that this was exactly the perspective of both Jesus and Paul, namely that they did not believe in a future beyond their own generation. Careful biblical scholarship, however, shows that both Jesus and Paul spoke of the certainty and the character of the end of human history but said almost nothing about the timing. While they were *ready* for the end to come at any moment they did not predicate their actions or even their ethics on the certainty that the end *must* come soon. Our way of life in this world, they would argue, must be influenced by the possible shortness of time, but the real reason for our living in this world differently from the thorough-going secularist, is the fact that the Kingdom has come and will come fully one day. So, capturing the emphasis of both Jesus and Paul, Luther is reported to have said, 'If I knew that tomorrow the world would perish, I would still plant a little apple tree in my back garden.'[2]

The New Testament encourages an eschatology with a *long-term* futurology. Believers are to be ready for the Lord to come back at any moment, but they are also to be ready to work in this world in the light of that glorious certainty for another thousand years if necessary. Like the wise virgins in the parable of the Wise and Foolish Virgins (Matt 25:1–13) they are waiting *now* but are prepared, if necessary, for a long wait. Possibly for a long, long wait. The long wait is not a futile wait. Nor is waiting inactivity. Rather the beautiful prospect of the end is a powerful motivation to do everything in this life with faith, hope and love. With great wisdom the theologian Jürgen Moltmann explained that eschatology feeds our faith and transforms living now. Eschatology is the most pastoral of all theological perspectives showing how the ending impinges on the present in such ways that the truth of the gospel is verified in life 'in the middle'. 'The believer is not set at the high noon of life, but at the dawn of a new day at the point where night and day, things passing and things to come, grapple with each other.'[3]

On the deck of a sinking ship

A vivid example of this is given in Acts 27:13–44 when Paul is being carried on a reeling ship, foundering in a storm. Though a prisoner on the ship he became its master by assuming a pastoral and prophetic ministry to the captain, the crew, the other prisoners, and even his travelling companion, Dr Luke, whose presence is signalled by the use of 'we' (27:18). First, Paul had a long-range plan for his life – in his case, to evangelise the whole Roman Empire. It did not matter whether he did this in chains, and he did not allow any negative present circumstance to overshadow his ultimate purpose for life in this world. Second, Paul expressed courage. 'So keep up your courage, men, for I have faith in God that it will happen just as he told me' (27:25). This was not merely whistling in the dark or pumping himself up. Paul was confident that God's purposes would not be thwarted and that all things would work for the good of those who love God (and even for those who do not!). Therefore he was able to tell them the hard facts that they must run aground on some island, but he did so with hope.

Third, Paul did the thing at hand as though he had an assured future. None of them had eaten for days, so sick, weary and hopeless were they. But, Paul 'took some bread and gave thanks to God in front of them all. Then he broke it and began to eat' (27:35). He made a eucharistic drama out of a normal meal and ministered to the practical needs of his fellow shipmates. Finally, Paul revealed that his hope was nurtured through his personal communion with God. 'Last night an angel of the God whose I am and whom I serve stood beside me and said, "Do not be afraid, Paul. You must stand trial before Caesar; and God has graciously given you the lives of all who sail with you"' (27:23–24). The modern Christian standing on the deck of a civilisation foundering in the storms of a post-modern world can live by, and proclaim, the same hope.

The Spirituality of Hope

The centrepiece of Christian hope is the second coming of Jesus Christ, a truth mentioned 318 times in Scripture. But the emphasis in the New Testament is always on readiness and longing rather than on calculating *when*. Jesus himself admonished his followers to watch for him, not to watch the calendar (Luke 12:36–40; Acts 1:6–7; Phil 3:20; Heb 9:28). The second coming of Jesus will be the personal and final visit of the groom to receive the bride, the church (Rev 21:2). But each of the other five 'peaks' in the panorama of Christian hope points to a Christ-centred reality.

Our future bodily existence has been guaranteed and demonstrated by the bodily resurrection of Jesus as the firstfruits of the grave. Resurrection is conformity to Christ bodily. Final judgment will not be an impersonal court-scene before an austere judge. Jesus is both judge and friend. Eternal life is life lived with Christ in the new age. Christ can properly be called, as he was by Irenaeus, the *autobasileia* – the Kingdom of God in person – since he embodied the rule of God as king and the service of his people. The New Testament suggests that the full coming of the Kingdom will be like the first coming of Jesus *and even more*! The new heaven and the new earth, the sixth 'peak,' is characterised not only by the renewal of creation but by the fact that the Lamb (Jesus) is in the centre (Rev 21:23; 22:3). What does this imagery mean?

The second coming

The second coming of Jesus will be personal (Rev 22:7), literal (Acts 1:10–11), glorious (2 Thess 1:7-9), and unexpected (1 Thess 5:2–3). This precious promise guarantees that our faith will become sight, and our partial and inadequate experience of Christ in this life will become consummated. Scripture does not use the metaphor of marriage for the Christian's relationship with Jesus in this life. That is reserved for the final wedding supper of the Lamb, so powerfully expressed in the last book of the Bible (Rev 19:6–9). Rather, the term 'betrothal' – which in the ancient world was presexual marriage, a more binding covenant than modern engagement – was the term Paul used to describe our present relationship with Christ (2 Cor 11:2). His coming again means a full marriage experience with the Lord! At the moment we can hardly say we know God at all. Indeed even Paul corrects himself and indicates that it is more proper to speak of God's *knowing us* (Gal 4:9). In spite of the impressive claims of some people to experience what they call 'spiritual marriage' with God in this life, we cannot expect a full and final mystical experience of Jesus until he comes again, unless we die first. But we can live hopefully with our betrothal experience because the marriage is absolutely certain.

The resurrection of the body

The resurrection of the body (1 Cor 15:12–58) promises that our future in Christ is not to become disembodied spirits floating around in heaven, but completely whole people, more whole than we ever were in this life with our 'psychological body'. When my daughter was an intern in the only hospital in our city which at that time received AIDS patients, she would sit on the beds of these modern lepers and, touching them, tell them about the resurrection of the body. What a glorious hope! Our hope is to be invested with a 'spiritual body' (1 Cor 15:44) which has both continuity with our present bodies and discontinuity because it will be transfigured. Resurrection is the end of incarnation. But far from merely projecting a sensuous and materialistic heavenly future, as is proposed in some religions, Christian hope looks forward to a life in full and final conformity to the likeness of God's Son, *even with regard to our bodies*. So the resurrection of Jesus is not only the visible proof that it can happen. More important, his resurrection is the first stage of our final taking on of the image of Christ. If the body is *for the Lord*, as Paul argues, then we must glorify God *now* in our bodily life even in such mundane things as eating, and such sensitive things as sexual activity. One can only imagine how shocking this was to the 'superspiritual' Corinthians who did not care what they did with their bodies. Equally shocking would be his assertion that the truly spiritual person would be one with a resurrection body.

Last judgment

Judgment is a theme hardly mentioned today even by Christian preachers. In contrast the psalmist longed for the judgment of God (Psalm 67:1–4; 96:10–13). The reason is that the psalmist lived in a topsy-turvy world in which there seemed to be no justice and he knew that God's judgment would mean restoration of justice and the vindication of the down-trodden. *We* imagine that we have justice in the world – at least a measure of it – and fear that the judgment of God will upset our applecarts.

But without judgment and the accountability it brings, life in this world does not make sense. There would be no final reckoning for the unjust suffering we experience, and no final reward for faithfulness (Heb 9:27–28).

The unique perspective of the Christian faith is that our judge is the same person as our Saviour-friend (John 5:22; Rom 2:16; Acts 17:30–31; 2 Cor 5:10), who has provided a covering for all our sins. Christians are not free from evaluation; but they are free from condemnation. Therefore question 52 of the Heidelberg Catechism asks: 'What comfort hast thou by the coming again of Christ to judge the quick and the dead?' The answer is this: 'That in all my miseries and persecutions I look with my head erect for the very same, who before yielded Himself unto the judgement of God for me and took away all malediction from me, to come as Judge from heaven.' This dimension of our future gives us hope because *God* will judge and restore all things. It is also a warning. If God is the final judge we should refrain from judging others now (James 4:11–12). There is also an invitation. God is withholding his final judgment to give the maximum possibility of repentance to his creatures. We should settle the issue now before we go to court.

Eternal life

Eternal life is simply life in the new age. As we discovered in the chapter 'Aware of the Struggle', the Christian person lives in the overlap of the ages. This can be represented graphically by the diagram on the next page.

Oscar Cullman has helpfully used terms from the Second World War to explain the realities of living in the overlap of the ages.

D-Day was 'departure day' when the Allied forces invaded enemy-occupied soil – so it was a brilliant analogy. It carried with it the certainty of final victory as the bridgehead at Caen was established, and the ensuing struggle made that fact increasingly plain, despite reverses in the war. V-Day would come – and it did three years later! The first coming of Jesus, his death

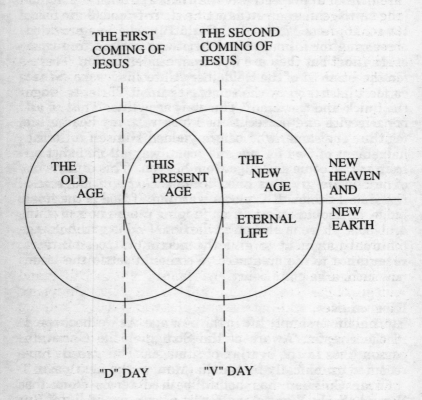

Figure 1

and resurrection, were D-Day. Sin and Satan were overcome and the principalities and powers which claim to dominate us were unmasked and disarmed (Col 2:13–15). A bridgehead was established. Victory is in sight. So we are invited to live in the overlap of the ages, in the light of the new age inaugurated by Christ. The powers of the age to come are substantially available now. So eternal life breaks into our present existence. As the poet Browning said, 'Earth's crammed with heaven.' There *are* reverses in the battle now. And like the Allies in Europe we face a foe that is substantially defeated but refuses to admit it. But V-Day is coming. One day, we will enter fully and finally into eternal life. It is not merely everlasting life, but life that has the quality of eternity – life *in* Christ.

Kingdom of God

The Kingdom of God, the fifth peak in the panorama of hope, is more than a realm. It is not a piece of territory. It is the rule of God as king, and the response of his subjects. It is much more than the church though, the church is an outcrop of the Kingdom. But there is more. There is the full influence of the regal claims of Jesus in such areas as education, family life, politics, and culture. Like iron filings lining up under the influence of a magnet, both nonhuman and human life is lining up under the influence of Christ as king. The hope of the full realisation of the kingdom of God is a powerful motivating reality in the Christian life. We already have the firstfruits of the Kingdom (Matt 12:28; 21:31; 23:13) and Jesus himself embodied both the rule of God as king and the response of God's people as subjects. But when Jesus comes again the Kingdom will come fully. All human systems and even the environment will be transformed into the perfect rule of God (1 Cor 15:24). That Kingdom will be truly international with Jews and Gentiles, indeed all kinds of people, sitting together at the great banquet of God (Luke 13:29). So our primary relationship in this life is not with the church but with the Kingdom. Nor is our primary relationship with this passing age but with a world without end. So we are delivered both from false hope and false pessimism: false hope that our puny efforts in this life to make changes will accomplish the irruption of the Kingdom; and false despair that our seemingly fruitless efforts in work and ministry have no eternal consequence. Anticipating these realities Paul said, 'Let nothing move you. Always give yourselves fully to the work of the Lord, because you know that your labour in the Lord is not in vain' (1 Cor 15:58).

New heaven and new earth

Place is part of our Christian hope. Our ultimate future is not to be immortal souls floating in a shapeless vacuum but to dwell in the place which Jesus has prepared for us. Nor is the future hope of the Christian merely 'heaven'. Our future is not dematerialised. We dare not drop 'earth' from a 'new heaven and a new earth', the subject of the last vision of the Bible (Rev 21–22). It is a place with shape, structure and exquisite beauty. This garden city fulfils both God's creativity – as suggested by the jewels – and humankind's creativity – as suggested by the description of kings of the earth bringing their splendour into the city (Rev 21:24–26). It is also a place where creation and people experience full and final healing (22:2). So Christian hope envisions the renewal by Christ of the entire cosmos (Eph 1:22). In this final vision, the Lamb is in the centre of the new creation. Lesslie Newbigin summarises this hope magnificently.

> The gospel is vastly more than an offer to men who care to accept it of a meaning for their personal lives. It is the declaration of God's cosmic purpose by which the whole public history of mankind is sustained and overruled, and by which men without exception will be judged ... It is the invitation to be fellow workers with God in the fulfilment of that purpose through the atoning work of Christ and through the witness of the Holy Spirit. It calls

men to commitment to a worldwide mission more
daring and more far-reaching than Marxism. And
it has – what Marxism lacks – a faith regarding the
final consummation of God's purpose in the power of
which it is possible to find meaning for world history
which does not make personal history meaningless,
and meaning for personal history which does not
make world history meaningless.[4]

What a glorious future! To make a final rendezvous with
Christ. To become like Christ in our resurrection bodies.
To be evaluated and rewarded by Christ. To participate
in Christ's eternal life. To experience the consummation
of the Kingdom of Christ. To live with Christ in a renewed
creation. To see his face! How far these thoughts are from
the instant gratification, this-worldly Christian culture
of today, is well illustrated by merely quoting Paul's
extraordinary confession in 1 Cor 15:19: 'If only for
this life we have hope in Christ, we are to be pitied
more than all men.' Most people today would say that
if in the next life only we had hope in Christ we are to
be pitied. Fortunately, Christian hope is both for this life
and the next. It is a hope to be lived now.

Living in Hope

But how can these convictions influence our lives? What
will it mean to live in hope?

First, Christian hope *calls for a life of radical discipleship*. Paul's letters are full of exhortations that arise
from the glorious future of believers. We are called to
live soberly and righteously (Tit 2:12–13), with patience
(James 5:7–8), with sincerity (Phil 1:10), showing brotherly love (1 Thess 3:12). 'May he strengthen your hearts
so that you will be blameless and holy in the presence
of our God and Father when our Lord Jesus comes with
all his holy ones' (1 Thess 3:13). Our characters should
express our ultimate fellowship with Jesus, ready not
only in longing but in life. The last book of the New
Testament is especially eloquent on this subject.

In the Revelation you are faced with a black-and-white choice: either worship Jesus by laying down your life, or destroy yourself by worshipping the beast. John transmits the heavenly call to 'come out of [Babylon], my people, so that you will not share in her sins' (Rev 18:4), but these people must be rescued while *in* Babylon. For until they are martyred there is nowhere else they can serve God. John invites his friends to find God in the centre of life, not at its circumference. In the Apocalypse (the word means 'revelation' or 'disclosure') of John there is no room for nominal Christianity. While the Revelation has more colour than any other book of the New Testament – jasper, carnelian, emerald, sapphire – discipleship is presented in stark black and white. Eugene Peterson says, 'Apocalypse is arson – it secretly sets a fire in the imagination that boils the fat out of an obese culture-religion and renders a clear gospel love, a pure gospel hope, a purged gospel faith.'[5]

Second, *our work in this world has meaning*. Obviously the work of witness and the ministry of God's word has great relevance when history is moving towards its final rendezvous and human beings are destined to meet their Maker. Though the verse is a little obscure, 2 Peter 3:12 hints that in some way beyond our complete understanding and certainly beyond our control, we may nevertheless have some part of 'speeding' the coming of the Lord, presumably by our work of witness and by the worldwide mission of the church. This first application of Christian hope – to the work of 'the' ministry – is so obvious that it hardly needs further comment. Less obvious, however, is the connection between Christian hope and projects of social justice and compassion. The Earl of Shaftesbury, one of Britain's most famous Christian reformers, wrote, 'I do not think that in the last forty years I have lived one conscious hour that was not influenced by the thought of the Lord's return.' It is literally true that those who have been of most earthly use have been the most heavenly-minded. To those who naively charge that Christianity has never done the world any good we point to the first three centuries of Christians, who were eagerly waiting for the Lord to come back, but left us with a splendid record of social action: rescuing abandoned and aborted babies, burying the dead at great personal risk during plagues, caring for prisoners and the shipwrecked, and being leaders in providing women with status and dignity.

Even less obvious is the connection between the panorama of Christian hope and ordinary daily work: cleaning house, selling cars, teaching school, collecting taxes, building homes, and working for the government. Paul obviously faced this problem in Thessalonica where some believers, convinced that time had run out and that nothing was worth doing in the world, stopped work completely and sponged off the others. It is in this context that Paul says, 'If a man will not work, he shall not eat' (2 Thess 3:10). His reason is not only that Christian love requires a person to provide for themselves if possible, but the fact that even ordinary work done for Jesus is never in vain (1 Cor 15:58). Humankind was made to make God's world work (Gen 1:28–30) and to take care of the world (2:5). Adam and Eve were priests of creation, a creation which one day will be transfigured. In some way beyond our understanding even the contributions we have made to life in this world, if done in faith, hope and love (1 Cor 13:13; 1 Thess 1:3) will outlast the world, and may even have a place in the new earth, while many so-called Christian activities may go up in smoke on the day and be burned with the hay and stubble (1 Cor 3:10–15). So even the most mundane activities take on meaning when the travail of history has in sight a worthy end.

Third, Christian hope invites us *to live the metaphors and symbols of the Christian life*. The word 'symbol' derives from a Greek word that means 'to throw, or put together'. In contrast the word 'diabolical' suggests 'to tear apart'. Obviously one of the most symbolic books of the Bible is the last. By using symbols, John intends to get his readers connected with another level of understanding and meaning: the spiritual and the divine. He is cultivating Kingdom-consciousness, another world-view that would empower us to live triumphantly in this world even when we appear to be losing battles. John does this through symbols. The Lamb, dragon, harlot, Babylon, pregnant woman, witness, and martyr are like the symbolic language of Orthodox icons. Speaking of the symbolism of the icons, Baggley says, 'The icons are not simply illustrations of Biblical themes or stories; rather they are an embodiment of a long tradition of meditation on these themes and incidents and their significance for man's soul ...'6 Similarly, John's Apocalypse is the fruit of inspired meditation on hundreds of symbolic Old Testament ideas, words, places and people in the light of Christ's first and second coming. Swete suggests that Revelation is a 'Christian rereading of the whole Jewish heritage'.7 But John's interest in a metaphorical interpretation of the Old Testament is pastoral not intellectual.

This pastoral interest is especially apparent in his choice of the central metaphor of the spiritual life in the Revelation: the martyr. After the first three chapters, all the Christians we meet in vision after vision are martyrs. The Greek word *martyr* (witness) is invested with its second meaning: the Christian is simply one who loses his life in order to find another life in Jesus. It is irrelevant whether one does this on the instalment plan, stage by stage, in face of direct opposition and indirect seduction, or in one extravagant act. The challenge of living this metaphor is simply this: either overcome with Jesus, or be overcome by the red dragon, beast, harlot and Babylon. Overcomers are not super-saints but simply Christians. John's apocalyptic approach dissolves nominalism in the furnace of transformation. But how can one live the martyr metaphor?

A Celtic text – an Irish homily of the seventh century – takes up the idea that martyrdom was the normal spiritual outlook of the early Christians and expresses some of the options in a society less hostile though more seductive: Red martyrdom consists in death for Jesus' sake. Green martyrdom consists of fasting and labour through which the believer flees from his evil desires and lives a life of repentance. White martyrdom consists of abandoning everything one loves for the sake of God.[8] Eugene Peterson shows that by cultivating the praying imagination, John helps us *see* enough to live the martyr metaphor whether red, green or white:

> The contribution of the Revelation to the work of witness is not instruction, telling us how to make a coherent apology of the faith, but imagination, strengthening the spirit with images that keep us 'steadfast, immovable, always abounding in the work of the Lord' (1 Cor 15:58). Instruction in witness is important, but courage is critical, for it takes place in the pitched battle.[9]

Fifth, Christian hope invites us *to worship God in the complexity of life in the world.* Martyr-candidates are invited to look into heaven (Rev 4:1) and to join the concentric circles of heavenly creatures enthralled by the glory of God. Before they encounter eschatological drama, they are invited to worship the God who is both creator and redeemer. In the last two chapters, when Christ makes all things new, John sees an endless environment of worship in which the highest privilege is to see God's face (22:4). God is beautiful. So worship is the dominating atmosphere of the Revelation. Every chapter directs us Godward instead of towards the pretentious and false worship of the Emperor. John's business as a pastor is to keep his people dealing with God, and worship does this better than anything.

Indeed, in this book *everyone* worships. Unless we worship God we shall inevitably worship the evil trinity: the beast, the harlot and the false prophet, joining those who choose to be sent to hell singing pseudo-hymns: 'Who is like the beast?' According to John it is impossible not to worship. Behind this choice for John's parishioners is the imperial cult which had worship centres located in each of the seven cities/towns in Asia where churches had been planted. To worship Christ or Caesar amounts to choosing between the Lamb and the harlot.

Faced with the temptations of idolatry and apostasy we must worship God (22:9). The best time and place to do this is in the thick of life, not simply in our leisure-time. Eugene Peterson sums up the crucial role of worship to the challenges of everyday life in these words:

> Failure in worship consigns us to a life of spasms and jerks, at the mercy of every advertisement, every seduction, every siren. Without worship we live manipulated and manipulating lives. We move in either frightened panic or deluded lethargy as we are, in turn, alarmed by spectres and soothed by placebos.[10]

Finally *we will live with Kingdom consciousness*. As we have already seen, evidences of hopelessness are not restricted to those without faith in Jesus. Among Christians one finds both short and long-range despair about the world (with a prayer for a speedy evacuation) as well as pathetic need to squeeze everything one can get out of this life (as if there were no other life and no other world). John invites a different approach.

In the Revelation we are invited to live with an open heaven. If we 'see' heaven, we will see earth the way it really is. Kingdom-consciousness is another way of speaking of this: living hopefully within the tension of the 'here' and 'not-yet-but coming' Kingdom of Jesus. This heavenly-mindedness is conspicuously lacking in Western Christians today. Kingdom-consciousness delivers us from false messianism (that our work, social action, ministry and compassionate ministry will save society), and from false pessimism (that our work in this world has to be successful and 'religious' to be meaningful). Like all contemplatives, Christians who live by this hope will seem a little bit irrelevant to the worldlings around.

So we have a glorious hope. We will see Christ face to

face. We will live with him forever. We will participate in a renewed creation with Jesus at the centre. We will live in the ultimate community of the people of God in a perfect environment. We ourselves will be transformed into his likeness bodily and spiritually. 'Dear friends, now we are children of God, and what we will be has not yet been made known. But we know that when he appears, we shall be like him, for we shall see him as he is' (1 John 3:2). Today, the greatest need is not to proclaim faith, or even love, but *hope*.

So we pray 'Come, Lord Jesus!' (Rev 22:20). But this prayer offered in the thick of life's duties, joys and disappointments is not a request to be evacuated from this life. Rather it is a commitment to be faithful to Christ unto death with the opportunities given to us to live and work for him in this world until he introduces us to a better world when he comes again.

CHAPTER TWELVE

AMBASSADORS OF LOVE

As we look at the spirituality of the first Christians, one quality stands out above all others. They were ambassadors of love. Love is the life of God himself. The holy Trinity is a relationship of constant self-giving in love, love which has overflowed upon the world God made and all the people in it.

There are many nuances to that much-misused word, love. The Greek language is full of them. The ancient world knew all about *storge*, family love: the love that binds together parents and children, and siblings in a family. They were deeply committed to *philia*, the bond that unites friends. They specialised in celebrating *eros*, sexual love. But the first Christians found none of these words satisfactory in describing the love of God. Instead, they made use of a very rare word; only occasionally had it been used before. It is the word *agape*. And they filled it with a profound and most unusual meaning. All other types of love are determined by the supposed worthiness of the one you love, be he or she a relation, a lover or a friend. You love them because you feel that in some way they merit it. It is utterly different with the New Testament word for God's love, *agape*. His love springs from the generous heart of the great Lover, not from any worthiness in the recipient.

The Love of God

That is the sort of love exhibited in John 3:16, the most famous verse in the Bible. God did not *like* the world, or

think it was attractive. No, he loved it, and was prepared
to make the ultimate sacrifice for it. That is the sort of love
which was fleshed-out in the life of Jesus. It is there in all
he did and all he said. He is God's *agapetos*, love child,
and *agape* characterises his lifestyle. Naturally therefore
he enjoined his disciples: 'A new commandment I give
to you, that you love one another; even as I have loved
you, that you also love one another. By this all men will
know that you are my disciples, if you have love for one
another' (John 13:34–35). Again and again this command
rings out: 'This I command you, to love one another' (John
15:17). In one sense, of course, this is an underlining of
his own summary of the whole Old Testament law: 'You
shall love the Lord your God with all your heart, and
with all your soul, and with all your mind. This is the
great and first commandment. And the second is like
it, You shall love your neighbour as yourself. On these
two commandments depend all the law and the prophets
(Matt 22:37–40). But it was not simply this double duty
of man which fired the teaching of Jesus. For God is love.
'Beloved, let us love one another; for love is of God, and he
who loves is born of God and knows God. He who does not
love does not know God; for God is love' (1 John 4:7–8).
That is the kernel of the matter. God is love, and if we
mirror that love we show our parentage. If we do not
love, that shows our parentage, too. It demonstrates that
despite our protestations we know nothing of the God we
claim to worship.

Love is the key to Christian discipleship. Love is also
its measuring rod. Such love is very demanding. It is
undiscriminating, like the rain which falls 'upon the just
and the unjust' with utter impartiality (Matt 5:45–46).
The falling of the rain is not in the least determined by the
recipient: neither must our love be. When Christians love
like that, people sit up and take notice. It is so unusual. So
other-worldly. That is why Mother Teresa has made such
an impact on this materialistic, selfish modern world.
Though we do not love like that, we know the authentic
article when we see it, and we know it comes from God.

Love in the Gospels

That is why Jesus encouraged his followers to love their
neighbours as themselves, even to love their enemies
(Luke 6:27). And that is what he himself did. He practised what he preached – perfectly. His love was always
flowing, to the women, the beggars, the lepers, the tax col-
lectors, the religious hierarchy, the prostitutes, the rich
young ruler, the Samaritans, Judas, and the men who
nailed him to the cross. Was there ever such love? Surely
not. In Jesus we have the supreme demonstration of what
God is like. God is the Father who loves the prodigal. He
is the wealthy party-giver who loves the street-people. He
loves the disciples who failed to understand him. He loves
their leader when he denies him. All he wants to know of
Peter after his fall is summed up in that thrice-repeated
question, 'Do you love me ... do you love me ... do you
love me?' Love is the acid test of Christian discipleship.
The path for the followers is the same path the Master
trod. We must love one another as he has loved us.
Thirty-four times in St John's Gospel alone this *agape*
word is stressed. It is the flower of Christianity.

Love in the Acts

Curiously enough the word is absent from Acts. And yet
we have the most wonderful examples of love brought
before us in that exciting book. Think of the love which
shared homes and possessions, which sold and shared out
the proceeds of their property, and gave great encouragement to one another (2:43–47 and 4:32–37). Think of the
fellowship meals between Jews and Gentiles, once they
had been reconciled to God through Jesus. Think of the
love which burst from the page as Paul said farewell to
his friends (20:36–38; 21:5 etc). Love is the language of
heaven. And it marks the citizens of heaven as with an
indelible stamp. It is the ultimate badge of belonging. It
is the essence of a truly Christian spirituality.

Love in 1 John

For love takes us to the very heart of God. All human love, however deficient and twisted, gives us some pale reflection of the love which makes the world go round, the love which marks the character of God. This is made very plain in 1 John. Love is personal (4:8). Love is searching (5:3). Love is generous (3:1). Love is sacrificial (4:10). Love lasts even beyond the day of judgment (4:17–18). Love is exclusive of all other commitments (2:15f). It challenges response to the great Lover (4:19–20) and to one and all who are objects of his love (3:16ff). And it goes without saying that love is not just a matter of talk; it involves costly, sacrificial self-giving (3:16–18). No wonder a marvellous story is told of John, when he was an old man – for he had deeply understood his Master's teaching on love. St Jerome tells us that St John was carried into the Christian assembly at an advanced age and was asked to give a message. 'Little children, love one another,' he said. When they asked for more, he repeated, 'Little children, love one another.' They then asked him why he gave no variation on this theme, and he replied, 'Because it is the commandment of the Lord, and if it is done, it suffices' (*Commentary on Galatians* 3.6.10). There is a man who had been permeated by the love of God: so much so that in extreme old age it was just love that shone through.

Love in 1 Peter

If we look at Peter's writings, love is no less central. He bids brothers and sisters in the Christian family to greet one another with the kiss of love (1 Pet 5:14). He urges them to extend deep love to one another, for love covers a multitude of failings (1 Pet 4:8). Indeed, it is the crown of all the virtues, as 2 Peter 1:7 makes very clear. There is something tremendously attractive and genuine in such love for the brethren (1 Pet 1:22; 2:17). And it all springs from loving the Jesus we cannot see, the Jesus who first loved us (1 Pet 1:8).

Love in James

James takes on the tension between law and love. He calls
the injunction 'You shall love your neighbour as yourself'
the royal law, the law of the kingdom of God (2:8). In
point of fact, law and love are friends, not enemies. They
come from the same source, the same God who is love,
and who created a law-governed world for law-abiding
citizens. Law without love becomes legalism, and Jesus
came to deliver men from that. But love without law
becomes soft and sentimental (if it does not degenerate
into licence). And Jesus came to deliver us from that,
too. But more: love itself *is* a law. 'This I *command*
you, to love one another' (John 15:17 italics mine).
Again 'If you keep my commandments, you will abide
in my love' (John 15:10), or 'If you love me, you will
keep my commandments' (John 14:15). The Jews had
613 commandments which they tried to keep. Jesus gave
only one. 'A new commandment I give to you, that you
love one another; even as I have loved you, that you also
love one another. By this all men will know that you are
my disciples, if you have love for one another' (John
13:34–35). If only we fulfilled that one commandment,
most of the subsidiary rules and regulations imposed by
churches would be utterly unnecessary.

Love in Hebrews

Hebrews has a lot to say about love, especially chapter 13.
It seems that the author wants to concentrate, at the end
of his letter, on the three great Christian virtues of faith
(chapter 11), hope (chapter 12) and love (chapter 13). It
is very challenging. For it is a love specifically directed
towards the Christian brotherhood (often not the easiest
people in the world!). It is a love which takes in strangers
and offers them hospitality. It is a love which profoundly
marks the marriage of Christians; it is warm and pure.
It is a love which shares possessions, and is content with
what it has (13:1–5). There is far more in the chapter
which springs from Christian love – obedience to church

leaders, the exchange of news and prayers, and so forth. But enough has been said to show how love runs through the spirituality of the first Christians like a silver thread in a tapestry.

Love in Paul

Nobody in the early church is more clear on the centrality and the power of love than St Paul. It has a dominant place in nearly all his letters.

Take, for example, his first, to the Thessalonians. He rejoices to recall the hard work that emerged from their love (1:3). He rejoices to hear that their faith and love are making an impact (3:6). He wants them to overflow in love towards one another (3:12). This will mean daily putting it on like a breastplate (5:8, for it does not form a natural part of our endowment, this supernatural *agape*). And that love is meant to reach and encourage their Christian leaders. Clearly love was an outstanding feature of this basically rather quarrelsome Greek city, once they had surrendered their lives to the Lord who loved them so much. Naturally, then, Paul confidently expects to see 'the love of every one of you for one another increasing'.

If we find such emphasis on love at the beginning of Paul's correspondence, it is even more apparent in his later writings. Take Ephesians, for example. He astounds them by informing them that God *chose* them to be blameless before him in love – chose them before the foundation of the world (1:4). He rejoices to have heard good news of their faith and love (1:15). He is overwhelmed at the great love God has poured out upon us, selfish rebels though we be, in giving us new life through Jesus (2:4–5). In his prayers he beseeches God that they may be 'rooted and grounded in love', as Christ is 'made at home' in their hearts (3:17). He wants them to experience the love of Christ which defies description (3:19). The Christian life is not easy: human hassles occur as much among us as among anyone else, and so he encourages them to put up with one another in love (4:2) and, later in that chapter, to tell the truth in love (or the Greek word may be translated 'act honestly' in love). Without that, the Christian community cannot hold together. And he longs for its coherence and growth into the very body of Christ which the Lord intends it to be, as it 'makes bodily growth and upbuilds itself in love' (4:16). Finally, he asks them to deliberately 'imitate God, whose children they are,' and live their daily lives in love, 'as Christ loved us and gave himself up for us' (5:2). They can never manage this by themselves, and the letter ends with clear awareness of the fact, and points to the source from which their love can be replenished: 'Peace be to the brethren, and love with faith, from God the Father and the Lord Jesus Christ. Grace be with all who love our Lord Jesus Christ with love undying' (6:23–24).

It is very evident that this humanly irascible, arrogant, activist man, Paul, has been suffused with the love of God, and longs to see it as the hallmark of all Christians. This is a major theme in all his letters, as we have seen in these two Epistles, the one drawn from his early writings and the other from his latest. But nowhere does he delve more deeply into it than in the famous hymn to love, 1 Corinthians 13.

1 Corinthians 13: the hymn to love
Any comment on this marvellous chapter runs the risk of spoiling it, but let us at least try to break through our familiarity with it by asking some pertinent questions.

What is the indication of God's presence?
That was a live issue in Paul's day, as it is in our own. Hebrews and Greeks both spoke with a divided voice.

On the one hand there were plenty who maintained that God showed his hand in the non-rational. That is where we should look if we want to see the Spirit at work. In the Old Testament you might think of Saul dancing like a dervish, or Samson smashing the Philistines. Among the Greeks, even so rational a thinker as Plato could maintain, 'It is by *mania* [ecstasy due to inspiration] that the greatest blessings have come to us,'[1] and the prophetess at Delphi worked herself up into a frenzy of possession by the god before uttering her oracles which had such an impact on ancient society. The Dionysius cult, the Cybele cult and many others sought divine inspiration in the non-rational.

On the other hand there were plenty to urge that the rational was the supreme mark of the divine in man. Socrates was the outstanding example of this in the Greek world, and in the Old Testament there was a strong emphasis on God revealing himself in a way that was intelligible, not incoherent.

But if we ask Paul how he discerned the presence of his Lord, he would have to tell us that it is neither in the rational, like the philosophers for whom the Corinthians sometimes mistook him, nor in the non-rational, like the Corinthians who were clear that God manifested himself supremely in charismatic gifts. It was in love that God was most clearly seen. Love takes us to his heart.

How important is love?

Love is the one indispensable ingredient in the use of the spiritual gifts which Paul is dealing with in chapters 12–14 of 1 Corinthians.

The tongues speaker cannot do without it (13:1). At Corinth this was happening, and it seems that some people were using this gift to make others feel small and to display their own supposed spirituality. Parading a spiritual gift in this way is horrible. It makes it sound less like the language of heaven and more like the clanging of an empty gong or the frenzied clashing of cymbals such as you might encounter in the Cybele cult. Tongues without love is disastrous. It concentrates on the non-personal and the non-ethical. It encourages pride. It is divisive. Unloving insistence on it has split many a church, just as dogmatic rejection of it has.

The man of knowledge cannot do without love either (13:2). Whether it is spiritual knowledge, depth of psychological insight or sheer learning – all branches of knowledge are disastrous without love. They give the misguided impression that God is interested in how much we know, not in how much we love.

The man of faith cannot do without love, either (13:2). Great heroes of faith are a tremendous challenge and inspiration to us. We love to read their stories. But what the biographers often omit to tell us is where there has been disaster in their family life: wives have felt neglected, and children deserted, because their dad has always been away on some hare-brained adventure of faith. Usually you find that such children rebel against Christianity when they grow up. That is because even faith without love is worth nothing.

The public benefactor cannot do without it (13:3). The millionaire may endow a research chair at the university, or a home for dispossessed cats. But without love, what is achieved in the long run? Our possessions, be they great or small, will all be left behind us one day, when we come to die. We shall only have our characters to take with us. And they are moulded by love.

The martyr cannot do without love (13:3). He may make the supreme sacrifice – perhaps (if the reading *kauthesomai* is right) by one of the most painful ways, being burnt. If *kauchesomai* is the right reading, it would mean that he does it in order to have something to be proud of. In either case, unless sacrifice is accompanied by love it is a cold, stoical thing. Without love, we gain nothing.

It is not what we know that matters; not how gifted we are; not how much we believe; not even what we do. It is what we *are* that is crucial. And that is valid in God's currency precisely insofar as it reflects his love.

Why is love so important?
Because love is the very heart of Jesus, as it is of his heavenly Father; and it is the supreme objective of the Holy Spirit to make us bear the family likeness.

In the Old Testament, as we have seen, the Holy Spirit very often appears as naked power. Moreover, he was restricted to special people, such as prophets, priests and kings. And he could so easily be withdrawn by the God who gave him in the first place, if the human recipients were presumptuous or disobedient, like Samson or King Saul.

But then Jesus came, Jesus the man filled by the Spirit. After Pentecost he became the supreme dispenser of the Spirit to his followers. No longer sub-personal, no longer limited to particular people, no longer here today and gone tomorrow, the Holy Spirit was the parting gift of Jesus to his church. The Spirit mediates to us the character of Jesus. If we want to know what the Father is really like, he is Christlike. If we want to know what the Spirit is really like, he is Christlike too. So always the measure of spiritual maturity in a church or an individual is likeness to Christ. And that means likeness to love. If people do not see love in us they will not see Jesus. That is why the supreme fruit of the Spirit is love (13:13, cf Gal 5:22).

How does it show?

It shows as the life of Jesus in us. In 1 Corinthians 13:4–7 Paul allusively sets the love of Jesus over against the failings which were so evident in the Corinthian church. They claimed to be following the 'higher' way of spiritual knowledge and experience. But Jesus beckoned them to the 'lower' way, the way of the Servant, the way of love.

Love is patient (13:4). The Corinthians were not. They were impatient for their rights in lawsuits, for their satisfaction in sex, for their chosen spiritual gifts.

Love is kind (13:4). The word means generous. The Corinthians were not like that. The rich ate all the supper at the love feast before the Holy Communion, so the poor slaves, who arrived late after work, had none.

Love is not jealous (13:4). Many at Corinth were jealous of their more talented friends.

Love does not make a parade of itself (13:4). Unlike many at Corinth, it is shy and self-effacing.

Love does not grow puffed-up with self-esteem (13:4).

Many of the Corinthian Christians seem to have been behaving like that, as they dined out on their spiritual experiences and achievements.

Love does not go fishing in the pool of shame[2] (13:5). It sets out to cover sins over, not to rake them up: unlike the Corinthians.

Love is unselfish (13:5). Jesus was supremely unselfish, but that was not mirrored in the lives of his disciples at Corinth.

Love is not irritable (13:5). The short-tempered, irritable, divisive Corinthians had a lot to learn from Jesus in this respect. Love foregoes the sharp retort and the snide comment.

Love is not moody (13:5). It does not brood over wrongs, real or imagined. There must have been a lot of that going on at Corinth in between the lawsuits and the adulteries.

Love does not revel in what is evil, but delights in what is true (13:6). That was the very opposite of the scurrilous gossip and the church divisions which prevailed at Corinth.

Love can put up with everything (13:7): loneliness, misrepresentation, pain, neglect, opposition. But the spiritual showmen at Corinth could not.

Love believes the best about people, not the worst (13:7) unlike the Corinthians, so ready to credit malicious rumours.

Love is experienced in the here and now: it is the sure platform for hope in what we cannot see (13:7). But there was little sign of that at Corinth. They were weak on future hope (ch 15) because they were so weak on present love (ch13).

Love endures whatever comes, without degenerating into cynicism (13:7). There was little of that stickability in volatile Corinth.

Finally, love never gives up (13:8), like the love of Jesus on the cross. It lasts into the life of heaven itself. Love at Corinth had clearly collapsed.

The contrast Paul is seeking to highlight is seen

very clearly from the following simple exercise. Try substituting 'I' for 'love', and see what it looks like.

> I am patient and kind. I am never jealous, give myself no airs. I am not puffed up with pride, and I do not dig in bins of other people's shame. I am unselfish, never irritable or moody. I turn my back on evil and revel in what is true. I put up with everything, believe the best about people, am full of hope, can keep on enduring whatever comes, and I never give up.

It sounds ridiculous, does it not? Pompous and totally untrue. But try it for size if you substitute Jesus instead of 'love'.

> Jesus is patient and kind. Jesus is never jealous, gives himself no airs. He is not proud, and does not dig in the bins of other people's shame. He is unselfish, and never irritable or moody. He turns his back on evil and revels in what is true. He can put up with everything, believe the best about people, remain full of hope, and he keeps on enduring whatever comes. Jesus never gives up.

That does not sound ridiculous or pompous, does it? It is the simple, unvarnished truth. Paul's whole picture of love in 1 Corinthians 13 is really a portrait of Jesus, and his longing is that it should be painted into the characters of his readers.

How does love wear?
Wonderfully well. Loving self-giving is the way of Jesus. When the days of all our earthly gifts and talents are over, when all prophecy has been fulfilled, when tongues are taken up into the song of heaven, when we know as we are known, when faith is swallowed up in sight and hope is fulfilled in complete possession by the Beloved – then love remains. The redeemed will still be united in

that glad self-offering to God and to the brethren which imperfectly marked their earthly pilgrimage. Love is the language of eternity.

John Wesley has a marvellous passage about the ultimacy of love, in his *Plain Account of Christian Perfection*[2]:

> It were well that you should be thoroughly sensible of this – the heaven of heaven is love. There is nothing higher in religion – there is, in effect, nothing else; if you look for anything but more love, you are looking wide of the mark, you are getting out of the royal way. And when you are asking others, 'Have you received this or that blessing?', if you mean anything but more love, you mean wrong; you are leading them out of the way, and putting them on a false scent. Settle it in your hearts that ... you are to aim at nothing more, but more of that love described in the thirteenth chapter of First Corinthians. You can go no higher than this until you are carried into Abraham's bosom.[3]

Did it continue?

The first Christians were very clear that this teaching on the supremacy of love was to be taken with the utmost seriousness. The earliest Christian book which has come down to us after the New Testament period is *1 Clement*, from the 90s of the first century. And there Clement, bishop of Rome, writes to rebuke the Corinthians for falling short of the love to which Christ called them, and of which Paul had written to them. They were schismatic and had deposed their leaders. Clement writes to tell them to practise what they preached:

> Let him who has love in Christ keep the commandments of Christ. Who is able to describe the bond of the love of God? Who is sufficient to tell the greatness of its beauty? The height to which love lifts us is inexpressible. Love unites us to God. Love

covers a multitude of sins. Love bears all things, is long-suffering in all things. There is nothing base, nothing haughty in love. Love admits no schism, love makes no sedition, love does all things in harmony. By love have all the elect been made perfect: without love nothing is well-pleasing to God. In love the Lord has taken us to himself. On account of the love he bore us, Jesus Christ our Lord gave his blood for us by the will of God; his flesh for our flesh, and his soul for our souls . . .[4]

Let us pray therefore and implore of his mercy that we may lead blameless lives in love, free from all human partisanship, free from blame.

And he goes on to challenge them to repent and to put right the divisions among them.[5]

Ignatius, his contemporary, shows that he has learnt this lesson equally well. 'The beginning of life is faith, and the end of life is love. When the two are joined together, it is God at work; all other requisites for a good life follow on from them.'[6] Significantly he quotes Jesus' words, 'The tree is known by its fruits' and concludes, 'so those who profess to belong to Christ will be seen by their deeds.'[7] And they were. Tertullian the Christian, and Lucian the pagan, corroborate one another on this point. Both had often heard on pagan lips the remark, 'Look how these Christians love one another.' It showed in so many ways. Tertullian describes some of them. 'Our giving is expended upon no banquets or drinking bouts or thankless eating-houses, but on feeding and burying poor people, on behalf of boys and girls who have neither parents nor money, in support of old people unable now to get about, as well as for people who are shipwrecked, or who may be in the mines, or exile, or in prison'.[8]

There is an enormous amount of evidence in the writings of the second and third century to show the phenomenal impact of the Christian cause: and love was the secret of their spirituality. A love which treated slaves as brethren, a love which supported widows and orphans, a love which formed trade unions to support the powerless, a love which cared for prisoners and those languishing in the mines, a love which poured itself out on those who were hit by natural disasters. A good example of this is recorded by the historian, Eusebius. A terrible plague had occurred.

> Then the Christians showed themselves to the heathen in the clearest light. They were the only people who amid such terrible ills showed their fellow-feeling and humanity by their actions. Day by day some would busy themselves by attending to the dead and burying them (for there were many to whom nobody else paid heed). Others gathered in one spot all who were afflicted by hunger throughout the whole city, and gave bread to them all. When this became known, people glorified the Christians' God, and, convinced by the deeds in front of their eyes, confessed that the Christians alone were truly pious.'[9]

We could go on. But the point is clear. The early Christians knew that the yardstick of their spirituality was love, love which derived from God, and love which therefore had to be reflected indiscriminately to all in need. Love was the badge they wore, and they were content to be judged by their display of it. All of which prompts, at the end of this book, a final question, drawing out the implications of Paul's hymn to love.

How do we Stand?

We Christians shall not be judged by our gifts or by our learning, but by our love. How shall we fare?

How shall we fare when *our churches* are judged in this light? Much that we do in our churches is totally irrelevant to the call of love, the needs of people around us, and the work of the Kingdom of God. We are preoccupied with our petty internal concerns, our constitutions and our

synods. We must look like an irrelevant Sunday School
for the pious, instead of the commando forces of the king
of love. Our churchy language and our introversion makes
it hard for others to join us. Our ineffectiveness and lack
of cutting edge alienates the young. Our divisions and
quarrels disgust the onlookers. Can our badge be said to
be love? Yet without it we are nothing.

How shall we fare when *as individuals* we are judged
by this standard of love? Our attitudes at work, in the
family, to our partner maybe. Our response to crying
needs all around us, to personal disappointments, to
being let down. How much do we really love the Lord?
A difficult question to answer, as St John realised. So he
gave us a helpful barometer: 'He who does not love his
brother whom he has seen, cannot love God whom he has
not seen' (1 John 4:20).

How shall we fare when *our suffering* is judged in this
light? We have all met sufferers who positively shine with
the love of God. It is a blessing to go and visit them. They
treat their sufferings like medals to be worn proudly on
their chest. How do we react in suffering, or towards those
who make life hard for us in the family or in the office?
Love is the standard God looks for.

How shall we fare when *our giving* is judged in the light
of love? The waste we contribute to, the opulence we enjoy
while others starve, will rise up in testimony against us.
So will the poverty of our actual giving to God's work.

How shall we fare when *our caring* is judged in this
light? Not many churches, at least in the West, are noted
for their involvement with the hungry, the prostitutes,
the AIDS victims, the alcoholics. We prefer to pass by on
the other side of the road, rather than display the love of
the good Samaritan. God will surely judge us for this.

How shall we fare when *our evangelism* is judged on
the same principle? The total lack of evangelism in many
churches, who never give the impression that they are
particularly anxious to introduce others to the Saviour
they profess to love. The hard, unloving evangelism in
other churches where there is a real attempt at outreach

but it is so strident, so complacent, so alien from the situation of those addressed that it savours more of marketing than good news. On the whole we do not tell people the gospel because we do not love them enough to bother. Or else we do it in a way they find hard to accept – because we do not love enough to learn a better way. We are driven back to St Paul's conclusion, 'Without love, I gain nothing.'

And how shall we fare when *we come to die*, and when the question is not how much we have known, or how much we have given, or how much we have done? The one question we shall be bound to answer is this. 'How much have you loved?' That is the core, the heartbeat of New Testament spirituality. How shall we fare then?

NOTES

CHAPTER ONE
1. Felix Minicius; *Octavius*, 10.
2. Eusebius *HE* 3. 31. 3.
3. Joachim Jeremias; *The Central Message of the New Testament*, (London, SCM Press).

I am indebted in this chapter to insights from my friend and erstwhile colleague Canon David Prior.

CHAPTER TWO
1. Dallas Willard; *The Spirit of the Disciplines: Understanding How God Changes Lives* (New York, Harper and Row, 1988), xii.
2. John Calvin; *Calvin, Institutes of the Christian Religion*, 2 vols., ed. John T. McNeill, trans. Ford Lewis Battles (Philadelphia, Westminster Press, 1960) 2:1063.
3. Paraphrased in Roland Bainton; *Here I Stand: A Life of Martin Luther* (Nashville, Abingdon, 1978), 156.
4. John Calvin; *Commentary on a Harmony of the Evangelists, Matthew, Mark, and Luke* trans. William Pringle (Grand Rapids, Eerdmans, 1956), 1:244.
5. Dietrich Bonhoeffer; *The Cost of Discipleship* (London, SCM Press, 1959), 79.
6. Thomas à Kempis; *The Imitation of Christ* (London, J.M. Dent and Sons Ltd., 1947), 1.
7. Ibid., 85.
8. Soren Kierkegaard; *For Self-Examination: Recommended for the Times*, trans. Edna and Howard Hong (Minneapolis, MN, Augsburg, 1940), 76–77.
9. Bonhoeffer, op. cit., 35–36.

CHAPTER THREE
1. Psalms of Solomon; 17. 37.

See my *I believe in the Holy Spirit* (Hodder & Stoughton) for further reading.

CHAPTER FOUR

1. Peter T. Forsyth; *The Soul of Prayer* (London, Independent Press, 1954), 15.
2. Ibid., 46 (emphasis mine).
3. John Baggley; *Doors of Perception: Icons and their Spiritual Significance* (New York, St. Vladimir's Seminary Press, 1988), 136.
4. Forsyth, op. cit., 29.
5. A. B. Bruce; *The Training of the Twelve: Passages Out of the Gospels* (New York, A.C. Armstrong and Son, 1902), 54–55.
6. Quoted in Leon Morris; *The Gospel According to John* (NICNT, Grand Rapids, Eerdmans, 1971), 716.
7. Tomas Spidlik; *The Spirituality of the Christian East: A Systematic Handbook* (Kalamazoo, Cistercian Publications, 1986), 45.
8. James Houston; 'Trinitarian Spirituality,' (unpublished paper, Regent College, Vancouver, 1989), 22.
9. Bruce, op. cit., 461.
10. Cheryl Forbes; *Imagination: Embracing a Theology of Wonder* (Portland, Multnomah Press, 1986), 46.
11. S. S. Fiorenza; *Invitation to the Book of Revelation* (Garden City, NY, Doubleday and Co., 1981), 18.
12. James Houston; *Transforming Friendship: A Guide to Prayer* (Oxford, Lion Books, 1989), 195–196.

CHAPTER FIVE

1. Tertullian; *Apologeticus* 39.
2. Tertullian; *Apologeticus*, Chapter 39.
3. Among the more useful studies of Christian fellowship are: A.R. George; *Communion with God*: David Prior; *The Church in the Home*: Edwin Judge; *The Social Pattern of the Christian Groups in the First Century* and Robert Banks; *Paul's Idea of Community*.

CHAPTER SIX

1. Hendrik Berkhof; *Christ and the Powers*, trans. John Howard Yoder (Kitchener, Ont., Herald Press, 1962/77), 29.
2. Ibid., 39.
3. Markus Barth; *Ephesians: The Anchor Bible* (Garden City, NY, Doubleday and Co., 1974), Vol. 1, 365.
4. Quoted in James S. Stewart; *A Faith to Proclaim* (London, Hodder and Stoughton, 1953), 77.
5. Gordon D. Fee; 'The Spirit against the Flesh: Another Look at Pauline Ethics' (unpublished lecture at New Orleans Baptist Theological Seminary, November 7, 1991), p. 17.
6. Anonymous; 'The War Within: An Anatomy of Lust,' *Leadership* (Fall 1982), 43.

7. Stewart; op. cit., 76–77.
8. Lewis Smedes; 'Forgiveness: The Power to Change the Past,' *Christianity Today* 27, no. 1 (7 January 1983): 26.
9. Quoted in Kenneth Leech; *True Prayer: An Invitation to Christian Spirituality* (San Francisco, Harper and Row, 1980), 68.
10. Blaise Pascal; *Pensees* (New York, The Modern Library, 1941), 166.
11. Quoted in Eugene Peterson; *Reversed Thunder: The Revelation of John and the Praying Imagination* (San Francisco, Harper and Row, 1988), 87.
12. James Houston; 'Lead Us through the Temptation: A Meditation on the Lord's Prayer,' (unpublished notes from the Ministry and Spirituality course, Regent College, Vancouver, B.C., 1990).

CHAPTER SEVEN
1. John Wimber; *Power Evangelism*, London, Hodder and Stoughton, 1985.
2. Francis MacNutt; *Healing*, London, Hodder and Stoughton, 1989, chapter 18, 'Eleven reasons why people are not healed'.
3. John Wimber; *Power Healing*, London, Hodder and Stoughton, 1986; chapter 8, 'Not everyone is healed'.
4. Michael Green; *I Believe in Satan's Downfall*, London, Hodder and Stoughton, 1988.
5. Justin Martyr; *2 Apol 6*.

CHAPTER EIGHT
1. Eugene H. Peterson; *A Long Obedience in the Same Direction: Discipleship in an Instant Society* (Downers Grove, InterVarsity Press, 1980).
2. Peter Davids; *Commentary on James* (New International Greek Testament Commentary, Grand Rapids, Eerdmans, 1982), 177.
3. John Chrysostom; *On Wealth and Poverty: Seven Sermons on Lazarus and the Rich Man* (Crestwood, St. Vladimir's Seminary Press, 1984), 50.
4. Dietrich Bonhoeffer; *Life Together*, trans. John W. Doberstein (New York, Harper and Row, 1954), 110–122.
5. Quoted in Howard A. Snyder; *The Radical Wesley and Patterns for Church Renewal* (Downers Grove, Ill: InterVarsity Press, 1980), 148.

CHAPTER NINE
1. *Didache*; 7:1
2. Joachim Jeremias; *The Eucharistic Words of Jesus* (London, SCM Press, 1970).

3. *Didache*; 10.

CHAPTER TEN

1. Oswald Chambers; *My Utmost for His Highest* (Toronto, McClelland and Stewart, 1953), 166.
2. Ibid., 219.
3. Andrew Murray; *Abide in Christ: Thoughts on the Blessed Life of Fellowship with the Son of God* (Fort Washington, PA, Christian Literature Crusade, 1989), 115.
4. Apol. XXIX; ANF, III, p. 46, quoted in Leon Morris; *The Gospel According to John* (NICNT, Grand Rapids, Eerdmans, 1987), 663.
5. LXXII. 5; pp. 266-267, quoted in Morris, op. cit., 663.
6. Quoted in Kenneth Leech; *True Prayer: An Invitation to Christian Spirituality* (San Francisco, Harper and Row, 1980), 103.
7. Murray; op. cit., 115.
8. James Stewart; *A Man in Christ: The Vital Elements of St. Paul's Religion* (London, Hodder and Stoughton, 1957), 165–166.
9. Adolf Deissmann; *Paul: A Study in Social and Religious History*, trans. William E. Wilson (London, Hodder and Stoughton, 1926), 150.
10. Ibid., 149.
11. Ibid., 152.
12. Michael Green; *The Meaning of Salvation* (Vancouver, Regent College Bookstore Reprints, 1992), 231–236.
13. Murray, op. cit., 31.

CHAPTER ELEVEN

1. Lesslie Newbigin; *Honest Religion for Secular Man* (Philadelphia, Westminster Press, 1966), 46.
2. This dictum has been ascribed to Luther but it is an apocryphon. It may stem from a grenadier of Frederick II of Prussia. Quoted by Markus Barth, *Ephesians, Translation and Commentary on Chapters 4–6*, vol 34A The Anchor Bible (Garden City, NY: Doubleday, 1981), 517.
3. Jürgen Moltmann; *Theology of Hope: On the Ground and the Implications of a Christian Eschatology*, trans. James W. Leitch (New York: Harper and Row, 1967), 31.
4. Newbigin; op. cit., 46.
5. Eugene H. Peterson; 'The Apocalyptic Pastor', *The Reformed Journal* 38, No. 2 (May 1988), 17.
6. John Baggley; *Doors of Perception: Icons and their Spiritual Significance* (Crestwood, NY, Vladimir's Seminary Press, 1988), 52.
7. John Swete; *Revelation* (New Testament Commentaries, Philadelphia: Trinity Press International, 1990), 40.
8. J. Ryan; *Irish Monasticism* (London, 1931), 197.

9. Eugene H. Peterson; *Reversed Thunder: The Revelation of John and the Praying Imagination* (San Francisco, Harper and Row, 1988), 112.
10. Ibid., 60.

CHAPTER TWELVE

1. Plato; *Phaedrus* 24c.
2. This is the probable meaning of *aschemonei*.
3. John Wesley; *Plain Account of Christian Perfection* (London, Epworth Press, reprinted 1955).
4. *1 Clement*, chapter 49.
5. *1 Clement*, chapter 50.
6. Ignatius; *Ephesians*, chapter 14.
7. Ignatius; *op. cit.*, chapter 14.
8. Tertullian; *Apologeticus*, chapter 39.
9. Eusebius; *History of the Church*, 9.8.